FAKE
NEWS!

MEDIA AND PUBLIC AFFAIRS

Robert Mann, Series Editor

FAKE NEWS!

MISINFORMATION IN THE MEDIA

EDITED BY **JOSH GRIMM**

Louisiana State University Press

Baton Rouge

Published by Louisiana State University Press
Copyright © 2020 by Louisiana State University Press
Foreword copyright © 2020 by Louisiana State University Press
All rights reserved
First printing

Designer: Barbara Neely Bourgoyne
Typeface: Minion Pro

These essays first appeared in the following publications:
Berkowitz, Dan, and David Asa Schwartz. "Miley, CNN and The Onion: When fake news becomes
    realer than real." *Journalism Practice* 10, no. 1 (2016): 1–17.
Gorbach, Julien. "Not Your Grandpa's Hoax: A Comparative History of Fake News." *American Jour-
    nalism* 35, no. 2 (2018): 236–249.
Johnson, Jessica. "The Self-Radicalization of White Men: 'Fake News' and the Affective Networking
    of Paranoia." *Communication Culture & Critique* 11, no. 1 (2018): 100–115.
Timmer, Joel. "Fighting Falsity: Fake News, Facebook, and the First Amendment." *Cardozo Arts &
    Ent. LJ* 35 (2016): 669–705.

Library of Congress Cataloging-in-Publication Data
Names: Grimm, Josh, 1980- editor.
Title: Fake news! : misinformation in the media / edited by Josh Grimm.
Description: Baton Rouge : Louisiana State University Press, 2020. | Series: Media and public
    affairs | Includes bibliographical references and index.
Identifiers: LCCN 2019052425 | ISBN 978-0-8071-7200-1 (paperback)
Subjects: LCSH: Fake news. | Misinformation. | Media literacy.
Classification: LCC PN4784.F27 F35 2020 | DDC 070.4—dc23
LC record available at https://lccn.loc.gov/2019052425

The paper in this book meets the guidelines for permanence and durability of the Committee
on Production Guidelines for Book Longevity of the Council on Library Resources. ∞

CONTENTS

CONTENTS

FOREWORD

The photograph on the CNN website showed a dark plume of smoke billowing above an immense chemical plant in rural South Louisiana. Residents were bombarded with text messages. Twitter was bursting with oddly worded warnings of hazardous chemicals engulfing towns and cities as far away as New Orleans and Baton Rouge.

Local security officials jumped on the phones. Was there a fire? An accident? A spill? The answer: No.

It turned out it was all fake. The CNN website? Fake. The photograph and the tweetstorm? Both fake. The Wikipedia page, the Facebook entry on louisiananews? All fake. Credit the New Orleans *Times-Picayune* for uncovering the hoax.

To this day, Homeland Security officials in St. Mary Parish can't explain it. They know of no motive or reason for pinpointing a fake news attack on a remotely located plant making carbon-black ingredients for polymers and plastics.

No one is absolutely sure of the culprit, but all signs point to the Internet Research Agency in St. Petersburg, Russia. The fake news attack was almost certainly manufactured by a small army of trolls and computer "bots" in Russia hoping to cause panic at a huge chemical plant in the small town. Why? Well, no one is really sure.

That was 2014, ancient history in the rapidly thickening annals of fake news in America. Since then, there have been have been a countless number of fake reports which became a popular issue during the 2016 presidential campaign. Besides the Russian "troll farm," as it's commonly called, which is closely linked to an associate of Vladimir Putin, a colony in Macedonia spun fake tales of campaign nonsense to profit from Google ad placements. When the election was over, they folded their tent, but not before reporting that the Pope had endorsed Donald Trump for president or that Hillary Clinton had sold weapons to ISIS.

Other fake news factories have dispensed fake news to sow confusion in the United States and threaten public safety, as with the attack in Louisiana, and undermine the integrity of American democratic institutions such as the media or voting.

Fakes, frauds and hoaxes have been a part of journalism for more than a century, as several excellent essays in this volume lay out. Conspiracy theories, fictional accounts, and faked kidnappings have long entertained readers everywhere. But the rise of social media, together with a host of other reasons in the last decade, has given made-up news the rocket fuel it long lacked.

Now, the pass-and-share culture of social media allows users to send anything—true or false—to countless friends who, like them, don't know if this is true, but it could be true. Confirmation bias is the diagnosis social scientists use. Gullibility is a close cousin.

Consider Cameron Harris, a young political consultant outside Washington, DC, who wanted to dip his toe into the steaming cauldron of bias and political division. He also wondered if her could make money doing it. Several weeks before the presidential election, Mr. Harris tried to confect two completely made-up stories while sitting at his kitchen table. Neither got any traction.

His third attempt was what the *New York Times* called "A Fake News Masterpiece." It described a discovery of thousands of paper ballots already marked for Hillary Clinton in a warehouse in Ohio, a battleground state. He found a photograph of a man standing behind a stack of storage boxes with "BALLOTS" stenciled on the side. Never mind that the photo had been taken in England. For Mr. Harris's purpose, it was perfect.

Within hours, the story soared through the Internet. Mr. Harris told his readers the story was still "developing" and to come back for the latest—all touches to keep the story orbiting the internet. Before it was over, more than six million people saw the story. Google attached random ads onto the article page, each paying a commission to Mr. Harris for every view of the story. His take: more than $20,000.

In less than a day, Ohio election officials knocked down the story. But Mr. Harris had confirmed his expectations about social media and profited from confirmation bias. Tracking polls showed that people tended to believe that Hillary

Clinton would try to win by cheating, and that she could not be trusted even in secret balloting. Social media, with billions of users bubbling in overheated echo chambers, or "filter bubbles," carried Harris's fake news into infamy.

Since the 2016 election, there has been a surge in discussion of fake news from academic halls such as MIT and Harvard's Shorenstein Center to a myriad of campus panels and investigative projects by leading newsrooms. These works have shown that fake news today travels faster—and sometimes farther—than real news, that greater educational efforts in media literacy are needed to fill gaps left behind by unmediated reports and shrinking ranks of experienced news editors, and that fake reports can influence opinion and possibly election results.

This book, a compendium of such scholarship, aims to dissect fake news not only because of its sudden resurgence but because of what it represents about our politically divided country, our social media culture, and our vulnerabilities.

—LEONARD APCAR

FAKE NEWS!

INTRODUCTION

Josh Grimm

May 21, 2016, was a warm, sunny Saturday in downtown Houston where, in front of the Islamic Da'wah Center, two groups were protesting. On one side of the street stood ten people waving Texas and Confederate flags, shouting against what they referred to as "the threat of radical Islam."[1] On the other side of the street, fifty to sixty people defending the Islamic center held signs denouncing Nazis, including one banner that read "Follow Your Leader: Kill Yourself" over a drawing of Hitler. Despite the rhetoric, the protest was relatively uneventful; as reported by the *Houston Chronicle,* "The event grew raucous at times but was mostly peaceful. Houston police made one arrest after one protester did not move out the way of a police vehicle."[2]

Houston has a population of roughly 2.3 million, and such a small protest shouldn't really draw too much attention given the lack of arrests and general disruption. However, it was the topic of US House and Senate Intelligence Committee meetings almost eighteen months later because of how the protests were organized. One side, a Facebook group called "Heart of Texas," had a folksy tagline—"homeland of guns, barbecue and your heart"[3]—and a fake news feed that declared, "Thanks to Obama's and Hillary's policy, illegals come here because they wait for amnesty promised."[4] The other side was a different Facebook group that called itself the "United Muslims of America" with the tagline, "I'm a Muslim, and I'm proud," to go with its 328,000 followers.[5] The Heart of Texas Facebook page organized a rally to "Stop Islamization of Texas," paying to promote the event, "which was viewed by about 12,000 people."[6] The United Muslims of America account organized the counterprotest by placing an advertisement calling to "Save Islamic Knowledge," which was viewed by 2,700 people on Facebook.[7] Both were to be held at the same time and place, but on that Saturday, the organizers on either side did not show.

That's because the organizers weren't in Texas. They were in St. Petersburg, Russia. Russian troll farms had created both the "Heart of Texas" and "I'm a Muslim, and I'm proud," pages and filled them with content created to drive traffic and followers to those Facebook groups. As for the protests themselves, the Russian operatives paid for Facebook advertising in order to get their calls for a protest (and counterprotest) seen by as many people as possible. The total cost for those advertisements? A whopping $200. This shockingly low price tag, along with the foreign intervention, is what brought this case to the attention of the US House of Representatives and Senate, but by the time of the hearings on these protests, fake news—by then as synonymous with disinformation, manipulation, and political agendas as the Houston incident—had long been engrained in the public consciousness.

The term "fake news" is often associated President Donald Trump, which is what tends to happen when you repeatedly tweet "FAKE NEWS!" However, the term didn't really manifest itself (in its current form) until after the election, and the first politician to use the term wasn't Donald Trump; it was Hillary Clinton. Speaking at the Capitol to honor Senate minority leader Harry Reid's retirement, Clinton spoke out against what she saw as a looming, bipartisan issue:

> Let me just mention briefly one threat in particular that should concern all Americans—Democrats, Republicans, and independents alike, especially those who serve in our Congress: the epidemic of malicious fake news and false propaganda that flooded social media over the past year. It's now clear that so-called fake news can have real-world consequences. This isn't about politics or partisanship. Lives are at risk—lives of ordinary people just trying to go about their days, to do their jobs, contribute to their communities. It's a danger that must be addressed and addressed quickly.[8]

Two days after Clinton's speech, Donald Trump used the term "fake news" in a tweet for the first time: "Reports by @CNN that I will be working on The Apprentice during my Presidency, even part time, are ridiculous & untrue—FAKE

NEWS!"[9] The *Fox & Friends* gang discussed the tweet on their show, and the rest is history.

The timeline for Trump popularizing the term "fake news" by warping its meaning is straightforward, and yet the motivation remains unclear, something we will likely never truly understand. The most convincing explanation comes from BuzzFeed media editor Craig Silverman, who believes Trump heard about the speech and saw an opportunity, particularly since many experts were still grappling with his victory:

> There were a lot of folks who were so shocked by Trump's victory, including Clinton, that they grabbed onto this a little bit as one [reason] or the main reason. And I think that caused a backlash from Trump and his supporters. You know, one of the stories of the 2016 election was how effective he and his supporters were at weaponizing information and at memeing [sic] and at owning part of the conversation. And I think that happened again with fake news.[10]

The *Washington Post* concurred, arguing that Trump likely "suspected that Clinton was trying to delegitimize his win, at least a little, so he counter punched (his term) by promoting the idea that fake news is actually something designed to hurt him, not help him."[11] Not surprisingly, this reappropriated definition of fake news tapped into the existing tensions and animosity toward mainstream news media that has been a fulcrum of the conservative movement since the New Right came to prominence during the 1980s. And just like that, the term "fake news" became weaponized.

This dramatic shift in meaning was particularly noteworthy, though after the last few months of the election, not exactly a surprise. Silverman became interested in fake news and actually revived the term in 2014. In an article aptly titled, "I Helped Popularize the Term 'Fake News' and Now I Cringe Every Time I Hear It," Silverman explains that he stumbled upon a false story on nationalreport. net that "was quickly racking up likes, shares, and comments on Facebook" by claiming that an entire Texas town was quarantined because a family living there had contracted Ebola.[12] Concerned, Silverman tweeted, "Fake news site National Report set off a measure of panic by publishing fake story about Ebola outbreak: [web address of news story posted in tweet]. Scumbags." By this time, Silverman had been tracking fake news for years, launching a website—Emergent—to verify or debunk various news stories, basically what the Snopes site would look like if had a web designer. The site tracked outrageous stories and classified them as true (British police really were looking for a man who slapped anyone who sneezed in public), unverified (whether a Russian cat recued an abandoned baby remains a mystery), and false (California KFCs are *not* selling marijuana and Willie Nelson is [thankfully] *not* dead),[13] all while also documenting the website where the story originated.[14]

In his original tweet and on his website, Silverman was using the term "fake news" the same way Clinton ultimately did, meaning "completely false information that was created and spread for profit."[15] However, Trump's re-brand of the term politicized the idea of fake news, possibly forever. It became a tactic used to cast doubt and discredit news stories and outlets. As Silverman put it: "Online misinformation, and the exploitation and manipulation of our information environment, are real, complex problems affecting global societies. By making the term 'fake news' ubiquitous and muddled, we lost a battle in the actual war against completely false information."[16]

And the effects could be far more detrimental than losing a single battle. In a massive media literacy study of over 7,800 students across twelve states, the Stanford History Education Group (SHEG) utilized a popular media–literacy curriculum to determine how adept students are at identifying inaccurate information online; the researchers were concerned that "democracy is threatened by the ease at which disinformation about civic issues is allowed to spread and flourish."[17] Students in middle school, high school, and college were given exercises to gauge their basic skills in this area. The results were startling, to say the least, with members of SHEG stating, "In every case and at every level, we were taken aback by students' lack of preparation."[18] For one test, students were given two Facebook posts announcing Trump's presidential candidacy; "one was from the verified Fox News account and the other was from an account that looked like Fox News."[19] Less than 25 percent of students recognized the verified account, and "over 30 percent of students argued that the fake account was more trustworthy because of some key graphic elements that it included."[20] These results were consistent across age groups and state lines, with many students not even bothering to check out sites like Craig Silverman's Emergent or the better-known Snopes site.

The truth was sobering, as Sam Wineburg, the lead author of the study, noted: "Many people assume that because young people are fluent in social media they are equally perceptive about what they find there. Our work shows the opposite to be true." The researchers' fears about democracy, it seems, are well founded.

The SHEG research team noted that, "For every challenge facing this nation, there are scores of websites pretending to be something they are not."[21] These sites are continuing to multiply—largely unchecked—with potentially dire consequences. In his 2016 article "Googling Is Believing: Trumping the Informed Citizen," Michael Lynch wrote that the Internet is "both the world's best fact-checker and the world's best bias confirmer—often at the same time."[22] These two roles were already at odds, but now, through the proliferation of fake news sites and stories, and the vast social networks that aid in their spread, dangerous biases can be reinforced by fabricated facts, muddling progress and stirring controversy. The issue of fake news has never been more important, which is why I've collected the pieces in this reader, as the best way to combat a problem of this magnitude is to better understand it.

This reader is divided into two sections, with each containing a mix of foundational pieces and original works published for this volume about various aspects of fake news. The first section focuses on the origins and evolution of fake news. Despite its recent popularity, the term dates back over a century, with the concept extending even further into the past. This historical context provides the backdrop for understanding how this seemingly unique phenomenon is far from restricted to the twenty-first century. The second section examines the impact and future of fake news. So many assumptions are made about fake news; assumptions about the audience, the medium, the message, and the intentions of all involved make for a muddled scene. The authors in this section examine different aspects of fake news to help determine to what extend people might be affected by fake news stories, while also expanding that understanding into the future of fake news, with discussions focusing on how outlets and organizations are handling the unique challenges surrounding this ongoing issue.

I highlighted the Houston protest case because it so perfectly encapsulates so much about fake news that remains true today, even though this was in the form of social media pages and sponsored ads rather than a news story. The two social media group had over half a million followers, but the advertised posts were themselves only seen by around fifteen thousand people, and most did not actually show up to a rally. The focus was on an issue that deeply divides various populations in this country, and those biases and prejudices were expertly preyed upon by a foreign party. And, of course, at least on the surface, there was a distinct lack of any large-scale consequences—no one was injured. And yet, the protest and counterprotest were treading close to a dangerous confrontation; after all, there was no real violence, but the Facebook post about protesting radical Islam encouraged everyone to bring their guns to the rally. Glenn, the *Houston Chronicle* reporter covering the protest, wrote that he saw at least one protester carrying an AR-15.[23] In other words, individuals were deliberately misled, the messages were inflammatory, people could have been seriously hurt, and the entire situation called attention to just how vulnerable people living in the United States are to this type of attack. All of these themes will be repeated in this volume and, unfortunately, in real life, at least for the foreseeable future.

NOTES

1. Jeremy Wallace, "Russians Duped Texans into Fake Rallies in Houston," *Houston Chronicle,* November 3, 2017, www.chron.com/news/politics/texas/article/Russians-duped-Texans-into-fake-rallies-in-Houston-12326774.php.

2. Wallace, "Russians Duped Texans."

3. Ryan Lucas, "How Russia Used Facebook to Organize 2 Sets of Protesters," NPR, November 1, 2017, www.npr.org/2017/11/01/561427876/how-russia-used-facebook-to-organize-two-sets-of-protesters.

4. Wallace, "Russians Duped Texans."

5. Lucas, "How Russia Used Facebook."

6. Natasha Bertrand, "Russian Organized 2 Sides of a Texas Protest and Encouraged 'Both Sides to Battle in the Streets,'" *Business Insider,* November 1, 2017, www.businessinsider.com/russia-trolls-senate-intelligence-committee-hearing-2017-11.

7. Bertrand, "Russian Organized 2 Sides."

8. Paul Kayne, "Hillary Clinton Attacks 'Fake News' in Post-Election Appearance on Capitol Hill," *Washington Post,* December 8, 2016, www.washingtonpost.com/news/powerpost/wp/2016/12/08/hillary-clinton-attacks-fake-news-in-post-election-appearance-on-capitol-hill/?utm_term=.739349e48522.

9. Donald Trump, Twitter post, December 10, 2016, 7:11 a.m., twitter.com/realDonaldTrump/status/807588632877998081

10. Callum Borchers, "How Hillary Clinton Might Have Inspired Trump's 'Fake News' Attacks," *Washington Post,* January 3, 2018, www.washingtonpost.com/news/the-fix/wp/2018/01/03/how-hillary-clinton-might-have-inspired-trumps-fake-news-attacks/?utm_term=.b3cde0db97f3.

11. Borchers, "How Hillary Clinton Might Have Inspired."

12. Craig Silverman, "I Helped Popularize the Term 'Fake News' and Now I Cringe Every Time I Hear It," *BuzzFeed News,* December 31, 2017, www.buzzfeednews.com/article/craigsilverman/i-helped -popularize-the-term-fake-news-and-now-i-cringe#.vxGRxZNy0A.

13. At least not as of the time of this being written. Hang in there, Willie!

14. www.emergent.info.

15. Silverman, "I Helped Popularize the Term."

16. Silverman, "I Helped Popularize the Term."

17. Brooke Donald, "Stanford Researchers Find Students Have Trouble Judging the Credibility of Information Online," *Stanford University,* ed.stanford.edu/news/stanford-researchers-find-students -have-trouble-judging-credibility-information-online (accessed December 15, 2018).

18. Sam Wineburg, Sarah McGrew, Joel Breakstone, and Teresa Ortega, "Evaluating Information: The Cornerstone of Civic Online Reasoning," *Stanford Digital Repository,* stacks.stanford.edu/file /druid:fv751yt5934/SHEG%20Evaluating%20Information%20online.pdf (accessed December 8, 2018).

19. Donald, "Stanford Researchers Find Students Have Trouble."

20. Donald, "Stanford Researchers Find Students Have Trouble."

21. Wineburg et al., "Evaluating Information."

22. Michael P. Lynch, "Googling Is Believing: Trumping the Informed Citizen," *New York Times,* March 9, 2016, opinionator.blogs.nytimes.com/2016/03/09/googling-is-believing- trumping-the -informed-citizen/.

23. Mike Glenn, "A Houston Protest, Organized by Russian Trolls," *Houston Chronicle,* February 20, 2018, www.houstonchronicle.com/local/gray-matters/article/A-Houston-protest-organized-by -Russian-trolls-12625481.php.

I

THE HISTORY OF FAKE NEWS

Within the last few years, fake news has taken on a fairly specific meaning, at least for the time being. This uniformity of meaning was not always the case, particularly not in terms of studying fake news. Tandoc, Lim, and Ling examined thirty-four academic articles studying fake news and found several categories of studies: news satire, news parody, news fabrication, photo manipulation, advertising and public relations, and propaganda.[1] While there is significant leeway in how fake news might manifest itself (depending on what category it would fall into), the public is more certain of what fake news is, though consensus does not always mean agreement. In reality, "fake news" has the unique position of being almost universally loathed, though for very different reasons. For some, fake news is a term that reflects a massive, concerted campaign on the part of mainstream media to cast doubt on President Trump's legitimacy. For others, it's simply a story that has been poorly reported or fabricated, often with a strong political bent aimed at praising the president and his agenda by manufacturing a favorable media environment surrounding him based on accomplishments that are, quite frankly, fake.

In order to cast as wide a net as possible (while still capturing the significance of the term), the closest definition of the phenomenon to this reader's design is as follows: "Fake news [is] information that is inconsistent with factual reality. In this sense, it is noise that needs to be removed before a signal can be properly interpreted. However, this noise has special properties in that it is biased in a specific way, unlike random noise."[2]

One reason it's difficult to define fake news is because it's something that has been around almost as long as mass media. Each of the pieces in this section focuses on a particular aspect of the rich, complex history of fake news. We open with an original piece for this volume by John Maxwell Hamilton and Heidi Tworek, which looks at the history of faking in news to understand what is truly new in our current moment and what merely lay undetected under the surface for a few decades. Hamilton and Tworek are interested in fake news published with the full knowledge and support of a news entity. This *institutional fake news,* as they call it, has been neither random nor errant. It has been an established feature of news throughout history. To illuminate this, they look at the three different types of fake news in history and the form of their reappearance today. First, they look at how fake news benefited the news business, for example by increasing subscriptions *inside* the news business; second, the history of medical advertising shows how fake news could financially benefit companies or sectors *outside* the news business. And finally, Hamilton and Tworek examine how fake news has had political consequences, whether foreign or domestic. They identify three differences from the past: faster, wider diffusion of fake information; less accountability for its creation; and greater powers of verification for individuals. Fake news has modern characteristics, but while it may pose a greater danger to governance than ever before, we can better assess the phenomenon if we see it in historical perspective.

This is followed by "Not Your Grandpa's Hoax: A Comparative History of Fake News," an essay by Julien Gorbach that first appeared in *American Journalism* in 2018. Gorbach focuses on hoaxes in newspapers, highlighting several over the course of the history of the press to note similarities "in editorial motive or public gullibility, not to mention the blurred lines between deliberate and accidental flimflam." He also explores reasons why they persisted throughout the early days of journalism and why people remain drawn to them today. Gorbach juxtaposes these stories and the reactions to them with the overblown concerns surrounding the role of fake news in the 2016 US presidential election, arguing against over-reaction while urging caution at underestimating the potential power of fake news. As for the concept of fake news itself, Gorbach does not mince words, advocating that we "should recognize the fake news of 2016 as a witches' brew of the worst elements from the very blackest episodes of our past."

Finally, Tworek and Hamilton return to place fake news in the historical, international context with another original piece, "From Early Modern Moon Hoaxes to Nazi Propaganda: A Brief Anthology of Fake News." Using publications dating back to the early 1600s, they highlight three pieces that help showcase the universal concerns surrounding fake news. Over two hundred years before the *Sun*'s moon hoax, playwright Ben Jonson performed for King James I of England, "satirizing the news and the news-hungry" while poking fun at "news consumers' and news producers' gullibility by suggesting they would believe fantastic tales about a world discovered on the moon." Tworek and Hamilton also include excerpts from a 1914 volume by Max Sherover titled *Fakes in American Journalism* and a 1939 talk by Joseph Goebbels on the *Lügenpresse,* all to better explore what they term the "soft underbelly of the Enlightenment: The wonderful opportunity to think independently and communicate widely is accompanied by the terrible opportunity to subvert discourse."

—JOSH GRIMM

NOTES

1. Edson C. Tandoc Jr., Zheng Wei Lim, and Richard Ling, "Defining 'Fake News': A Typology of Scholarly Definitions," *Digital Journalism* 6, no. 2 (2017): 137–53.

2. Emerging Technology from the arXiv, "A mathematical model captures the political impact of fake news," *MIT Technology Review,* www.technologyreview.com/s/612004/a-mathematical-model -captures-the-political-impact-of-fake-news/ (accessed December 2, 2018).

FAKE NEWS

A USABLE HISTORY

John Maxwell Hamilton and Heidi Tworek

I n October 2018, the government of the United Kingdom banned the term "fake news." One of President Donald Trump's favorite phrases now cannot be used in policy documents or official papers produced by one of the United States' closest allies. UK officials have jettisoned the term in favor of "misinformation" or "disinformation." They decried "fake news" as "a poorly-defined and misleading term that conflates a variety of false information, from genuine error through to foreign interference in democratic processes."[1] There are many reasons why this decision makes political sense. But as fraught as the term has become, "fake news" has a long, rich history that is not entirely nefarious and should not be banished from scrutiny by journalists and historians, even if it should be by politicians. At times, faking could be seen positively as a type of embellishment of real-life events.[2] History shows how faking served different political and economic purposes. It reminds us that the real and the fake have never been so easily disentangled as our current political discourse suggests.

Paradoxically, we are in the golden age of studying the history of news. This is a paradox because our age is anything but a golden age for the practice of journalism. Journalism is under assault. Journalists, once secure financially and uncontested in the provision of news, are engaged in intense self-reflection and adjustment. No longer is it a given that advertising revenue will sustain high-quality journalism. No longer, either, is it a given that high-quality editing will fence back blatant misinformation and rumor. Thanks to new liberating technologies, anyone can be a reporter, one's own editor, and one's own newspaper delivery boy or girl. In this welter of half-baked rumor and deliberately planted misinformation, news has become a hazy fungible concept that alters civic discourse. Political leaders around the world discredit inconvenient reports from reputable news media by calling it "fake news."[3] In January 2018, President Donald J. Trump announced his fake news awards, which he amplified with his own assiduous tweeting. That same month Pope Francis called for reflection on fake news's rending of the social and political fabric of modern life. In May, Trump tweeted that "91% of the Network News about me is negative (Fake)," making it clear that he equated media criticism with faking.[4] Tweets like these are why a European High-Level Expert Group on fake news recommended using the term "disinformation" instead.[5]

But the upending of the days when professional journalism was secure opens the way to a more profound historical understanding of it. As Friedrich Hegel observed, "The owl of Minerva only spreads its wings with the falling of dusk." We clearly understand phenomena when they fade into history. With the old verities of journalism under duress, we can ask questions about the past that only a few years ago were considered irrelevant, if not rank heresy.

For much of the twentieth century, Anglo-American journalism was not only clearly established as a profession but also considered a model for other countries to follow if they wished to have a wholesome democracy. That model of journalism took reporting to its highest reaches ever, but was historically anomalous.[6] Journalism arose from a special set of circumstances that were out of sync with its prehistory. Much of what we see today is the past returning in slightly altered versions. The original foreign correspondents of colonial America, for instance, were letter writers whose missives ended up in newspapers. No such thing as a paid reporter existed. Today citizen journalists post stories from all over the world while doing something else for a living, such as working for an NGO or a government. Understanding history helps us see the present in a richer context.

Fine-grained historical analysis can push back against overblown panic about new developments; it can show us what is truly new and what merely lay undetected under the surface for a few decades. To give one example, the division between urban and rural provision of news stretches back at least to the early modern period. Urban centers were the hubs for information and often the main spaces for innovations in news. This was as true in the seventeenth century as it was in the late 1800s.[7] For a few decades in the mid- to late-twentieth century, television and radio compensated for these divisions because they reached almost every American. Over the last decade, the increasing concentration of journalists in major cities and comparatively poor Internet penetration rate in many rural areas have created media conditions that often look more like the early nineteenth century than the 1960s.

As Michael Schudson and Barbie Zelizer recently put it, "To act as if today's fake news environment is fundamentally different from that of earlier times misreads how entrenched fake news and broader attitudes toward fakery have been."[8] The history here can offer a sense of what Frank Gavin has called "chronological proportionality."[9] The current concerns about news that dominate headlines are not necessarily the most important in the long run. It may not be bots or particular items of fake news that matter. It might be the cumulative effect on institutions that is happening behind the scenes. This does not mean we should do nothing about our present moment. But it encourages us to be circumspect and consider where the novelty really lies.

News thus has a usable past, to borrow a phrase Van Wyck Brooks coined in 1915 on the importance of looking at antecedents.[10] Such history helps us to understand the role of news in society in the short and long terms. As Robert Danton has pointed out, public opinion became important in France well before the concept was recognized or defined. Nor did philosophical discussions of public opinion, as expressed in subversive songs about the king, "coincide with the social reality."[11] The same can be said of fake news, which has acquired enormous, but undefined, political power.

Scholarly debates about news and politics long circled around Jürgen Habermas's concept of the "public sphere," meaning the development of places like a coffeehouse where reasoned men would gather in the late eighteenth century to debate public affairs. Habermas argued that the public sphere had been severely weakened in the nineteenth century by the rise of commercial communications technologies like telegraphy and news agencies. He believed that both the technology and the content producers were oligopolistic and stifled wide-ranging debate.[12]

The history of news suggests that another approach may be more fruitful. Rather than thinking about public spheres or publics, we might do better to think about institutions. French sociologist Pierre Bourdieu argued that institutions were the key to linguistic credibility. Words only exerted certain types of power if they were uttered within certain institutions. The words "I do," for example, only marry two people if they are spoken before a person licensed by the state to marry couples.[13] Similarly, institutions have long undergirded the credibility of the media. The declining trust in institutions helps to explain the current concern with fake news as much as other factors like social media platforms.

We agree that fake news has modern characteristics. It may pose a greater danger to governance than ever before. But faking is a long-standing practice that has been pervasive and routine—and a matter of deep concern to those who care about the importance of facts in healthy political discourse.[14] To illuminate this, we look at the three different types of fake news in history and the form of their reappearance today. First, we look at how fake news has benefited the news business—for example, by increasing subscriptions *inside* the news business. Second, the history of medical advertising shows how fake news could financially benefit companies or sectors *outside* the news business. Third, we examine how fake news has had political consequences, whether foreign or domestic. Historical examples help us to differentiate between different types of fake news and understand why they emerged at certain times.

Our frame of reference is not hoaxes and fakes by journalists who made innocent mistakes, although the term "fake news" has been used to cover this. Nor are we concerned with individual journalists who make things up because they are lazy or because they are eager to burnish their reputations with a better story than what they actually have found. We are not interested in William Frances Mannix or Janet Cooke. Mannix was unmasked by a fellow correspondent for concocting stories for the *New York Times* on Cuban rebels while sitting in his Havana hotel room during the Spanish-American War.[15] Mannix made a career of hoaxes as well as diamond swindles. For her part, Cooke made up a heart-wrenching Pulitzer Prize–winning story about an eight-year-old heroin addict. When the Janet Cooke fake was unmasked, the *Washington Post* returned the Pulitzer. We are interested in fake news published with the full knowledge and support of a news entity. This *institutional fake news,* as we call it, has been neither random nor errant. It has been an established feature of news throughout history, as our three examples show.

In May 1902 Ellery Sedgwick, editor of *Frank Leslie's Popular Weekly*, published "A Modern Voyage to Liliput." The story related a curious quirk of nature—that horses bred over long periods in environments of extreme temperatures evolve into "diminutive creatures."[16] The idea for the story, as Sedgwick told it in a charming autobiography, arose from a visit to his editorial offices by one Frank Buffum, who had a theory about how to produce small horses. The theory would not make much of a story, the editor said, but it would be compelling to readers if turned into an account of finding the "kittenish horses" that purported to be real. Tongue in cheek, he wrote in his autobiography that this was a stunt, not a hoax.

"Not for worlds," Sedgwick said, "would I bridge that gap, but to keep that story from falling flat it must be absolutely realistic."[17] The story on Buffum's discovery of the animals on the island of Lliani was full of vivid detail. The horses were, he said, "about the size a Scotch collie dog and weighed, as we judged by lifting them, about fifty pounds each."[18] Long before the word "photoshop" existed, Sedgwick created photographs that, as he put it, "bore lying and emphatic witness."[19] The author claimed to have imported these tiny animals to his Rhode Island farm, and Sedgwick confected a legal attestation on their existence from the made-up "State Committee on Livestock."

The article seems clumsily preposterous today, and Sedgwick thought it would seem so then. The incredible photographs of the horses are reduced images of large, sleek thoroughbreds pasted onto pictures of men and normal horses for putative comparison. To make sure it would seem a farce, Sedgewick introduced an anecdote about a thief running away with a horse under each arm. A postscript said *Leslie's* editors "expressed some incredulity" over the story.[20] The title of the article, "A Modern Voyage to Liliput," with Lilliput misspelled, hollered out that this was a joke.

Alexander Graham Bell, not a man disposed to credulity, was close to being taken in. He wrote his daughter about the article, noting it was highly interesting although he detected "a fishy aspect" that called out for verification.[21] No doubts at all crept into Sedgwick's mail. "In the deluge of letters that followed," he recounted, "there was not a suggestion that the story was a 'spoof.'" Most correspondents were interested in the scientific details. Only one complaint landed on the editor's desk. A man in the horse state of Kentucky took out a bank loan so he and his family could travel to Rhode Island to see the tiny creatures. "The

American mouth is always open," Sedgwick said. "The monstrosities it gulps down outstrip the confines of credulity."[22]

To understand the significance of this story, we need to know three things. First, Sedgwick was one of the great editors of his age. He went on to purchase one of the most esteemed journals in the United States, the *Atlantic Monthly*. No one thought of him as a sleazy editor, even when in 1928 and 1929, as editor of the self-consciously respectable *Atlantic Monthly*, he published—and aggressively promoted—a three-part series on love letters between Abraham Lincoln and Ann Rutledge that were fascinating *and* forgeries. This was not an institutional hoax, but a case of sloppy editorial oversight. Some suspect the perpetrator was William Francis Mannix. Perhaps out of embarrassment at bungling such a serious topic, Sedgwick did not recount this episode in his memoir.

Second, Sedgwick's motivation for running the horse hoax was the need to grow readership. The magazine was sagging financially. The word "popular" in its title, he said, was not even funny as a joke. His rush to publish the "Lincoln the Lover" series seems to have been driven similarly by the thought that the sensational story would add subscriptions during the Christmas gift-giving period. The series, Sedgwick said in an advertisement, "will make an *Atlantic* subscription for the coming year a life-long keepsake –and incidentally a most appropriate Christmas remembrance."[23]

Third, Sedgwick was not an outlier. In rationalizing the *Leslie's* story, he placed himself squarely in a tradition of the journalism that thrived at the time: "Yellow journalism has no law. It lives by two simple rules: first, when there is news, transform it; second where there isn't, make it. There was no news so I made it."[24]

Sedgwick claimed his miniature-horse story was a temporary descent into the yellow journalism that was prevalent at the time. To be sure, sensational newspapers filled their pages with hoaxes, some quite inventive. In 1835, one of the first, suitably with the first penny newspaper, the *New York Sun*, told of the discovery of life on the moon. The *New York Herald* reported the mass escape of all the wild animals in the Central Park Zoo. (The last paragraph gave away the hoax by pointing out that the story aimed to draw attention to the zoo's inadequacies.)[25] But faking was not strictly the province of the yellow press. Sedgwick was engaged in a time-honored activity that extended for many years afterward, as the case of K. Jason Sitewell illustrates.

Saturday Review editor Norman Cousins was as esteemed as Sedgwick when he published on April 1, 1971, a letter to the editor under the name of K. Jason Sitewell. Sitewell called on readers to oppose HR 6142, asserting the legislation was a secret attempt to eliminate golf courses. He claimed the author of the legislation was influenced by tragic deaths in his family. His grandfather died of exhaustion trying to get his golf ball out of a sand trap, and his father perished after hitting nineteen balls into a pond.[26]

Cousins was Sitewell. He often wrote what he called "spoofs" under that name. In his letter, Cousins planted hints, as Sedgwick had done with his tiny horses. The article appeared, after all, on April Fool's Day, and the alleged legislator was named A. F. Day. Yet the response was overwhelmingly credulity, so much so that Cousins thought the episode warranted "a serious major sociological study."[27] Across the country boards of golf clubs held emergency meetings. A leading golf journal reprinted the letter under the headline, "A Frightening Bill." No one challenged Cousins's made-up statistics about the high rate of heart attacks, ulcers, and golf-cart fatalities on the links. So it went until the *Wall Street Journal* exposed the spoof.

Cousins's motivation was also akin to Sedgwick's. He made up an entertaining story to satisfy and build audience. Cousins regarded his fake letter to the editor as the same thing as a humorous cartoon. He was not seeking to fool readers. He was entertaining them, and it worked. He published a book devoted to his hoaxes, *K. Jason Sitewell's Book of Spoofs*.

Alongside faking to raise subscriptions, much fake news in newspapers was meant to boost sales for products outside the news business. We often mistakenly separate advertising too cleanly from news. Modern newspapers relied fundamentally on advertising as well as subscriptions to turn a profit. Historians have generally focused on the news items in newspapers. But advertisements often took up half of the newspaper's space and sometimes even more. The ads themselves often told stories about their products that were akin to news items. Advertisements, including classifieds, were as integral to newspapers as the news.

Newspapers were under no obligation to quality-control their advertisements, and fakery abounded. This was particularly true of medical advertising in the late nineteenth and early twentieth centuries. At this time in the United States, there were two classes of medicine: standard drugs listed in the US Pharmacopoeia and patent medicines, that is, medicines with unknown ingredients and trademarked names. Patent medicines included products like Lydia Pinkham's Vegetable Compound, Hamlin's Wizard Oil, and Kickapoo Indian Sagwa.

The standard drugs were later called "ethical" drugs by the American Medical Association and were not generally advertised to consumers. By contrast, advertisements for patent medicine accounted for around half of newspapers' advertising income around 1900.[28] These advertisements made exaggerated and often knowingly false claims about their products. They also did not disclose ingredients. An advertisement in a newspaper from Salt Lake City in 1881 claimed that Lydia Pinkham's Vegetable Compound could "cure entirely the worst form of female complaints, all ovarian troubles, Inflammation and Ulceration, Falling and Displacements."[29]

Patent medicine advertisements tried to claim that their products were superior to "ethical" drugs and doctors because they were cheaper and easier to understand. Fake medical advertising resonated because it offered simpler, quicker, less painful solutions. Why waste time going to a doctor and getting a complicated prescription written in Latin when Hamlin's Wizard Oil could "break up a cold on the lungs in a night," as one advertisement claimed in a West Virginia paper in 1904.[30]

Medical advertising around 1900 laid the groundwork for men like Edward Bernays, who became known as the "father of public relations" in the interwar period. Bernays claimed to use more sophisticated advertising techniques based on psychoanalysis—he was a double nephew of Freud—to sell products to consumers. Bernays used doctors as experts to claim health benefits for all sorts of products, including bacon as a breakfast food. Bernays also launched major campaigns to persuade women to smoke cigarettes in public. Many of the advertisements claimed health benefits for cigarettes, such as curing coughs.[31]

In this period, others created demand for products to solve problems that did not quite exist before advertising invented them. Advertisers like J. Walter Thompson turned to American behavioral psychology to play on the public's fears and urge them to buy goods. Listerine, for example, started life as a disinfectant for the battlefield and a floor cleaner. In the 1920s, the manufacturer advertised the liquid as a cure for "halitosis," an "ominously clinical-sounding" condition that was "largely unheard of" before Listerine's advertising campaigns.[32]

Relief from the more egregious ads came with federal regulation. The Pure Food and Drug Act of 1906, the first federal drug legislation, provided guidelines for product labeling so that consumers could receive more reliable information. The Sherley Amendment of 1912 outlawed labels with false therapeutic claims that were meant to defraud consumers. Of course, it was hard to prove prior intent, and these regulations initially had little effect on medical advertising.

After one hundred people died taking a drug called elixir sulfanilamide, the Food, Drug, and Cosmetic Act (FDCA) was passed in 1938. Now, manufacturers had to prove that a drug was safe, and drugs needed FDA approval before being marketed. Drug labeling was also required to be more extensive.

The 1938 act drastically changed medicine, and medical advertising. "Ethical" drugs, or what we now call prescription drugs, increasingly dominated the market, rising from 32 percent of consumer spending on pharmaceuticals in 1929 to 57 percent in 1949 to 83 percent by 1969.[33] Medical advertising saw an inverse development. Pharmaceutical companies moved away from direct advertising to consumers and focused ever more on doctors, who could prescribe medicine. In the early 1930s, before the passage of the FDCA, pharmaceutical companies aimed over 90 percent of marketing at patients rather than doctors; the inverse was true by the 1960s.[34] This affected how medical advertising functioned (though it hasn't completely stopped false claims, as we have seen with assertions about the nonaddictive nature of opioids made by pharmaceutical companies in the 1990s). Regardless, the FDCA removed many of the false claims that newspaper consumers had long encountered in their daily perusal of the paper.

Late-nineteenth- and early twentieth-century consumers prized their "sacred right" to self-medication and self-information, mainly through word of mouth and medical advertising. Federal regulation in the first decades of the twentieth century fundamentally changed both consumers' understanding of medicine and advertising in news. This has to stand as a benchmark of what can be done when there is a will to make a correction. Regulation alone was insufficient; societal attitudes had to change, too. The emergence of a professional advertising profession played a role in this. Wanting respectability for itself and for the branded products they sold, they fought against spurious product promotion. They also prized high-quality, fact-based news because it also lent validity to their products by association. Faking does not always have to beget more faking.

Although news and advertising often misrepresented or falsified events and claims for financial gain, news could be faked for political purposes, too. Just like today, faked news could have domestic or international ramifications.

In the United States in 1942, tens of thousands of white southerners believed the rumor that First Lady Eleanor Roosevelt was organizing black women into secret "Eleanor clubs." These clubs were purportedly planning to force white women in the future to cook and clean for black women, who were the main domestic servants at the time. Although the rumors were wholly false, they appeared in multiple regional newspapers. An undereducated and inward-looking population fearful of demographic change coupled with a fractured political system made the South ripe for rumormongering.[35]

Fake news spread internationally at least as early as fifteenth-century blood libel accusations.[36] Though the amount has ebbed and flowed ever since, states and groups have long used fake news to try to influence international politics.

Journalists were fed disinformation about the Bolsheviks in the form of the Sisson Documents in 1918, named for the US government propagandist who acquired them from anti-Bolshevik elements in Petrograd and then oversaw their distribution in the United States and abroad, the latter through fellow American propagandists. These forged papers aimed to delegitimize the Soviet government by purporting that Lenin and his comrades were German agents. Like the best fake news, the papers contained an element of suspected truth, namely that the Germans did give financial support to the Bolsheviks. It left out the nuance that virtually every Russia party had taken foreign money and that the Bolsheviks were seeking to spark a revolution in Germany. The documents were endorsed by leading news organizations across the country. Their release by the Wilson administration coincided with and helped validate the United States' decision to join with the Allies in launching an invasion of Russia. It also oxygenated the administration's communist witch hunt immediately after the war.[37]

The outbreak of World War II two decades later also relied upon an elaborate scheme to falsify news. To provide a pretext for invading Poland, Gestapo director Reinhard Heydrich ordered SS troops to disguise themselves as Poles and attack the German radio tower at Gleiwitz. This attack on August 31, 1939, became known as the Gleiwitz Incident. The organizer of the incident, Alfred Naujocks, revealed at the Nuremberg trials after the war that Heydrich had justified the false flag attack by saying that "actual proof of these attacks of the Poles is needed for the foreign press, as well as for German propaganda purposes."[38]

Much of the fake news put out today on the Web, especially health advertising, combines commercial and political incentives. Right-wing agitator Alex Jones came to prominence with claims that the Sandy Hook Elementary School massacre was a hoax. On his website, *InfoWars,* and his accompanying talk radio show, Jones has propagated multiple conspiracy theories. He was a fringe character until the 2016 presidential election, when Donald Trump validated Jones by appearing on his show. Jones has continued to spread conspiracy theories, including Pizzagate, and he still seems to have the ear of the president. Jones's political clout curiously has facilitated a throwback to overhyped nineteenth-century medicine advertisements. The sale of vitamin supplements is his chief source of income. "It's like QVC for conspiracy," a former Jones employee said, referring to a popular television shopping channel. Estimates of Jones's sales ranged between fifteen and twenty-five million dollars over two years. They were also sold at a massive markup and mostly contained "ineffective blends of vitamins and minerals that have been sold in stores for ages," a BuzzFeed investigation found in October 2017.[39] This is less novel than it at first appears.

These historical precedents and parallels should not obscure that we face somewhat different challenges today. Rather, it helps us to look at our current problems from a new perspective. We identify three differences from the past: faster, wider diffusion of fake information; less accountability for its creation; and greater powers of verification for individuals.

Fake news has become a sophisticated weapon in domestic and foreign politics, though it often worked that way in the past as well. Still, the diffusion of fake news today is much easier and faster. Previous communications technologies were generally one-way, or at least it took a while for readers or consumers to send their opinions back to news producers. They came to Sedgwick in the mail. Television and radio were one-to-many technologies with a central network disseminating information to many consumers. Now, the Internet and social media have enabled many-to-many diffusion of information.

This development has given the audience much more power than it had in the past. News consumers have many more choices. Before, they read local papers—and those decreased in most communities to one or perhaps two dailies in the last half of the twentieth century. They had local radio news, fed by a small number of networks that also controlled the three national television outlets until the rise of twenty-four-hour TV news channels in the 1980s. They could subscribe to a national magazine. The term "exponential growth" is often just an exaggeration, but in the case of media choices available today, it is an understatement.

The wider range of choice allows space for a wider range of voices. But many-to-many information infrastructure also offers simpler methods to spread or amplify false material. Users are influenced by the popularity of a news item or headline, whether through the number of comments, likes, or retweets. Russian-affiliated groups can, for example, easily create or purchase pro-Trump bots on Twitter. Celebrities can (and do) easily buy fake followers on the social media black market to boost their apparent popularity.[40] Estimates vary, but between 15 and 20 percent of Twitter users may be fake or bots. Because Twitter's business model relies on user numbers and engagement, the company has less incentive to root out all the bots. Huge numbers of followers and large numbers of retweets provide apparent social proof for a statement that amplifies its effects. Rather than relying on neighbors, friends, or colleagues to decide what to read (the classic two-step model of communications influence), many users rely on social proof engineered by technology. In contrast, we can find no evidence that Sedgwick's horse story was picked up. The more sensational moon hoax got a little more play (it appeared in pamphlet form in Europe), but that took many weeks, and key players involved were unaware of this.[41]

Our current technological engineering extends to the algorithms providing news. If you have a propensity for some bias, subsequent disinformation comes to you without your asking for it. The very structure of social media platforms also seems to enable false news to spread faster than truth. Cathy O'Neil called algorithms "weapons of math destruction" for a reason.[42] Still, human nature also plays a role. A study by MIT scientists on Twitter stories from 2006 to 2016 showed that false stories were 70 percent likelier to be retweeted than true ones. This was due to human retweeting rather than bots.[43]

While these developments are concerning, historical precedents caution us not to assume that every aspect is utterly brand-new. Often it is a matter of degree.

News spread quickly in cities in the early twentieth century. Newspapers used to print one-sheet extras when important breaking news occurred. An extra could make it onto the streets within ten to fifteen minutes of a newspaper receiving the bulletin. News hawkers stood on the street, screaming out the breaking news to encourage passersby to purchase their bulletins. Newspapers in major cities like Berlin might have four or more editions a day. It was possible to buy a newspaper with the latest reporting at any time of day. The key difference was between rural and urban areas. There might have been multiple editions of newspapers every day in cities; some rural areas had only one newspaper, printed once a week.

The distinction between urban and rural areas remains relevant today. Around 20 percent of the US population is "ruralized" as far as the Internet is concerned, mostly older people, or citizens in rural areas. (Indeed, the demise of local news is also pronounced in towns and small cities across the country, making 1,300 communities "news deserts.")[44] Journalists and communications scholars also tend to forget the basic, but crucial, fact that only about 20 percent of the US population are active monthly users of Twitter. One study on the 2016 election indicated that many voters listened to the radio and watched TV more than using social media. Only 14 percent of voters in one survey listed social media as their most important source of news. Television (cable, network, and local) was much more important for many people. Thus, framing on "traditional" media had much more effect in determining voting patterns.[45] Talk radio in particular deserves more attention. It's hard to estimate the total number of listeners on talk radio, but Rush Limbaugh alone attracts around 14 million weekly listeners.[46] While there are many top-rated conservative talk radio hosts like Limbaugh, Glenn Beck, and Laura Ingraham, there is only one popular progressive host—Thom Hartmann.

While we know who the major talk radio hosts are, the Internet creates online spaces with far less accountability and far more anonymity. In media organizations, people who put out the information—and editors—had to take responsibility. The sources of fake news don't have to reveal themselves. Much of the most despicable fake news originally appears without any obvious patrimony. Sedgwick could not hide after his midget-horse hoax. He took furious abuse from the man who took out a bank loan in order to visit Rhode Island. He was accountable. Sedgwick had an investigation done of the Lincoln fakes and published it and published a critique of the forgeries by one of his toughest critics.

Journalists still assiduously correct mistakes, even if Trump has conflated correction with fake news. One journalist quickly corrected his mistaken assertion that Trump had removed the Martin Luther King bust from the Oval Office. Trump gave the incident a fake news award.

Despite this, it is far easier for readers to find out whether Trump is right. Readers can graze through multiple media to check out a story for other perspectives. They can rely on specialized media fact-checking sites. Again, such efforts to correct the record are not new. *Newsbook,* created in 1908, was one of many publications designed to help readers "pick the truth form the mass of reports that were not true."[47] Similar efforts were made in the *Columbia Journalism Review* and the *Washington Journalism Review.* But they are dwarfed by the media-checking outlets that exist today.

Of course, the value of such availability is predicated on citizens using the tools to fact-check the news. This is not done enough, and it is not easy. While it is easier to fact-check, few people possess the time, skill, or, frankly, the desire to identify what is true. In every case where public intellectuals critique the news—from Walter Lippmann in *Public Opinion* to modern calls for media literacy—the same solution always emerges: better education. If it may seem too facile at times, it is nevertheless an essential ingredient in combatting fake news. Better intermediaries—Lippmann spoke of this too—helps. But someone has to press a button to see what the fact-checkers say—and then double-check *them.*

In thinking why this matters, it is worthwhile to point out that aggressive self-policing by news media has perversely given its critics new cudgels with which to beat responsible journalists. "Ah-ha," critics say, often when they are the object of the erring article, "the whole story is fake news." It is no coincidence that the Trump "fake news awards" were given to news organizations' reporting that had swiftly corrected their errors.[48] (Seventh on Trump's list was one CNN story about Anthony Scaramucci's meeting with a Russian that led to three reporters being fired. Subsequently the *New York Times* found the CNN reporters had been right.)[49]

There is deep irony in this situation. Users have more ability to verify the news than ever. Theoretically any reader of any article can swiftly find secondary sources to check claims in an article. This empowers "the people formerly known as the audience," as Jay Rosen calls news consumers. But it may also make them overly skeptical of media institutions. A greater awareness of errors (for example, corrections at the bottom of online articles rather than separated by several days' worth of printed newspapers) means that media seem less reliable when the very opposite is probably true.

The BBC's media editor, Amol Rajan, gave a lecture in March 2018 on the role of journalism in the twenty-first century and how journalists might address the "crisis of trust" in the media. Rajan proposed that fake news was "a genuine and relatively new phenomenon," which he defined as "deliberate lies told for political or commercial purposes transmitted around the world through social media." Rajan drew a distinction between "fake news" and what he called "false news"—the bogus stories circulated for decades by the tabloid press, often about celebrities. The main difference between fake and false news, Rajan argued, was the "deployment of digital technology."[50]

It's understandable why Rajan made this distinction between past and present. It's what almost everyone is arguing. As we have shown, however, the sentiment is fundamentally flawed. Yes, there is novelty in how falsified news operates today. But much unites it with the past.

Ironically, a BuzzFeed journalist swiftly uncovered that Rajan himself had "delivered fake news in a lecture about fake news." One of Rajan's key anecdotes about the easy manipulation of internet algorithms was untrue.[51] Prior to this discovery, various Twitter pundits were touting Rajan as a possible next director of BBC News. Now, we will have to wait and see if an apparent genuine mistake—not real fake news, as it were—undermines Rajan's credibility in general. Regardless, it illustrates our point that the Internet provides swifter verification processes and that media-literate readers might need to learn what journalists are supposed to know—proportionality. They need to know that a mistake is not fake news and that correction is a sign of reliability, not perfidy. They need skill in discriminating a fake story from a mistaken one.

We have old-new problems that have caused some entertaining journalism in the past but which also can sunder a democracy. What people know and how they know it go to the heart of the democratic process. So does a belief that one must have access to facts on which to base judgments. The rat-a-tat-tat of fake news, some of it not fake at all, but described that way by those who find legitimate news inconvenient, is eating away at the institutions that sustain our democracy. Not just serious journalism has lost credibility, so have the judiciary, the legislature, and the executive branch as a result of fake news tactics. In a profound sense, media literacy is not just *media* literacy, it is *political* literacy as well.

A useful way to think about this is in terms of growing information disequilibrium. First, institutional credibility is harmed by the massive ability to lie. When lying is massive and highly diffused, it tends to crowd out legitimate information and call legitimate institutions into question. In this environment, it is easier for new fake news to find purchase. Second, the massive ability to target groups effectively "atomizes" society, as Tom Rosenstiel has noted.[52] This paradox—wide diffusion to narrow audiences—has changed the public square, where people had to pass each other in their daily news wanderings, to colonies of like-minded people who want nothing to do with each other. The political purveyors of fake news have a far greater ability to divide us, though recent evidence suggests that most people online are exposed to a wide variety of news sources.[53]

"In journalism," Sedgwick said, "the standard is everything." But standards are under assault. News gates manned by editorial gatekeepers still exist in legacy media. David Manning White conducted a seminal study on gatekeeping in 1950. He noted the subjectivity that crept into the process.[54] But it was never as bad as now, when putative journalists operate on vast fields where there are neither gates nor fences. Governments have also elevated various types of fakery to a common practice as part of foreign policy. Because they are governments, they have tremendous firepower. The Internet has also enabled a far lower barrier to entry for fakery.

Still, some of our examples from the past offer glimmers of hope. Institutions have acted in the past to shore up credibility. Governments reacted to the peddling of bogus products by regulating medical labeling and creating new agencies for control such as the Food and Drug Administration. And now the British government has mounted an attack on the expression "fake news." This and other efforts to combat the modern phenomenon are a start in shoring up institutional credibility by the institutions that must be preserved if democracy is to function. We need to remember that the old interventions took years to formulate, and so will these new ones.

NOTES

1. Digital Culture, Media and Sport Committee, "Disinformation and 'Fake News': Interim Report: Government Response to the Committee's Fifth Report" (October 9, 2018), publications.parliament .uk/pa/cm201719/cmselect/cmcumeds/1630/163002.htm (accessed October 25, 2018).

2. Andie Tucher, "'I Believe in Faking': The Dilemma of Photographic Realism at the Dawn of Photojournalism," *Photography and Culture* 10, no. 3 (2017): 195–214.

3. On definitions, see Edson C. Tandoc Jr., Zheng Wei Lim, and Richard Ling, "Defining 'Fake News': A Typology of Scholarly Definitions," *Digital Journalism* 6, no. 2 (2017): 137–53.

4. Dara Lind, "President Donald Trump finally admits that "fake news" just means news he doesn't like," *Vox,* May 9, 2018, www.vox.com/policy-and-politics/2018/5/9/17335306/trump-tweet -twitter-latest-fake-news-credentials.

5. European Commission, "Final Report of the High Level Expert Group on Fake News and Online Disinformation," March 12, 2018, ec.europa.eu/digital-single-market/en/news/final-report -high-level-expert-group-fake-news-and-online-disinformation.

6. John Maxwell Hamilton and Heidi J. S. Tworek, "The Natural History of the News: An Epigenetic Study," *Journalism: Theory, Critique, Practice* 18, no. 4 (2017): 391–407.

7. On the role of cities, see Terhi Rantanen, "The Cosmopolitanization of News," *Journalism Studies* 6 (2007): 843–61. On journalistic innovation in urban environments in the late nineteenth century, see David Paul Nord, "The Urban Newspaper and the Victorian City," in Richard R. John and Jonathan Silberstein-Loeb, eds., *Making News: The Political Economy of Journalism in Britain and America from the Glorious Revolution to the Internet* (Oxford, UK: Oxford University Press, 2015), 73–106. On how cities and media mutually constituted each other in a German context, see Peter Fritzsche, *Reading Berlin 1900* (Cambridge, MA: Harvard University Press, 2000).

8. Michael Schudson and Barbie Zelizer, "Fake News in Context," in *Understanding and Addressing the Disinformation Ecosystem,* firstdraftnews.org/wp-content/uploads/2018/03/The -Disinformation-Ecosystem-20180207-v2.pdf, p. 2.

9. Frank Gavin, *Five Ways to Use History Well* (San Francisco: Long Now Foundation Lecture Series, 2010).

10. Van Wyck Brooks, "On Creating a Usable Past," *The Dial,* April 11, 1918, 337–41.

11. Robert Danton, *Poetry and the Police: Communication Networks in Eighteenth-Century Paris* (Cambridge, MA: Harvard University Press, 2010), 134.

12. Jürgen Habermas, *Structural Transformation of the Public Sphere: An Inquiry into a Category of Bourgeois Society* (Cambridge, UK: Polity, 1962).

13. Pierre Bourdieu, *Language and Symbolic Power,* ed. John B. Thompson (Cambridge, UK: Polity, 1991). On Bourdieu, Habermas, and journalism, see Heidi Tworek, "Oligopolies of the Past? Habermas, Bourdieu, and Conceptual Approaches to News Agencies," *Journalism: Theory, Criticism, Practice* (forthcoming).

14. Two books by journalists who were concerned with the problem are George Bronson Rae's *Facts and Fakes About Cuba* (New York: George Munro's Sons, 1897), which looks at bogus reporting of the Spanish-American War, and Max Sheerover's *Fakes in American Journalism* (New York: Buffalo Publishing Co., 1914).

15. Rae, *Facts and Fakes,* 163–64.

16. David Buffum, "A Modern Voyage to Liliput," *Frank Leslie's Popular Monthly,* May 1902, 40.

17. Ellery Sedgwick, *The Happy Profession* (Boston: Little, Brown, 1946), 118.

18. Buffum, "A Modern Voyage to Liliput," 44.

19. Sedgwick, *The Happy Profession,* 121.

20. Editor's note, Buffum, "A Modern Voyage to Liliput," 49.

21. Bell to Marian Bell Fairchild, July 22, 1902, Alexander Graham Bell Family Papers, Manuscript Division, Library of Congress.

22. Sedgwick, *The Happy Profession,* 125.

23. Madelyn K. Duhon, "Journalist and Hoaxer: William Francis Mannix and the Long History of Fake News," MS thesis, Louisiana State University, May 2017, 86.

24. Sedgwick, *The Happy Profession,* 116.

25. Curtis D. MacDougall, *Hoaxes* (New York: Ace Books, 1958), 240.

26. The hoax along with the letter to the editor and the responses to it are in Norman Cousins, *K. Jason Sitewell's Book of Spoofs* (New York: E. P. Dutton, 1989), chap. 3.

27. Norman Cousins, "The Decline and Fall of Congressman Day," *Golfdom,* June 1971, 33.

28. James Harvey Young, *The Toadstool Millionaires: A Social History of Patent Medicines in America before Federal Regulation* (Princeton, NJ: Princeton University Press, 1961).

29. Julie Donohue, "A History of Drug Advertising: The Evolving Roles of Consumers and Consumer Protection," *Milbank Quarterly* 84, no. 4 (2006): 664–66.

30. *Sistersville* (WV) *Daily Oil Review,* July 11, 1904, *Chronicling America: Historic American Newspapers,* chroniclingamerica.loc.gov/lccn/sn86092356/1904-07-11/ed-1/seq-4/.

31. Edward Bernays, *Propaganda* (1928; Brooklyn, NY: Ig Publishing, 2005).

32. Tim Wu, *The Attention Merchants: The Epic Scramble to Get Inside Our Heads* (New York: Knopf Doubleday, 2017), 55.

33. Peter Temin, *Taking Your Medicine: Drug Regulation in the United States* (Cambridge, MA: Harvard University Press, 1980), 4.

34. Donohue, "A History of Drug Advertising," 668–69.

35. Joshua Zeitz, "Lessons from the Fake News Pandemic of 1942," *Politico,* March 12, 2017, www.politico.com/magazine/story/2017/03/lessons-from-the-fake-news-pandemic-of-1942-214898.

36. Jacob Soll, "The Long and Brutal History of Fake News," *Politico,* December 18, 2016, www.politico.com/magazine/story/2016/12/fake-news-history-long-violent-214535.

37. George F. Kennan, "The Sisson Documents," *Journal of Modern History* 28, no. 2 (1956): 130–54.

38. *Nuremberg Trial Proceedings,* vol. 4, 24th Day, December 20, 1945, Morning Session, 242, avalon.law.yale.edu/imt/12-20-45.asp.

39. Charlie Warzel, "We Sent Alex Jones' InfoWars Supplements to a Lab. Here's What's in Them," *BuzzFeed,* August 9, 2017, www.buzzfeed.com/charliewarzel/we-sent-alex-jones-infowars-supplements-to-a-lab-heres?

40. Nicholas Confessore, Gabriel J. X. Dance, Richard Harris, and Mark Hansen, "The Follower Factory," *New York Times,* January 27, 2018, www.nytimes.com/interactive/2018/01/27/technology/social-media-bots.html.

41. Paul Maliszewski, "Paper Moon," *Lapham's Quarterly,* 2018, 93.

42. Cathy O'Neil, *Weapons of Math Destruction: How Big Data Increases Inequality and Threatens Democracy* (New York: Crown, 2016).

43. The study examined only stories that had been featured on fact-checking websites; Robinson Meyer, "The Grim Conclusions of the Largest-Ever Study of Fake News," *The Atlantic,* March 8, 2018, www.theatlantic.com/technology/archive/2018/03/largest-study-ever-fake-news-mit-twitter/555104/.

44. Tom Stites, "About 1,300 U.S. Communities have Totally Lost News Coverage, UNC News Desert Study Finds," *Poynter,* October 15, 2018, www.poynter.org/business-work/2018/about-1300-u-s -communities-have-totally-lost-news-coverage-unc-news-desert-study-finds/.

45. Hunt Allcott and Matthew Gentzkow, "Social Media and Fake News in the 2016 Election," National Bureau of Economic Research, www.nber.org/papers/w23089.pdf. On how *New York Times* coverage focused on Clinton's e-mails as a scandal far more than any Trump scandal and how coverage of scandals far outweighed coverage of policies, see Duncan Watts and David Rothschild, "Don't Blame the Election on Fake News: Blame It on the Media," *Columbia Journalism Review,* December 5, 2017, www.cjr.org/analysis/fake-news-media-election-trump.php.

46. On the history of talk radio, see Brian Rosenwald, *Talk Radio's America: How an Industry Took over a Political Party that Took over the United States* (Cambridge, MA: Harvard University Press, 2019).

47. George Creel, *Rebel at Large* (New York: G. P. Putnam, 1947), 74. The alert reader will note that Creel became a leading American propagandist in World War I.

48. Jen Kirby and Libby Nelson, "The 'Winners' of Trump's Fake News Awards, Annotated," *Vox,* January 17, 2018, www.vox.com/2018/1/17/16871430/trumps-fake-news-awards-annotated.

49. Sonam Sheth, "There's Been a New Twist in a Controversial CNN Story That Led to the Firing of 3 Journalists Last Year," *Business Insider,* March 7, 2018, www.businessinsider.com/cnn-russia -scaramucci-dmitriev-meeting-new-details-2018–3?r=UK&IR=T.

50. Amol Rajan, "The Tortoise and the Share," *BBC News,* March 5, 2018, www.bbc.com/news /amp/entertainment-arts-43230640?

51. Mark Di Stefano, "The BBC's Media Editor Appears to Have Delivered Fake News in a Lecture about Fake News," *BuzzFeed,* March 6, 2018, www.buzzfeed.com/markdistefano/one-direction?

52. Tom Rosenstiel, "The 2018 John Breaux Symposium: An Anatomy of Fake News," May 3, 2018, gspm.gwu.edu/sites/g/files/zaxdzs2286/f/downloads/2018BreauxSymposium%5B1%5D.pdf.

53. Joshua Tucker et al., "Social Media, Political Polarization, and Political Disinformation: A Review of the Scientific Literature" (Rochester, NY: Social Science Research Network, March 21, 2018), papers.ssrn.com/abstract=3144139.

54. David Manning White, "The 'Gate Keeper': A Case Study in the Selection of News," *Journalism Bulletin* 27 (1950): 383–90.

NOT YOUR GRANDPA'S HOAX

A COMPARATIVE HISTORY OF FAKE NEWS

Julien Gorbach

O n October 20, 2016, *BuzzFeed* broke the story of a twenty-first-century media phenomenon that appeared to be as disturbing as it was transforma-tional: the onslaught of "fake news" during a presidential election.[1] At first, *BuzzFeed*'s report garnered little attention. But the election of Donald Trump three weeks later, followed within forty-eight hours by CEO Mark Zuckerberg's assertion that it was "a pretty crazy idea" to suggest Facebook had delivered Trump's victory, opened the floodgates. Hundreds of articles and editorials over the next two months clanged the alarm that fake news was the *Götterdämmerung* of democratic societies in the Information Age.[2]

In an interview with the *New Yorker,* President Barack Obama decried a media ecosystem where "everything is true and nothing is true," in which the capacity to spread lies and wild conspiracy theories and to caricature political op-ponents without any rebuttal made it nearly impossible to have a rational discus-sion.[3] That ecosystem "seems to have evolved into a near-perfect environment for fake news to thrive," *New York Times* CEO Mark Thompson said in December.[4] "This year, the adage that 'falsehood flies and the truth comes limping after it' doesn't begin to describe the problem," the *New York Times* editorial page noted abjectly. "That idea assumes that the truth eventually catches up."[5]

Yet fake stories are hardly new to journalism, and a sense of historical per-spective is clarifying. Fiction disguised as a fact dates back to what some media historians consider the very birth of the journalistic report in 1722, when readers mistook Daniel Defoe's *A Journal of the Plague Year* to be a true memoir. Perhaps the most wildly successful hoax in American history caught fire just as the Penny Press of the 1830s was first introducing "news" as we now understand it—as everyday stories written for popular consumption.[6]

Writing for *Columbia Journalism Review* in mid-December of 2016, David Uberti surveyed this history and cautioned doomsayers to take a deep breath. "A little bit of brake-tapping may be in order," he wrote. "It's worth remembering, in the middle of the great fake news panic of 2016, America's very long tradition of news-related hoaxes. A thumbnail history shows marked similarities to today's fakery in editorial motive or public gullibility, not to mention the blurred lines between deliberate and accidental flimflam. It also suggests that the recent fixation on fake news has more to do with macro-level trends than any new brand of faux content."[7]

To drive home the point that there is nothing new under the sun, Uberti quoted an 1807 letter from the original champion of the American press himself, Thomas Jefferson: "Nothing can now be believed which is seen in a newspaper. Truth itself becomes suspicious by being put into that polluted vehicle." Sure, Uberti argued, people now recovering from the shellshock of the 2016 election are alarmed about today's "polluted vehicle"—that great powerhouse known as "the media" of the twenty-first century. It is true that wild conspiracy theories whip between social networks at the speed of light. But this is really just a return to a longer-term norm, to life without a mainstream media controlling the conversation. "The existence of an independent, powerful, widely respected news media establishment is an historical anomaly," Georgetown Professor Jonathan Ladd wrote in his 2011 book, *Why Americans Hate the Media and How It Matters*. "Prior to the twentieth century, such an institution had never existed in American history."[8]

Months later, Uberti was eager to walk back his anodyne assessment, but it is still worth testing his original hypothesis. Is all this hand-wringing an overreaction? The following thumbnail history reveals three key insights. First, in contrast to other incarnations of fake news—or hoaxes, as they have traditionally been known—the flood of it in 2016 was of a far more *deliberate* than accidental kind of flimflam. Second, comparably dark periods in American media history illustrate why our recent and ongoing fake news is a highly toxic cocktail of the worst spirits we have seen, and thus poses a multiplicity of threats to democracy.

Finally, and most crucially, while Uberti stressed similarities to the past, it is also worth considering *the difference* in stakes now: nineteenth-century societies did not have to reckon with the same risks of global catastrophe.

While one might naturally have assumed that political ideology was the driving force behind the recent spate of what *BuzzFeed* called "hyperpartisan" fake news, investigative reporting by the *Guardian, Wired,* and other outlets revealed that, from Macedonia to California, profit was the primary motive.[9] Another theme common among the entrepreneurs, however, was: "I don't call it fake news; I call it satire."[10] *Denver Guardian* creator Jestin Coler, who said he pays twenty to twenty-five writers, claimed that he started out intending to expose the extremism of the alt-right.[11] In other words, according to some culprits, spreading fake news is a way of telling the truth. But if that was the case, why was so much investigation required to track down Coler and the others, and get them to come clean?

Analyses of fake news published both before and after 2016 have emphasized a distinction between more innocent varieties and outright fraud. In a 2010 study titled "The Art of the Hoax," Chris Fleming and John O'Carroll argued: "One useful way of dividing varieties of hoax is in terms of their relationship to deception. We call anything that seeks to deceive a hoax, despite the fact that some are structured to make a point (and can only do this by being revealed or discovered), whereas others are more akin to fraud, and are designed to conceal their very existence from discovery at any stage." As for the former, more benign variety: "The hoax *lies in order to tell the truth.*"[12] Similarly, "Defining Fake News: A Typology of Scholarly Definitions," published in 2017 by Tandoc, Lim, and Ling, identified six varieties of false news that had been examined in thirty-four studies since 2003, and distinguished between high and low levels of "intent to deceive." Fabricated stories and propaganda rate high in deception, for example, whereas parody and satire rate low.[13]

Whether the intent to deceive is high or low, however, money is always a primary motivator. Given the rich tradition of parody and satire in journalism, literary hoaxing is, at first blush, clearly distinct from more naked grabs for profit. The humorous and curious stunts of such luminaries as Benjamin Franklin, Edgar Allan Poe, and Mark Twain would seem to bear little resemblance to the notorious journalistic frauds perpetrated by Janet Cooke, Stephen Glass, and Jayson Blair or phony sensations concocted to sell newspapers. The six-part moon hoax of 1835, which is possibly the most successful ploy in history and certainly among the most legendary, was a straightforward bid for newsstand sales, the pre-digital, print-era version of clickbait. But in fact, the literary hoax was also a purely commercial endeavor, even if the most talented writers were able to make readers forget that. Franklin, Twain, and Poe all straddled the line between journalism and literature, and hoaxing was their stock and trade.

Profitable or not, some of the earliest known examples of hoaxing were also actually impressive feats of truth-telling. To expose London astrologers as charlatans, eighteenth-century British satirist Jonathan Swift soberly prophesied the imminent death of the city's most prominent seer, John Partridge. While Partridge angrily insisted that he was very much alive, the popularity of Swift's comical soothsayer, Isaac Bickerstaff, flourished across Europe.[14] Benjamin Franklin's career as a hoaxster started in much the same vein. His "Witch Trial at Mount Holly," published in the *Pennsylvania Gazette* on October 22, 1730, reported dancing sheep and Psalm-singing hogs to ridicule superstitions about witchcraft.[15]

Franklin, a man with peerless business acumen, achieved a fortune through hoaxing, stealing a page from Swift in doing so. He adopted the Bickerstaff-like identity of impoverished scholar Richard Saunders to pen *Poor Richard's Almanack,* in which he foretold the demise of rival almanac author Titan Leeds. Like Swift's poor victim astrologer, Leeds furiously protested that he was not dead, while sales of *Poor Richard's* brought Franklin wealth and fame.[16] Franklin directed the same caustic satire at business rivals to build the *Pennsylvania Gazette* into the most popular newspaper of the colonies.

In the nineteenth century, hoaxes would prove an effective means of generating both cash and the right kind of notoriety. Edgar Allan Poe devised six hoaxes for income, but although they displayed his genius for macabre storytelling, his record of monetary success was mixed. Few people were fooled by his moon hoax, perhaps because as he later admitted, it was "a sketchy trifle," written "in a tone of banter."[17] But he was also the victim of bad luck. After Poe's June 1835 installment of "The Unparalleled Adventures of One Hans Pfaal" appeared in the *Southern Literary Messenger,* the rest of the series never made it to print because, in late August, Richard Locke's moon hoax created an unprecedented sensation. As Poe himself acknowledged, Locke's hoax caught on because it was a far more cunning contraption. Even to the modern reader, the careful, realistic details of the early installments made it seem believable.[18]

By the time the story grew truly outlandish, readers were hooked. *Sun* publisher Benjamin Day had anticipated a huge demand for Locke's moon hoax story, but the first installment quickly sold out—a copy could not be found at any price. The press was soon running at full capacity, ten hours a day, as sales increased with each new installment, and it still could not keep up with the demand. The world's first penny paper, the *Sun* had originally achieved a circulation of 4,000 in 1833, outpacing all other New York papers. By the time Day published the article describing an alien race of bat-men fornicating on exotic moon tundra, circulation had shot up to 19,360, making the *Sun* the most popular newspaper on Earth. The rival and more respectable six-cent papers were embarrassed and rushed to catch up with the important story, reprinting it without crediting the original. European newspapers picked up the news as well, thus exciting and deceiving "almost the whole reading world."[19]

The *Sun* confessed to their ploy by mid-September, and until the end of the century, newspaper hoaxsters seemed to have mostly maintained faith with the public. A comparably effective ruse by the *Herald* contained an admission of guilt within the story itself. The November 9, 1874, headline announced: "AWFUL CALAMITY," "The Wild Animals Broken Loose from Central Park," "TERRIBLE SCENES OF MUTILATION." In 10,000 words of white-hot prose, the story reported carnage that ensued after an enraged rhinoceros broke free from his cage, trampled and impaled zoo keepers, and smashed open dozens of other cages. Police and crowds fell back as herds of deadly beasts assaulted them. Elephants went on rampages, monkeys clinging to their backs. The National Guard was called in. The story included a tally of casualties: thirty-two people killed, eighteen injured, and fifty-nine animals slaughtered. Then the final paragraph of the lengthy article explained: "Of course, the entire story given above is a pure fabrication. Not one word of it is true." The *Herald* warned, however, that the zoo was in such poor condition that a true calamity might happen at any time.[20]

If the moon story had shown the tolerance of readers for a good-natured hoax, the zoo story revealed their capacity to forgive. It also demonstrated the power of fake news to sow chaos. The *Herald*'s tacked-on justification in the name of public safety had hardly made a difference, as the paper learned a new lesson: People rarely read to the bottom. Managing Editor Thomas B. Connery found that his own wife had kept his children from school that morning as panic swept the streets. One of the writers, Joseph I. C. Clarke, recalled mothers rushing to take crying, terrified children from school. The police were overwhelmed by calls. Fury rained on the newspaper, but despite the criticisms and vows to cancel subscriptions, the *Herald* did not lose a single subscriber, and circulation actually increased.[21]

The *Herald*'s Central Park Zoo misadventure may have been wildly irresponsible, but in these final years of the honorable literary newspaper hoax, pranksters were stunned and often horrified by the extent of their own successes. This was even true for western tall-tale pioneer Mark Twain, who along with close friend Dan De Quille, spun the yarns for the Virginia City *Enterprise* in the early 1860s. The humor was absurd, but also sardonically reflective of the culture of fraud, swindle, and violence that had mushroomed with the California Gold Rush and subsequent silver boom of Nevada's Comstock Lode.

Twain cooked up hoaxes as jokes on friends and coworkers, but naturally found himself the butt of them as well. After an editor broke his nose in a boxing match, he was so embarrassed that he left town, and in Twain's absence, De Quille published stories about his face. One reported that a huge bloody red nose had attempted to jump aboard a stagecoach, terrifying the passengers.[22]

Twain's hoaxes were equally outrageous, yet first to his amusement, and then shock and dismay, they caught fire like a torch to desert sage. Just a few weeks after joining the *Enterprise,* he reported that a roughly hundred-year-old petrified man had been discovered in the mountains. The image was meant to mock a local fascination with petrifications. Twain maintained that he had never meant to fool anyone, but one paper after another began reprinting it. The news spread despite Twain's strong clue that it was bogus: the stone-faced man was holding one thumb up to a nostril with fingers splayed out—literally thumbing his nose at posterity.[23]

Twain's "masterpiece"—though he hardly saw it as one—was the "Empire City Massacre." It reported that a man named P. Hopkins rode into town on horseback with his throat slit from ear to ear, carrying the dripping scalp of his murdered wife, and then collapsed dead at the door of the Magnolia saloon. Back at Hopkins's house, a sheriff's posse discovered six of nine children butchered with an ax.[24] Once again, Twain thought he had left plenty of clear indications of a hoax, but instead the vivid, gory details alarmed locals and nonlocals alike.

"Well, in all my life I never saw anything like the sensation that little satire created," he later recalled. "It was the talk of the town, it was the talk of the territory." Nevada papers angrily denounced the story as "cruel and idiotic," and in "shockingly bad taste." Twain published a contrite retraction titled "I take it all back." He was upset about the incident for weeks, and according to De Quille, had trouble sleeping. "Mark," De Quille advised him, "never mind this bit of gale. It will soon blow itself out. This item will be remembered and talked about when all your other work is forgotten." And in Nevada at least, that turned out to be true.[25]

Sixty years later, columnist Dorothy Thompson argued that Orson Welles and the Mercury Theater should be awarded a congressional medal for demonstrating the power of the hoax in the age of mass media, with their "War of the Worlds" broadcast. "They have shown up the incredible stupidity, lack of nerve and ignorance of thousands," she wrote. "They have proved how easy it is to start a mass delusion."[26] Yet the hoaxes of the previous century had already exposed the remarkable gullibility of the public, and the capacity of absolute bunk to "go viral," long before mass media or the Internet ever existed.[27]

The reasons hoaxes succeed have remained the same. Many tell people what they want to hear, and fictional stories are often more compelling than the truth. One notorious example of a story that reinforced what people already believed was an 1856 London *Times* report about a train trip across Georgia that became a bloodbath. It drew great excitement because many Brits were already convinced Americans were violent savages.[28] Reports about Hillary Clinton assassinating an FBI agent or operating a sex-trafficking ring out of a pizza parlor went viral both because they offered far spicier details than typical news and affirmed people's opinions. As in the days of the Georgian train ride from hell, other journalists debunked the hoaxes, but perversely, that only made the tales more popular and powerful. Studies of fact-checking and debunking have documented this phenomenon, known as "confirmation bias."[29]

Where Twain had seen cause for alarm, others in increasingly urban, competitive, and cynical newspaper markets saw opportunity. By the late nineteenth century, the journalist that Norman Howard Sims has called "the backwoods sketch artist" and the literary hoax were dying out. This was nowhere more evident than in Chicago of the 1890s where, as Sims observed: "The hoax took a twist. It became invisible. Or else it was a joke which could be detected only by a few fellow reporters. Instead of a perfectly visible absurdity, the hoax actually became an unrecognizable deceit."[30]

This "twist" was driven by market competition that grew increasingly intense over the next thirty years, the apex of the Industrial Revolution. During the early twentieth century, Chicago newspaper reporters distinguished themselves with a roguish and wild approach to journalism that the writer Ben Hecht immortalized in *The Front Page,* his 1927 hit Broadway comedy. By then, the American Society of Newspaper Editors was adopting a code of ethics that would stamp out the hellfire of the Chicago press.

Hecht recalled in his autobiography that, as a sixteen-year-old "picture chaser" for the *Journal,* his first job in journalism had been to beg, borrow, or—mostly—steal newsworthy photos, and this he did with talent and a sense of mission. After his Aunt Chasha sewed large pockets into his jacket to conceal burglary tools and the loot, Hecht "clambered up fire escapes, crawled through windows and transoms, posing when detected as everything from a gas meter inspector to an undertaker's assistant," recalled one friend.[31] Soon Hecht graduated to part-time cub reporter and full-time professional hoaxer. Collaborating with photographer Gene Cour, he delivered splashy scoops on police pursuits of riverboat pirates, and the Great Chicago Earthquake, which tore a terrific fissure through Lincoln Park. His career came to an end, however, with publication of a riches-to-rags tearjerker about a Romanian princess found slinging hash on Wabash Avenue. *Journal* publisher John C. Eastman was laughed out of his smoking club for running the photo of a well-known local prostitute—Hecht's "princess"—on the front page.[32]

Though they seem fantastic, Hecht's tales explain the traditions of Chicago journalism through a kind of narrative shorthand. The idea that newspapers paid young men to break into homes and steal photographs may seem hard to believe, but Theodore Dreiser and Vincent Starrett cite it as a common practice in their own memoirs. Hecht's claim that his promotion to reporter afforded the opportunity for a short-lived, madcap career as a hoaxer recalls this other dubious journalistic sport that Chicago reporters adopted and made peculiarly their own.

The Chicago hoax went beyond being a mere genial prank: it became one more ploy in the reporter's bag of tricks, put to use in the bare-knuckle fight for scoops. In the 1890s, Finley Peter Dunne of the *Herald* and Charles Dillingham of the *Times* brought it into play against the *Tribune*'s Frank Vanderlip, their competitor on the hotel beat. The hapless Vanderlip could not understand how his rivals kept grabbing exclusives with famous and exotic personages who stopped in town overnight and then vanished without a trace. Unable to keep pace, Vanderlip was fired for incompetence, without ever realizing that these extraordinary hotel guests had never come or did not exist. In Chicago, the hoax was now a hustle pulled on the competition and public alike.[33]

Ironically, the same bottom line that compelled a swarm of young men to gather facts also honed their talents for deception and misdirection, creating the cutthroat culture portrayed in *The Front Page*. "'Get the news! Get the news!'—that was the great cry in the city editorial room," recalled Theodore Dreiser, who was struck by the "pagan or unmoral character" of newspaper work.

> Don't worry much over how you get it, but get it, and don't come back without it! . . . Don't let other newspapers skin us—that is, if you value your job! . . . While a city editor might readily forgive any form of trickery he would never forgive failure. Cheat and win and you were all right; be honest and lose and you were fired. To appear wise when you were ignorant, dull when you were not, disinterested when you were interested . . . these were the essential tricks of the trade. . . . And I soon encountered other newspaper men who were as shrewd and wily as ferrets.[34]

Tales of scooping are legion. Reporters were known to toss false tips that sent the competition on wild goose chases. *Collier's* celebrated Harry Romanoff of the *Herald & Examiner* as Chicago's greatest telephone reporter because of his talent at impersonations. Once calling a barroom where a murder had occurred, Romanoff identified himself as Sgt. Donohue of the coroner's office. "That's funny," said the voice on the other end. "So is this." Stepping things up a notch, city news alum and ex-editor Frank Carson staged a collision of two circulation trucks in front a police station, a diversion that enabled his operatives to steal the diary of the alluring murderess Ruth Randall out of the evidence room.[35] Sometimes reporters planted evidence. "If it occurred to us that a janitor's missing mother-in-law might have been lured into the janitor's furnace, and the clues did not fit that attractive hypothesis," wrote Starrett, "we helped the story to headlines by discovering incinerated bones that somehow the police had missed."[36]

When Chicago crime reporters were not breaking into places or pulling a con, they were busy deputizing themselves with the local law enforcement. "Murder mysteries fascinated readers, and the reporters, not the police, would solve them," wrote John J. McPhaul. Papers supplied badges that reporters would flash to pass themselves off as detectives or assistant coroners. Carson, who was always ready to push things to an extreme, invented "muscle journalism," manufacturing phony badges, warrants and other documents, and installing wiretaps.[37]

Much of this roguish behavior is amusing in hindsight, but it is worth also keeping in mind that these were grim days for news, and for the city of Chicago. Determined to gain an edge on the local competition with the launch of the *American* in 1900, William Randolph Hearst hired Max Annenberg, an immigrant from East Prussia and a Chicago West Sider, to organize crews of sluggers who strong-armed newsboys into ditching stacks of rival newspapers. The *Tribune* and *Daily News* soon rose to the challenge, and what started with knives and brickbat brawls between gangs of neighborhood toughs evolved into shooting sprees that claimed the lives of newsboys and residents alike. In 1921, *Chicago Tribune* publisher Robert McCormick testified that twenty-seven newsboys had been killed in the violence between 1910 and 1913. More than a dozen of the young thugs hired by the Circulation Department would later graduate to become the gunmen of the Al Capone era, after the passage of Prohibition.

Another casualty of the newspaper wars was *real* news. During the same period when Max Annenberg and his brother Moe first signed on with the *American*'s Circulation Department, the city's ten dailies ignored fire-code violations in the graft-ridden First Ward that routinely had lethal consequences.[38] Finally, on December 30, 1903, a blaze at the Iroquois Theatre claimed some six hundred lives, mostly children. Over the next three years, it would take a series of exposés in the *Lancet,* a British journal, to break arguably the biggest story in the city's history: the disgusting and dangerous conditions of the stockyards, which became the focus of Upton Sinclair's 1906 novel *The Jungle.*[39]

The city was so corrupt that, each year, the alderman of downtown's First Ward would parade with underworld bosses, common criminals, pimps, and prostitutes at a Gangster's Ball. With the ascendance of Al Capone in the 1920s, "the parasite that had once been the Levee had begun to consume the city that had once been its host," noted historian Michael Lesy.[40] In the face of all this, the cynicism of the press was summed up neatly by Walter Howey, the reigning Hearst editor whom Hecht and Charles MacArthur immortalized as the Machiavellian genius Walter Burns in *The Front Page.* Howey collected dirt on all the officials in the city, but he used the material as leverage for access, rather than for crusading news stories. As *Herald-Examiner* veteran Charles Murray explained of his boss: "Howey knew that such exposés would do no good, as far as reform is concerned. He was under no illusions about the intelligence of the ordinary citizen, or his capacity to remember from one day to the next which politicians are gypping him and how they are going about it. . . . Howey did not operate his paper by any code of ethics dreamed up at journalism school in an ivory tower full of idealistic professors. He ran it on the same basis as other businesses in the community operated."[41]

Hecht thought that the best example of public obliviousness was the support for Capone's toady, Mayor William Hale Thompson: "Every paper was a blood-hound baying after Thompson. The headlines never let up during Big Bill's long roost in the city hall. Scandal on scandal was 'bared.' The looting of the city's treasury was constantly exposed and documented. Tales of thievery by Thompson and his henchmen, of collusion between the city hall and the town's 'inferno of vice and crime' were offered daily to the citizenry. In the teeth of this constant exposure as a political ogre, Thompson offered himself biannually as a candidate for mayor—and was elected five times."[42]

Chicago's Front Page Era is instructive not just because of its pivot toward devious hoaxing, but also because of its Hieronymus Bosch panorama of shenanigans and mayhem. Similarly, fake news was not the only disturbing feature of the recent presidential contest, and context is crucial.

Observers have since offered at least two other historical comparisons to 2016, and what is most striking and disturbing is how well *all of these* combine and apply. Eleven months after the election, David Uberti no longer scoffed at "the recent hyperventilating." Adopting a more dour view, he likened today's media to the Partisan Press, that era of vicious mud-slinging and tribal truth-twisting so distasteful that it drove President John Adams to sign the Alien and Sedition Acts, rolling back the First Amendment only a decade after the Constitution had been ratified. Uberti no longer shrugged off "a shift back to historical norms," but instead now wrote that the disintegration of a dominant twentieth-century news media establishment had sucked us down a wormhole, into a fragmentary, illusory realm with few agreed-upon standards, shadowy actors, and evaporating trust. "No one really knows what's out there or where it comes from," he concluded. "Professional journalists, bullshit artists, advertisers, and foreign propagandists all exist on the same plane. . . . It's chaos, in other words, and some dynamics mirror those of the nineteenth century."[43]

The fragmentation most benefits those from Macedonia to California ready to cash in on the targeting and tribalism. Back in 2011, Tom Rosenstiel had observed the emergence of a "neo-partisan press." He called some of the cable news and radio talk shows the "journalism of affirmation" because they profit by reinforcing their audience's preconceptions, though he noted that this was actually a marked change from the original Partisan Press, which did not exist to make money.[44]

In other words, today's media are even more toxic, because divisions and subterfuge are further distorted by greed. They are also worse than that of the Front Page Era, because Chicago's madness had not been ideological. And it is more corrupt than even the partisan and Chicago eras added together, because neither was also warped by the cunning manipulations of authoritarian apparatchiks. The goal of Russian propaganda, according to those who have studied it, is not so much to convince anyone of their side of a story, but rather to create an environment where, to return to Obama's phrase, "everything is true and nothing is true." Putin's trolls kick up enough dust that the truth feels unknowable. One telling example of the topsy-turvy, disorienting reality we inhabit today is President Trump's denunciations of fake news, so routine that we hardly even register the outbursts anymore. He pollutes our atmosphere with fake news that mislabels real news as fake.

The specter of totalitarian propaganda inspired Adrian Chen's comparison in the *New Yorker* to the radio days of the 1930s. "The Fake-News Fallacy" begins with a montage of images—recently the object of scrutiny—of panicked listeners to the Orson Welles broadcast: a seventy-six-year-old millworker grabbing for his shotgun, thirty men and women rushing for cover at the West 132nd Street police station, two people who reportedly suffered heart attacks, a man in Pittsburgh who claimed he just barely stopped his wife from gulping poison. Dorothy Thompson was among those who had immediately drawn the unnerving connection to the demagogues then so effectively tapping into the new technological power of radio: Hitler, Father Charles Coughlin, Huey Long. Similarly, Chen argues: "Trump used Twitter less as a communication device than as a weapon of information warfare. . . . Yet the Internet didn't just give him a megaphone. It also helped him peddle his lies through a profusion of unreliable media sources that undermined the old providers of established fact. Throughout the campaign, fake-news stories, conspiracy theories, and other forms of propaganda were reported to be flooding social networks."[45]

Chen adds that, as with debates about radio, we are experiencing a similar freefall from our original utopian hopes for the Internet to dystopian fears. Struck by the new mass medium's reach from the inner-city slums to remote ranchlands, John Dewey had proclaimed radio "the most powerful instrument of social education the world has ever seen." But intellectuals soon grew alarmed by the skill with which dictators bent America's pioneering advertising techniques to their ends. In recent years, observers of the Arab Spring hailed Twitter and Facebook as great gifts to democracy, until ISIS YouTube videos and online chats began luring Western teenagers to Syria. Google was supposed to unlock the vast stores of knowledge in the world's libraries; now the tech companies have been shutting down neo-Nazi websites, while they struggle to dam up the electronic torrents of deception.[46]

So which of the historical comparisons—the Partisan Press, Chicago, 1930s radio—is the most apt? None of them, and all of them. American media historians should recognize the fake news of 2016 as a witches' brew of the worst elements from the very blackest episodes of our past. Between the multipronged meddling of Russian intelligence, the armies of trolls and bots, the WikiLeaks hack and strategic dumps, the hyperpartisanship, memes, filter bubbles, flame wars, Pizzagate and other conspiracy theories spun by professional cranks like Alex Jones, the bullying tweets and neo-Nazi retweets, the false narratives and pathological lying of a reality television demagogue, and the unregulated flood of advertising money in the new, post–Citizens United era, in addition to the customary corporate cynicism, superficiality, short-sightedness, blind spots, distortions, and sundry other failures that we have come to expect from American election coverage, the media of the presidential race served up a smorgasbord of demonic delights, as if Lucifer had invited Hitler, Stalin, and Mussolini over for potluck. It succeeded in nothing so well as to completely unmoor the American public sphere from rational argument, reality, and truth.

All this has happened at a time when clear thinking and smart stewardship are needed more than ever to solve the world's increasingly complex and intractable problems, as the stakes couldn't get higher and the margin for error gets narrower. I write this from Hawaii, "the endangered species capital of the world," which like every mile of US coastline faces an uncertain future of hurricanes, floods, and rising sea levels. Early on a sunny day in January here, our phones lit up with the warning of an incoming North Korean missile attack. One scene in an apartment that morning suggests the range of panic detonated by this recent fake news broadcast, from the comic—a student told me he desperately tried to tape his windows shut, as if duct tape could shield against a thermonuclear attack—to the tragic: his roommate meanwhile sat weeping in the other room, saying her goodbyes to her mother over the phone. Finally, a bit of fact-checking broke this spell of mass delusion.

NOTES

This essay was originally published as "Not Your Grandpa's Hoax: A Comparative History of Fake News" in *American Journalism* 35, no. 2 (2018): 236–49.

1. Craig Silverman et al., "Hyperpartisan Facebook Pages Are Publishing False and Misleading Information at an Alarming Rate," *BuzzFeed,* October 20, 2016, www.buzzfeed.com/ craigsilverman /partisan-fb-pages-analysis?utm_term=.lnn1PJpX9#.pulP7wZbl.

2. Results of a national Nexis news search corroborates this chart produced by a Google Trends search for "fake news": trends.google.com/trends/explore?date=today%2012-m&q=%22fake%20 news%22 (accessed March 2017).

3. David Remnick, "Obama Confronts a Trump Presidency," *New Yorker,* November 11, 2016.

4. David Uberti, "The Real History of Fake News," *Columbia Journalism Review,* December 15, 2016.

5. "Facebook and the Digital Virus Called Fake News," *New York Times,* November 19, 2016.

6. Norman Howard Sims, "The Chicago Style of Journalism," PhD diss., University of Illinois at Urbana-Champaign, 1979, 32. On the invention of news in the 1830s, see Michael Schudson, *Discovering the News: A Social History of American Newspapers* (New York: Basic Books, 1978), chap. 1.

7. Uberti, "The Real History of Fake News."

8. Jonathan M. Ladd, *Why Americans Hate the Media and How It Matters* (Princeton, NJ: Princeton University Press, 2011), 6.

9. Dan Tynan, "How Facebook Powers Money Machines for Obscure Political 'News' Sites," *Guardian,* August 24, 2016. Craig Silverman and Lawrence Alexander, "How Teens in the Balkans Are Duping Trump Supporters with Fake News," *BuzzFeed,* November 3, 2016. Samantha Subramanian, "Inside the Macedonian Fake News Complex," *Wired,* February 15, 2017.

10. Andrew Higgins, Mike McIntire, and Gabriel JX Dance, "Inside a Fake News Sausage Factory: 'This Is All About Income,'" *New York Times,* November 26, 2016.

11. Laura Sydell, "We Tracked Down a Fake-News Creator in the Suburbs. Here's What We Learned," *All Things Considered,* National Public Radio, November 23, 2106. Laura Bradley, "Samantha Bee Tracked Down a Fake-News Mogul to Ask, 'What the F**k?'" *Vanity Fair Hollywood,* December 6, 2016.

12. Chris Fleming and John O'Carroll, "The Art of the Hoax," *Parallax* 16, no. 4 (2010): 45–59.

13. Edson C. Tandoc Jr., Zheng Wei Lim, and Richard Ling, "Defining 'Fake News': A Typology of Scholarly Definitions," *Digital Journalism* 6, no. 2 (2017): 137–53.

14. Lynda Walsh, *Sins against Science: The Scientific Media Hoaxes of Poe, Twain, and Others* (Albany: State University of New York Press, 2006), 18; Fred Fedler, *Media Hoaxes* (Ames: Iowa State University Press, 1989), 3–5.

15. Benjamin Franklin, *Satires & Bagatelles* (Detroit: Fine Book Circle, 1937), 22–24.

16. Fedler, *Media Hoaxes,* 10–11.

17. Edgar Allan Poe, "The Unparalleled Adventures of One Hans Pfaal," *The Works of Edgar Allan Poe,* Raven Edition, 2008, www.gutenberg.org/ebooks/25525#download. See note 1 at the end.

18. Walsh, *Sins against Science,* 50–97; Fedler, *Media Hoaxes,* 17–33.

19. Fedler, *Media Hoaxes,* chap. 4.

20. "Awful Calamity," *New York Herald,* November 9, 1874.

21. Fedler, *Media Hoaxes,* chap. 6.

22. William R. Gillis, *Memories of Mark Twain and Steve Gillis,* 2nd ed. (Sonora, CA: The Banner, 1924), 78–79.

23. Sims, "The Chicago Style of Journalism," 35.

24. "Empire City Massacre," Museum of Hoaxes, hoaxes.org/archive/permalink/empire_city_massacre (accessed March 31, 2017).

25. Fedler, *Media Hoaxes,* 47.

26. Dorothy Thompson, "On the Record: Mr. Welles and Mass Delusion," *New York Herald Tribune,* November 2, 1938, 21.

27. Douglas Rushkoff, *Media Virus: Hidden Agendas in Popular Culture* (New York: Ballantine Books, 1994). Rushkoff is often credited with inventing the media term.

28. "Railways and Revolvers in George," (London) *Times,* October 15, 1856, 9.

29. Brendan Nyhan and Jason Reifler, "Misinformation and Fact-Checking," *Research Findings from Social Science,* New America Foundation, 2012, www.dartmouth.edu/~nyhan/Misinformation_and_Fact-checking.pdf. Science journalist Elizabeth Kolbert summarizes some of the broader research in "Why Facts Don't Change Our Minds," *New Yorker,* February 27, 2017.

30. Sims, "The Chicago Style of Journalism," 39.

31. William MacAdams, *Ben Hecht: The Man Behind the Legend* (New York: Scribner, 1988), 14. See also Hecht's own account of picture chasing in *A Child of the Century* (New York: Primus, 1985).

32. Hecht, *A Child of the Century,* 134–35.

33. Sims, "The Chicago Style of Journalism," 34–39.

34. Theodore Dreiser, *Newspaper Days: An Autobiography,* 7th ed. (New York: H. Liveright, 1922), 152–53.

35. A. A. Dornfeld, *Behind the Front Page: The Story of the City News Bureau of Chicago* (Chicago: Academy Chicago, 1983), 39, 119–20; George Murray, *The Madhouse on Madison Street* (Chicago: Follett Pub. Co, 1965), 189; Wayne Klatt, *Chicago Journalism: A History* (Jefferson, NC: McFarland & Co, 2009), 125; Ben Hecht, *The Front Page: From Theater to Reality* (Hanover, NH: Smith & Kraus, 2002), 153–55. note 170.

36. Vincent Starrett, *Born in a Bookshop; Chapters from the Chicago Renascence* (Norman: University of Oklahoma Press, 1965), 101.

37. Dreiser, *Newspaper Days,* 77–78; May Mann, "Going Hollywood" column, *Ogden* (Utah) *Standard-Examiner,* December 5, 1940, 9; "Muscle Journalist" (obituary), *Time,* March 31, 1941, 40; Murray, *Madhouse,* 194–201; Klatt, *Chicago Journalism,* 119.

38. Matthew C. Ehrlich, *Journalism in the Movies* (Urbana: University of Illinois Press, 2004), 22; Klatt, *Chicago Journalism,* 77.

39. Klatt, *Chicago Journalism,* 72–74, 83.

40. Michael Lesy, *Murder City: The Bloody History of Chicago in the Twenties* (New York: W. W. Norton & Co, 2007), 306–7. Lloyd Wendt, *Lords of the Levee: The Story of Bathhouse John and Hinky Dink* (Indianapolis: Bobbs-Merrill Co., 1943). 294.

41. Murray, *Madhouse,* 178.

42. Ben Hecht, *Gaily, Gaily* (Garden City, NY Doubleday, 1963), 213–14.

43. David Uberti, "Fake News and Partisan Blowhards Were Invented in the 1800s," *Splinter,* October 6, 2017, splinternews.com/fake-news-and-partisan-blowhards-were-invented-in-the-1-1819219085 (accessed January 2018).

44. "As Media Lines 'Blur,' We All Become Editors," Neal Conan interview with Tom Rosenstiel, *Talk of the Nation,* National Public Radio, September 1, 2011.

45. Adrian Chen, "The Fake News Fallacy," *New Yorker,* September 4, 2017.

46. Chen, "The Fake News Fallacy."

FROM EARLY MODERN MOON HOAXES TO NAZI PROPAGANDA

A BRIEF ANTHOLOGY OF FAKE NEWS

Heidi Tworek and John Maxwell Hamilton

F ake news" has had many names. The "pasquinade" derived from efforts of sixteenth-century author Pietro Aretino to sway a papal election. He posted sonnets lambasting all but his favorite candidate on a battered Hellenistic statue called "il Pasquino," named for a local wit when it was unearthed in the sixteenth century. Pasquinades carried on as disparaging and mostly false assertions about public figures and political opponents. The "canard," which came along later, was a printed and more popular version of Aretino's trick that sold on the streets of Paris from the seventeenth century. Pictures and wild stories about people and magical creatures kept gullible readers buying.[1]

A parallel aspect of fake news is the anxiety that it arouses. With greater freedom to publish one's thoughts came greater unease about the freedom people had to spread false information. This alarm about fake news expressed itself in satire, political commentary, and later, serious scholarship.

In a paradoxical way, worry about fake news became a sign of a healthy skepticism about truth and knowledge. No institution, including the press, can be trusted at all times. Up to a point, concern about the quality of our news is essential for a robust democracy. The problem is that demagogues can leverage those anxieties for their own censorious and authoritarian purposes. We may think of this as the soft underbelly of the Enlightenment: the wonderful opportunity to think independently and communicate widely is accompanied by the terrible opportunity to subvert discourse.

There is no shortage of examples of this phenomenon. Three of them, from England, the United States, and Germany, illustrate the range of faking that has taken place over the centuries. They also show how authoritarian figures can use accusations of faking as a cudgel to crush protest and press freedom.

We start with English satirist Ben Jonson at the dawn of newspapers. The first newspapers appeared in continental Europe in the early 1600s with the Strasbourg *Relation* (1605) and the *Frankfurter Postzeitung* (1615). Somewhat regular news periodicals emerged in England in 1620 to inform the English about the Thirty Years' War between Catholics and Protestants which had started on the continent two years before. These "corantos" were initially printed in the Netherlands and began to appear in England in 1622 thanks to printers such as Nathaniel Butter.[2]

The steadily growing popularity of newspapers dovetailed with the Age of Enlightenment. This is remembered as a time of scientific discovery and increasing enthusiasm over the ability of people to discover the truth for themselves. But this unshackling from the previously uncontested authority of the church and state also opened the possibility that false information would find its way into civic discourse. In his *Novum Organum,* published on the cusp of the Enlightenment in 1620, scholar and Lord Chancellor Francis Bacon produced a list of impediments that made it difficult for people to sift the true from the false. The book prefigured Lippmann's classic *Public Opinion,* published almost exactly three hundred years later. "Human understanding," Bacon wrote with Lippmannesque flair, "is like a false mirror, which receiving rays irregularly, distorts and discolors the nature of things by mingling its own nature with them."[3]

Playwrights and artists were as concerned as scholars and politicians about these developments. Although Ben Jonson is far less known than his contemporary William Shakespeare, the two playwrights were equally well regarded at the time. Jonson's works were often performed in front of then King James I of England (and VI of Scotland). The pieces performed were known as masques, a type of courtly entertainment with music, singing, acting, and dancing that often displayed strong satirical elements. Popular in other European courts, masques were sometimes performed by the monarchs themselves.

If Jonson wanted the king to know about his political and social concerns, it made sense for him to choose a masque. Jonson began satirizing the news and the news-hungry in his masque, *News from the New World Discovered in the Moon.* The masque was first performed the year Bacon's *Novum Organum* was published. Jonson poked fun at news consumers' and news producers' gullibility by suggesting they would believe fantastic tales about a world discovered on the moon. This short masque foreshadowed Jonson's longer play *The Staple of News,* first performed in 1625 and published in 1631.

The world was of course a very different place in the seventeenth century. Literacy rates were very low. Comparatively few people could read the newspapers that Jonson satirized. Much news still came in the form of newsletters handwritten by people called "factors" who served a select circle of interested elites (the authors of e-mail newsletters today are somewhat equivalent). Another source of news was spread orally through gossip, rumor, and song. Nevertheless, many of the dynamics satirized by Jonson have continued up to the present. The extract below from Jonson's masque shows that six of our current concerns existed at the very start of mass-printed news provision.

First, we worry that news organizations propagate falsified news for profit. The printer in Jonson's masque tells the audience right at the start that he will "give anything for a good copy now, be't true or false, so't be news."

Second, we worry that news is falsified or disinformation spread for political purposes. Much of the news entering England came from Europe and discussed the Thirty Years' War. At least implicitly, this news pushed for England to enter the war on the Protestant side. Jonson seems to have agreed with King James's hesitation about involving England in a continental war. His news satires may have been meant to raise doubts about the veracity of news and to question the motives of those supplying it. Note how the factor refers to letters from people of different religions as evidence of his broad base of sources. The factor then wishes to create a central news office essentially to fact-check news before sending it out to the rest of the country, or shires.

Third, we worry that audiences are gullible and enjoy believing lies. "Why should they [the common people] not ha' their pleasure in believing of lies are made for them?" the printer asks rhetorically.

Fourth, we worry that it is harder to correct false news once it has spread. The chronicler similarly muses that it is more difficult to retract falsehoods than to gather news in the first place. He says he has "been so cheated with false relations i' my time as I ha' found it a far harder thing to correct my book than collect it."

Fifth, we emphasize the importance of trust in news. The first herald bringing news of people on the moon asks the printer, factor, and chronicler to "dare take upon trust" what he and his fellow heralds are saying. The printer, factor, and chronicler ask questions to try to verify; the masque satirizes how they still have to trust unreliable narrators for news.

Finally, we worry that newer methods of news dissemination create a greater preponderance of falsity. In Jonson too, the factor writes news by hand and condemns the still comparatively new technology of printing. He is "offended" at the printing of news, even arguing that printed material is not even really news. If news items are written by hand, he declares, "though they be false, they remain news still." The printer retorts that many people "believe nothing but what's in print." The fights between new and old technologies are as old as technologies themselves.

Here is the excerpt from Jonson's masque.

> *Enter first herald, second herald, printer, chronicler, factor.*
>
> *First Herald.* News, news, news!
> *Second Herald.* Bold and brave news!
> *First Herald.* New as the night they are born in—
> *Second Herald.* Or as the fant'sy that begot 'em.
> *First Herald.* Excellent news!
> *Second Herald.* Will you hear any news?
> *Printer.* Yes, and thank you too, sir. What's the price of 'em?
> *First Herald.* Price, cockscomb! What price but the price o' your ears? As if any man used to pay for anything here!
> *Second Herald.* Come forward. You should be some dull tradesman by your pigheaded sconce [head] now, that think there's nothing good anywhere but what's to be sold.
> *Printer.* Indeed I am all for sale, gentlemen, you say true. I am a printer, and a printer of news, and I do hearken after 'em wherever they be, at any rates; I'll give anything for a good copy now, be't true or false, so't be news.

First Herald. A fine youth!

[. . .]

Factor [newsletter columnist] Gentleman, I am neither printer nor chronologer, but one that otherwise take pleasure i' my pen: a factor of news for all the shires of England. I do write my thousand letters a week ordinary, sometime twelve hundred, and maintain the business at some charge, both to hold up my reputation with mine own ministers in town and my friends of correspondence in the country. I have friends of all ranks and of all religions, for which I keep an answering catalogue of dispatch wherein I have my Puritan news, my Protestant news and my Pontifical news.

Second Herald. A superlative, this!

Factor. And I have hope to erect a staple [main office] for news ere long, whither all shall be brought and thence again vented under the name of staple-news, and not trusted to your printed conundrums of the serpent in Sussex, or the witches bidding the devil to dinner at Derby—news that, when a man sends them down to the shires where they are said to be done, were never there to be found.

Printer. Sir, that's all one, they were made for the common people, and why should not they ha' their pleasure in believing of lies are made for them, as you have in Paul's that make 'em for yourselves?

First Herald. There he speaks reason to you, sir.

Factor. I confess it, but it is the printing I am offended at. I would have no news printed; for when they are printed they leave to be news. While they are written, though they be false, they remain news still.

Printer. See men's divers opinions! It is the printing of 'em makes 'em news to a great many, who will indeed believe nothing but what's in print. For those I do keep my presses and so many pens going to bring forth wholesome relations, which once in half a score years (as the age grows forgetful) I print over again with a new date, and they are of excellent use.

Chronicler. Excellent abuse, rather.

Printer. Master Chronicler, do you not talk; I shall—

First Herald. Nay, gentlemen, be at peace one with another. We have enough for you all three, if you dare take upon trust.

Printer. I dare, I assure you.

Factor. And I, as much as comes.

Chronicler. I dare too, but nothing so much as I ha' done. I have been so cheated with false relations i' my time as I ha' found it a far harder thing to correct my book than collect it.

Factor. Like enough. But to your news, gentlemen; whence come they?

First Herald. From the moon ours, sir.

Factor. From the moon! Which way? By sea? or by land?

First Herald. By moonshine, a nearer way, I take it.

[. . .]

Second Herald. Certain and sure news—

First Herald. Of a new world—

Second Herald. And new creatures in that world—

First Herald. In the orb of the moon—

Second Herald. Which is now found to be an earth inhabited!

First Herald. With navigable seas and rivers!

Second Herald. Variety of nations, polities, laws!

First Herald. With havens in't, castles and port towns!

Second Herald. Inland cities, boroughs, hamlets, fairs and markets!

First Herald. Hundreds, and wapentakes! Forests, parks, cony-ground [rabbit warrens], meadow-pasture, what not?

Second Herald. But differing from ours.

Factor. And has your poet brought all this?

Chronicler. Troth, here was enough; 'tis a pretty piece of poetry as 'tis.

First Herald. Would you could hear on, though.[4]

The rest of the masque describes the world on the moon in more detail, including language and animals. It takes a ribald turn, as the heralds describe the women in this other world. The heralds sing four songs about the world on the moon and end by praising King James as a truthful and renowned king. This was all part of the effort in Jonson's satire of fake news to shore up loyalty to the king and persuade him not to engage in the war on the European continent, even if newspapers were now full of news about it.

Jonson's masque only took aim at foreign news. He chose the moon because it was the most foreign place he could imagine. Satirizing foreign news made eminent sense at the time, because only foreign news could be printed fairly freely in England. The printing of domestic news, and particularly of parliamentary debates, became a key point of contention in 1641 during the buildup to the English Civil War. Printers rebelled against Charles I, son of James I, by printing the proceedings of Parliament for the first time. In 1665, shortly after the restoration of the monarchy, the first newspaper printing domestic news appeared as the *London Gazette*.

Fake news about the moon did not end with Jonson. One of the greatest fake news stories ever was "The Great Moon Hoax." A bogus series of six articles in the *New York Sun* in 1835 sensationally reported that a Scot astronomer had found lunar life replete with winged human beings. That story was an example of fake news to boost sales in the news business. The flip side of such faking is that people today deny that actual landings have been made on the moon. These conspiracy theorists believe these are NASA-perpetrated hoaxes. Such is the corrosiveness of fake news. It makes it easier to discredit the truth.

In the nineteenth century, newspapers became the main vehicle for news. In the United States, cheap, penny newspapers started in New York and other major cities in the 1830s. A variety of factors lay behind this expansion of the newspaper franchise. Press freedom came to be seen as a state-guaranteed right in North America and parts of Europe. Stamp taxes and other taxes on knowledge were revoked in Britain and other European countries from the 1850s onwards. Germany created a press-freedom law in 1874. In addition, economic and technological constraints disappeared. Until the late nineteenth century, paper was made from rags. There was a fairly small supply, and the paper was very costly. In the nineteenth century, paper started to be manufactured from the much cheaper and more accessible wood pulp. Steam presses and other industrial equipment to mass-produce newspapers emerged in the nineteenth century. Millions moved to cities and started to buy cheap urban newspapers to learn about their new homes. During the nineteenth century, newspapers became products for the masses in Europe and North America.

These changes opened the sluice gates for news of all kinds, including that which was faked. One artifact from this time is a poorly printed book on low-grade paper that appeared in 1914 under the name of Max Sherover. The young reporter-editor is largely forgotten—or was until recently. The one-time editor of the equally obscure *New Age of Buffalo* is occasionally mentioned now on account of the highly relevant title of his little lost volume, *Fakes in American Journalism.* The book stands, perhaps, as the ultimate example of President Donald Trump's casual association with accuracy, his false claim that he invented the term *fake news.* The contribution Trump may have made through his nearly daily use of the term has been to encourage the editors of Dictionary.com to add it to their database in the fall of 2017. (Merriam Webster has declined to do that since the term is self-explanatory.)

Criticism of journalism like Sherover's is a good barometer of evolving press attitudes about the standards for the profession. But lamentation over fake news or its equivalent has been a constant refrain, possibly reaching a pre-Trump high point of paroxysms at the turn of the last century. When journalism ran amuck during the coverage of the Spanish-American War, correspondent George Bronson Rae wrote *Facts and Fakes About Cuba.* For the exasperated Rae, the trouble with fake news was professional and personal:

> The "intrepid war correspondent" of a leading New York daily who never leaves the safe environments of the city, and who sees the most marvelous battles, and celebrates astonishing interviews with unknown Cuba chiefs, and mixes names and geography in such a manner as to cause the insurgents to jump one hundred and fifty miles in an hour, has also had the affrontery to invent the story about my being expelled from the camp of [insurgent leader Máximo] Gomez for lying.[5]

Sherover's book is worth remembering not simply because it is a vivid reminder that the "fake news" phenomenon today has literal antecedents. It was overlaid with political motivations that are common today as well. Sherover made it clear that fakes came in many flavors—that some were there for the purpose of selling more papers and some were there to promote a political agenda. While he had a chapter on "Harmless Fakes," his political opinions prompted him to write the book. Sherover was a socialist and believed the capitalist-owned press was suppressing news in order to maintain and enlarge its power. As Sherover put it, "The fact that a 'kept' press is a menace to democracy inspired the compilation of the data contained herein." A decade before Walter Lippmann wrote about the "manufacture of consent," Sherover wanted to show "how public opinion is manufactured."[6]

Socialist Upton Sinclair's famous critique of the press in *The Brass Check* gives a shout-out to Sherover's "excellent little pamphlet." In Sinclair's words, the nation had "a class-owned press, representing class-interests, protecting class interests with entire unscrupulousness, and having no conception of the meaning of public welfare."[7] Indicating the establishment forces against whom he inveighed, Sinclair published the book himself. Shereover's book, which went through several editions, was published by the Free Press League, which is as forgotten as he is.

Although Trump has a much larger stage and more powerful megaphone than Sherover enjoyed, he and Sherover are alike in decrying "fake news" to discredit their opponents. This is not to say that both men rely equally on facts in making their case. Sherover is tendentious but provides a more detailed analysis for his claims than Trump normally does. In any event, as often happens in an assessment of "fake news," one tends to accept as fake that which wars with one's own beliefs as to what is fact.

Here is a sampling of Sherover's *Fakes in American Journalism*:

INTRODUCTION

American journalism holds the record for faking. In its masterful manner of misleading the public it has yet to be surpassed. Its ingenuity in this direction asserts itself in every phase of the news. Whether it be an imaginary voyage to a heretofore unexplored or unheard of region; a pipe dream interview with a dead man; a detailed account of a battle that was never fought, or a riot by strikers that never took place; the author of the fake is invariably surprised at the unusual credence given his fake. Which goes to prove that the majority of us are not Missourians.[8]

We believe what we read. When we learn that we were stung we have nothing but admiration for the stinger.

Fakes may be divided into several groups. There are those which are called "harmless"; then there are those that are deliberately harmful; those that are engineered with the purpose of profiting the faker, or the interests he represents; those that creep into the paper through carelessness; the fakes that will provoke a sob in the woman reader; those that are inspired by the advertisers; those that are influenced by the interests of the owners of the paper; those whose purpose it is to create a certain kind of public opinion, and finally those which affect the conflict between capital and labor. Worse than faking is suppression of news. Every paper has a policy. And one rule of that policy is either "soft-pedal" or entirely suppress certain news. . . .

THE WAY OUT

The foregoing chapters must have made clear the power of the press and how it is used, with several praiseworthy exceptions, in the interests of the powerful few. It is not too much to say that the press can plunge the people into war; can make and unmake individuals and institutions; insidiously prepares the masses to unprotestingly, even willingly, submit while Big Business goes through their pockets. The press can impeach governors, and elect presidents, create national hysteria or popular indifference; it can lift heavenward an unworthy cause or kill by silence a sacred one.

Seldom has the truth been stated so eloquently as by Sheridan in the English Parliament:

Give me but the liberty of the press, and I will give to the minister a venal house of peers—I will give him a corrupt and servile house of commons—I will give him the full sway of the patronage of office—I will give him the whole host of ministerial influence—I will give him all the power the place can confer upon him to purchase up submission and overawe resistence—and yet armed with the liberty of the press I will go forth to meet him undismayed—I will attack the mighty fabric he has reared with that mightier engine—I will shake down from its heigh corruption, and bury its amidst the ruins of the abuses it was meant to shelter.

BUT THERE IS A WAY OUT.

The people must recognize that in the struggle between the Plutocracy and the Masses They must realize that the press of the Plutocracy can never be the mouth piece of the Masses. They must understand that a press which is owned outright by the beneficiaries of Organized Greed and Legalized Plunder or subsidized through the medium of large advertising grants from the same sources will not, *or cannot afford to,* champion the interests of the multitude.

The masses, if they would have a press that will be truly theirs, must subsidize it even as the press of the Interests is subsidized by the Interests.[9]

Let the reader pledge himself that he will not only support in every way within his power the struggling Socialist and labor press, but let him urge as many others as he can to do likewise.

In this way, and this way alone, can a press be established which will not be beholden to the Interests.

Until the coming of the classless society, this, and this alone, is the remedy.

Sherover was part of the broader questioning of authority during the Progressive Era in the United States. Muckraking became a new genre of reporting around the turn of the twentieth century. Some of it, like Sherover's, was tendentious. Some was not. Jacob Riis's and Ida Tarbell's investigations of urban slums and monopolistic trusts led to social welfare programs and antitrust laws. And reporters like Ray Stannard Baker exposed "bought" newspapers that failed to tell the truth about these problems. Serious American press criticism can be said to have emerged at this time.

In the twentieth century, accusations of faking and lies did not always herald positive developments or display a healthy skepticism. When driven too far, these accusations could have terrible repercussions for press freedom and civil rights. A famous (or infamous) example occurred in Nazi Germany, which alarmed citizens about falsified facts (which were actually true) to incite hatred and disguise its intentions.

Over the past few years, we have seen the reemergence of a German term forgotten by everyone but historians: *Lügenpresse* or lying press. Resurrected mainly by the far-right Alternative for Germany (AfD) party in Germany, it has also become a tactic for the far right in the United States to condemn journalism it does not like. This term started to circulate in the Weimar Republic, the democracy created in Germany after World War I. The term *Lügenpresse* drew on longer-standing anti-Semitic and anti-Marxist ideas in German society.

The term was tied to two major political developments. First, it drew from myths about Germany's defeat in World War I. Prominent generals and many on the right believed that Germany had not lost the war militarily. They believed that Germany had been stabbed in the back by the Jews and Social Democrats who had signed the armistice with the Allies on November 11, 1918, and later the Treaty of Versailles. This stab-in-the-back myth (*Dolchstoßlegende*) became a key thread in German right-wing revanchism in the interwar period. Building on older, prewar anti-Semitic beliefs that Jews controlled the media, many on the right thought that Jews controlled the Weimar press and were lying about the state of Germany. It was true that many of the major German newspaper publishing companies like Ullstein and Mosse were founded and run by Jewish families. It was also true that many other prominent publishers were not Jewish.

Second, the term came to more prominence once the Nazi Party started to gain political salience in the late 1920s, when the Great Depression rocked the country. The Nazis did not use the term *Lügenpresse* extensively before 1933. Their ideology was, however, infused by similar sentiments. Nazis also decried the press as a *Systempresse* (system press) that only produced conformist thought and did not support nationalist German ideals and particularly the idea of a *Volks-gemeinschaft* (people's community) bound together by ethnic German heritage.

When the Nazis came to power in January 1933, Joseph Goebbels became the minister for propaganda at the new Ministry of Public Enlightenment and Propaganda (*Reichsministerium für Volksaufklärung und Propaganda*). Nazis like Goebbels had ideas about how citizens interpreted news that were rather different from those of scholars and democratic politicians in the Weimar Republic. While Weimar scholars such as Ferdinand Tönnies had debated the concept of "public opinion" (*öffentliche Meinung*), the Nazis rejected the idea of public opinion on the grounds it was a "rallying cry of liberalism."[10]

Instead, Goebbels believed that there were two ways for people to understand the world. Individuals had both a *Stimmung* (mood) and a *Haltung* (attitude). *Stimmung* was more temporary and fluctuated depending on daily news. *Haltung* was formed from a person's long-term attitudes and behaviors that could only change gradually over time. Goebbels aimed to use propaganda to create and maintain a Nazi mood and attitude. Goebbels believed that the best propaganda "exclusively serves the truth," as he put it in June 1941.[11] That "truth" meant convincing Germans that all sources of information other than the Nazis were liars.

In this speech of February 1939, we see many themes common to Goebbels's addresses and to Nazi worldviews. Goebbels decries the foreign press as liars and hate-mongerers in order to cover up the Nazis' own falsehoods. He blames external enemies for German woes, particularly the Treaty of Versailles. He points the finger at three groups in particular whom he paints as foreign to "real" Germans: Jews, Marxists, and Freemasons. The Nazis frequently tied anti-Semitism to anti-Marxism, accusing both groups of producing false press reports to undermine national socialism. These sentiments would later combine to justify the immense violence of the Holocaust on the Eastern Front to "eradicate" so-called "enemies of the Third Reich."

Goebbels's speech took place a few months after the Munich Conference in 1938, when the United Kingdom, France, and other European countries acquiesced to German annexation of the Sudetenland, which had been part of Czechoslovakia. The Nazis had justified this annexation by claiming that the Czechoslovak state was mistreating the large German minority in the region. Goebbels insists the Nazi state was not looking for war, but merely wished to defend its own national interests. This was itself a lie: The Nazi state had been secretly preparing for war for several years on Hitler's orders. Nazi Germany would annex the rest of Czechoslovakia in March 1939 and then invade Poland in September 1939, unleashing World War II on the European continent.

Here is part of what Goebbels said on February 25, 1939.

Whoever leafs through the smearing and lying press [*Hetz- und Lügenpresse*] abroad in these days and weeks could easily conclude Europe is on the brink of a new world war. [. . .] Once again like with all the big global political events in the past few years, the democracies have the doubtful pleasure of being behind this development.

Why the noise? What do these democracies really want? One could almost conclude that they sporadically create a big outcry to project certain inferiority complexes.

What danger do authoritarian states really pose to democracies? We do not want to attack them. We do not want to convert them to National Socialism. But still we threaten them. They demand from us a gesture of friendship or willingness to cooperate internationally. Now that means turning things on their head. The democracies tortured, humiliated, and tormented Germany from 1918 to 1933 in a manner that was unique in world history. Germany's hopeless situation has changed thanks solely to its own strength, the courage and far-sightedness of its leadership as well as the discipline and decisiveness of its people. But the democracies have not raised a finger to alleviate our desperate situation. Who then should make a gesture of friendship or willingness to cooperate internationally—Germany or the democratic states?

They hope to succeed again one day in sowing discord between the German leadership and the German people. That would be the only way to defeat and humiliate Germany again. A few days ago, a big English newspaper let the cat out of the bag when discussing German news programs on English radio. The *News Chronicle* wrote on February 20 that continuing these programs might "drive a wedge between the German people and their rulers who tried to keep the people in the dark."

So that is what is meant! In this audacious hope, the enemies of the German people abroad align with the small clique of intellectuals and professional naysayers at home. As hard as this judgement may seem, they comprise the International of the enemies of the Reich. Whether consciously or unconsciously, they are playing into each other's hands and together doing the business of the enemies of the German people. That is why, for example, the anti-German papers in Paris, London, and New York adore [Martin] Niemöller and the Confessing Church [a movement within the Protestant Church that opposed the Nazis]; that is why they protect political jokers; that is why they plead for the right to freedom of opinion and fight for the intellectuals who are supposedly vilified and tortured in Germany. They already know to whom they can turn when it comes to opposing the freedom, prosperity, and interests of the German people.

But they do not have it as easy as they did in the past. For the leadership of the Reich is on guard and determined to radically exterminate all tendencies that could harm the freedom and honor of the German people. A few examples will show the lengths of this international smear and its absurd consequences: [. . .]

On February 14, the Washington correspondent of the London *Times* reports that the German armed forces will be fully mobilized by March 6. Although not a single word of this report is true, it still contributes to triggering international agitation and panic-mongering. [. . .]

These examples are just a small anthology. They could be expanded at random. The peoples themselves are plunged into the most terrible unrests and nervous crises, just so that irresponsible journalists have something to write and similarly irresponsible statesmen can use malicious shibboleths to distract the eyes of their peoples away from domestic concerns to supposed foreign policy dangers.

All this debris comes from a single source. The backers of this agitation are well known to us. They are to be found in the circles of international Judaism, international Freemasonry, and international Marxism. But as always, they lack the necessary imagination to at least lie in a sophisticated way. One notices the aim and is annoyed. They want to make us nervous and only make themselves nervous with their own yelling.

In contrast, there is only one rallying cry for the German people: look to the Führer and punish the lies of our enemies with sovereign contempt. This is not the first time that the international world conspiracy has tried to damage Germany by poisoning public opinion.

When a prominent Frenchman asked us a little while ago if it was not already too late to calm Europe internally, we could only give one answer: it is never too late for peace. One must support peace, and not with words, but deeds. [. . .]

For the peoples want peace. The German people want it too. But it also wants something more that other peoples have long possessed: the security of its national life and justice.[12]

Nazi propaganda fanned the flames of prejudice that led to the Holocaust and millions of deaths in World War II. Many Germans accepted these views because the Nazis had argued for years that sources of news other than themselves could not be trusted. "Truth will out," as Shakespeare wrote in the *Merchant of Venice*. But in the case of Nazi Germany, truth came late. Even today there are Holocaust deniers.

At the beginning of the Enlightenment, when the individual no longer had to heed the state and the church, expression became a matter of free choice—and inevitable wild comment. The rise of professional journalism in the late-nineteenth century gradually brought some order to public discussion. The high economic barriers to starting a new newspaper left the press in the hands of a few owners who increasingly sought to establish norms that called for fact-based reporting.

While this was far from perfect, editors fenced back much that was silly hoax or vicious falsehood. And still, there was room for Goebbels and people like him.

Now we are in many respects back at the beginning. The Internet, which broke the hegemony of professional journalists over news, began with great hope, expressed in Facebook's claim, which found its way into the company's securities filings: "Our mission is to make the world more open and connected." The result, however, has been a fraught free-for-all world of expression by the frivolous and the malevolent. Mark Zuckerberg, Facebook's chief executive, is not called to testify before congressional committees in order to take bows. He spends his time there trying to explain what went wrong and promising to make amends. To borrow from Ben Jonson, faking *is* a staple of the news.

NOTES

1. Robert Darnton, "The True History of Fake News," *New York Review of Books,* February 13, 2017, www.nybooks.com/daily/2017/02/13/the-true-history-of-fake-news/.

2. On early modern news, see Andrew Pettegree, *The Invention of News* (New Haven, CT: Yale University Press, 2014).

3. Francis Bacon, *The Essays* (New York: Penguin, 1985), 277.

4. Ben Jonson, *Ben Jonson: Selected Masques* (New Haven, CT: Yale University Press, 1970).

5. George Bronson Rae, *Facts and Fakes About Cuba* (New York: George Munro's Sons, 1897), 22.

6. Walter Lippmann, *Liberty and the News* (New York: Harcourt, Brace and Howe), 37; Max Sherover, *Fakes in American Journalism* (Brooklyn, NY: Free Press League, 1916), 22.

7. Upton Sinclair, *The Brass Check* (Pasadena, CA: published by the author, 1919), 282, 318.

8. This is a reference to Missouri's nickname as the "Show Me State."

9. The idea here is that advertisers can use their power to distort the news. If readers cover the costs of news, this will not happen.

10. *Meyers Lexikon,* 1939, qtd. in Stefan Krings, *Hitlers Pressechef: Otto Dietrich (1897–1952): Eine Biographie* (Göttingen: Wallstein, 2010), 243.

11. Joseph Goebbels, "Nachrichtenpolitik," June 6, 1941, rpt. in Bernd Sösemann and Marius Lange, eds., *Propaganda: Medien und Öffentlichkeit in der NS-Diktatur: eine Dokumentation und Edition von Gesetzen, Führerbefehlen und sonstigen Anordnungen sowie propagandistischen Bild- und Textüberlieferungen im kommunikationshistorischen Kontext und in der Wahrnehmung des Publikums* (Stuttgart: Franz Steiner, 2011), 770. On Nazi attitudes to news, see Heidi J. S. Tworek, *News from Germany: The Competition to Control World Communications, 1900–1945* (Cambridge, MA: Harvard University Press, 2019), 39–40.

12. Joseph Goebbels, "Krieg in Sicht. 25. Februar 1939," in Joseph Goebbels, *Die Zeit ohne Beispiel: Reden und Aufsätze aus den Jahren 1939/40/41* (Munich: Zentralverlag der NSDAP, 1941), 39–47 (translated into English by Heidi J. S. Tworek), archive.org/stream/DieZeitOhneBeispiel/GoebbelsJoseph -DieZeitOhneBeispie11941852S._djvu.txt.

II

THE IMPACT AND FUTURE OF FAKE NEWS

It's rare that academic research makes a splash beyond the scientific community, but in April 2018, one study grabbed the attention of the press and social media. A team of researchers from Ohio State University released a study titled "Fake News May Have Contributed to Trump's 2016 Victory," which was an analysis of survey data that focused on voters who voted for Barack Obama in the 2012 election.[1] While the paper was unpublished, it didn't stop the news outlets from running with it. Leading the charge was the *Washington Post* with the headline, "A new study suggests fake news might have won Donald Trump the 2016 election."[2] Many outlets followed suit, with equally stunning headlines, such as National Public Radio's "Did fake news on Facebook help elect Donald Trump? Here's what we know."[3] The *Post* story was careful not to suggest that this proved anything, noting: "This alone does not prove that fake news made a difference, of course. A recent Princeton-led study of fake news consumption during the 2016 campaign found that false articles made up 2.6 percent of all hard-news articles late in the 2016 campaign, with the stories most often reaching intense partisans who probably were not persuadable."[4]

The Princeton study referenced was a study conducted by Guess, Nyhan, and Reifler that compared survey responses with Internet search histories to study selective exposure to news content. They found that over a quarter of Americans had visited either a pro-Clinton or a pro-Trump fake news website during the last weeks of the 2016 election campaign, which the researchers note might not seem like a large number, but it was actually the equivalent of more than 65 million people of voting age.[5]

Granted, there are qualifiers in many of the news articles—and even the headlines—in order to avoid suggesting causality, but that didn't stop the story from tearing through social media, where it was soon treated as fact. While it makes for a compelling narrative, the idea that so many people saw fake news during the election does not mean that this influenced their votes. This belief that people will read a fake news piece and suddenly change the way they vote presupposes a powerful media effects model.

Originally referred to as the magic bullet or hypodermic needle theory, the idea was that whatever message the sender intended to convey would be lodged within the (metaphorical) bullet or needle, with the media outlet embedding that message deep within the subconscious of the audience member; think *The Manchurian Candidate*, but instead of assassinating leaders in the service of a communist conspiracy, it's about children viewing sex and violence in gangster movies. The most popular manifestation of this was the infamous "War of the Worlds" radio broadcast. On the night before Halloween in 1938, in New York City, twenty-three-year-old Orson Welles's program aired on *Mercury Theatre on the Air,* a radio series created by Welles where he and other actors/actresses would perform hour-long dramas. This particular episode featured a script by *Casablanca* screenwriter Howard Koch and had a unique style; following an announcement at the top of the hour that this would be an "original dramatization" of the "War of the Worlds" story, the program featured an orchestral performance that was quickly interrupted by fake news broadcasts of the invasion.[6] At the end of the hour, after aliens had destroyed New York City, Welles closed the show by stating:

> This is Orson Welles, ladies and gentlemen, out of character to assure you that "The War of the Worlds" has no further significance than as the holiday offering it was intended to be. The Mercury Theatre's own radio version of dressing up in a sheet and jumping out of the bush and saying "boo!" . . . We annihilated the world before your very ears, and utterly destroyed the Columbia Broadcasting System. You will be relieved, I hope, to learn that we didn't mean it, and that both institutions are still open for business.[7]

The question of Welles's intent followed him "for the rest of his life, and his answers changed as the years went on—from protestations of innocence to playful hints that he knew exactly what he was doing all along."[8] Welles spent little time on the early process of revising the script, and in fact, when the rehearsal was recorded for him (Welles was rehearsing a play at the time), everyone who listened to the recording agreed it was "an unmitigated disaster."[9] Welles wanted to try something different through the use of the program's "breaking news" format, but he most likely had no idea how effective it would be.

The program elicited strong responses, at least from a few. The Trenton, New Jersey, Police Department reported receiving over two thousand phone calls in two hours. In Schwartz's excellent book, *Broadcast Hysteria: Orson Welles's War of the Worlds and the Art of Fake News,* he includes accounts of individuals fleeing New York City in fear. Other accounts tell of individuals frantically trying to get ahold of loved ones: "Listeners with relatives living anywhere near the placid village of Grover's Mill tried desperately to telephone them, only to find that all circuits were jammed. One man finally managed to get through to a cousin of his who lived in the town of Freehold, N.J. 'Are the Martians there?' he gasped. 'No,' came the cool reply, 'but the Tuttles are, and we're about to sit down to dinner.'"[10]

And yet, despite the random stories, "the supposed panic was so tiny as to be practically immeasurable on the night of the broadcast."[11] Overall, the reaction was sporadic at best, and the headlines that touted panicked masses terrified of invaders from the stars were largely exaggerated. In a study titled *The Invasion from Mars* (credited to Hadley Cantril but more accurately a collaborative effort of the Princeton Radio Research Project, a team that included mass communication pioneers Paul Lazarsfeld and Herta Herzog),[12] interviews and surveys revealed that few people actually believed an actual alien invasion was taking place in Grover's Mill, New Jersey. The "War of the Worlds" broadcast and the ensuing reactions have become something of a legend, though the reasoning behind those (very limited) overreactions is sound. Unique listening circumstances was cited as a reason for the overreaction. For example, a significant portion of the city was not tuned in to the *Mercury Theatre on the Air* program that night—in fact, most had tuned into the *Chase and Sanborn Hour,* a very popular variety show that at the time featured Edgar Bergen and his wooden dummy Charlie McCarthy (you read that correctly; they had a ventriloquist act that aired on a radio broadcast). That night, many *Chase and Sanborn* listeners decided to change the station (likely due to an unpopular guest or sketch) and turned the dial to CBS, only to be dropped into the "War of the Worlds" broadcast already in progress.[13] Audiences were also under a great deal of stress at the time, having dealt with the ongoing Great Depression and fears of the spread of Nazism overseas.

The "War of the Worlds" broadcast was not exactly the fake news we know today although, as with the media hoaxes discussed in the previous section, it shared a great deal of its DNA, particularly when it comes to determining effects. For instance, we can comfortably say that fake news did not cause Trump to win the 2016 election. However, it would be naive to suggest that fake news played *absolutely no role* in the election, likely through reinforcing ingrained political beliefs and biases. Furthermore, individuals fixated on particular aspects of fake news might have a startling impact. While Welles's radio play strongly affected a very small number of people, those listeners *did* take action. Anecdotal evidence of fake news influencing decisions are frightening, particularly if it's a man entering a family-friendly pizza restaurant with an assault rifle to break up a nonexistent pedophile ring.

While the first section looked at the history of fake news, this section aims to examine the current landscape of fake news, particularly how fake news is being used and what effect (if any) it might be having. This section also focuses on proposed solutions to the fake news problem. Again, attitude changes are incredibly difficult when it comes to exposure to mass communication messages, and behavioral changes are far, far rarer. However, given the uncertainty surrounding the actual impact of fake news, this section is an attempt to flesh out what fake news looks like now, and under what conditions it might be more likely to influence individuals. The first entry is a piece by Jacob L. Nelson, written for this reader, titled "Connecting Partisan Selective Exposure and Fake News." Nelson explores what fake news consumption looked like leading up to the November 2016 election, noting that fake news constituted a small portion of the total online news audience in both size of audience and amount of time audiences were willing to engage with the content. In other words, not as many people saw fake news as previous studies have suggested.

In "Can Media Literacy Reduce Biases in Beliefs about Susceptibility to Fake News? Evidence from a Survey Experiment," Tryfon Boukouvidis, Pamela Labbe, and Michael Henderson explore fake news consumption in a piece written for this

reader. They find that, while individuals tend to overestimate their ability to identify fake news content (leaving them susceptible to those messages), but telling
those individuals how to identify fake news while reminding them that they rarely
engage in such practices can have a positive outcome by reducing overconfidence
and reducing skepticism of citizens on the other side of the political spectrum.

The next entry is an article from *Journalism Practice* titled, "Miley, CNN, and
The Onion: When Fake News Becomes Realer than Real." Written by Dan Berkowitz and David Asa Schwartz, the piece discusses the social media and news
media reactions to Miley Cyrus after she twerked at the 2013 MTV Video Music
Awards. Following her performance, the *Onion* (no stranger to fake news) noted
the amount of news coverage Cyrus was receiving and penned a commentary
piece (by a fictionalized managing editor at CNN), "Let Me Explain Why Miley
Cyrus' VMA performance Was Our Top Story This Morning," detailing why the
story had received so much media attention. The piece is particularly salient,
even for the *Onion,* and Berkowitz and Schwartz argue that the response to the
response actually demonstrates how the "Fifth Estate" of bloggers and columnists
can hold traditional news outlets responsible through the use of satire.

Joel Timmer's "Fighting Falsity: Fake News, Facebook, and the First Amendment" provides a legal component to the argument surrounding fake news. Timmer explains that "political speech, . . . even when false, is highly protected by
the First Amendment, making it unlikely a valid law against fake news could
be crafted." As a result, candidates are unlikely to be able to successfully pursue
defamation action, particularly because sites that post fake news are protected by
the Communications Decency Act. Timmer also discusses actions that Facebook
has taken to fact-check posts, and he makes recommendations for what can be
done to help curb the spread of fake news.

The next piece was written for this reader by Fred Vultee, and it examines
fake news through an ethical lens. In "Potato Chips, Botulism and Carbon Monoxide: The Lying-Bullshitting Distinction in 'Fake News,'" Vultee argues that
deciding what to do about an apparent epidemic of fake news requires both a
definition of fake news and an understanding of what it does wrong. Drawing
on the philosophical distinction between lying and bullshit, his entry seeks to set
falsity apart from fakery, categorize the potential impacts of different varieties
of fake news, and suggest an ethics-based framework for countering them. The

practice of journalism can address some of these challenges as a craft and some as a profession; the paper concludes by suggesting that those approaches bring complementary benefits to journalism and its audiences.

The final essay, by Jessica Johnson, titled, "The Self-Radicalization of White Men: 'Fake News' and the Affective Networking of Paranoia," examines "how paranoia is affectively networked through digital technologies, political performances, and social media to radicalize white men," analyzing the ways in which "acts of domestic terrorism perpetrated by white men are triggered beyond rationales of self-interest through the circulation of paranoia as affective value." Johnson is interested in connecting online violence with offline violence, and explains the connection between counterterrorism, fake news, accusations of fake news, and algorithms. She argues, "rather than an individual pathology or self-contained anomaly, paranoia is an ecology that is affectively networked by state and non-state actors, materializing in processes of digital communication such that the radicalization of white men has violent physical and structural effects."[14]

It is my hope that this section helps capture the complicated nuances of media literacy as a technique to combat the relentless barrage of false information. In a report to the European Parliament's Committee on the Internal Market and Consumer Protection, Dr. Žiga Turk noted the need for "citizens to become aware that the internet is a different media environment than TV and newspapers. There are no editors and no gatekeepers."[15] Ultimately, the report argued for technological solutions, writing that fake news needed to be stopped at all stages of the news process: "creation, editing, publication, amplification, and consumption."[16] However, even in such a sweeping report, Turk acknowledges that the most difficult part of this approach is the "speedy detection of fake news," pointing out that the "most promising are the methods that rely on the provenance and social footprint of a news item."[17] In other words, it's easiest to detect those pieces of fake news that have already spread to news audiences, which kind of defeats the purpose of trying to stop fake news.

And yet, solutions must be found. The fake news problem is likely to get even worse, specifically because of an "explosion of video, audio and photos" aided by increasingly sophisticated software, not to mention more sophisticated search algorithms that are more likely to find the answers you *want* to hear, as "search engines strongly favor a particular, usually positive perspective, irrespective of the truth."[18] The term "media literacy" can be used as something of a catchall, vague enough to deflect blame from media outlets while simultaneously allowing audience members to believe that others—rather than themselves—are the irresponsible ones. Lurking beneath each of these issues is the fact that this is all relatively new to us, not necessarily the content but rather the distribution of that content. Average news consumers simply are not equipped to combat fake news on their own. As Stanford University psychologist Sam Wineburg explained, when it comes to consuming information online, "We are all driving cars, but none of us have licenses."[19] And while we collectively put off going to the media equivalent of the Office of Motor Vehicles, the problem is only going to continue to grow.

—JOSH GRIMM

NOTES

1. Richard Gunther, Paul A. Beck, and Erik C. Nisbet, "Fake news may have contributed to Trump's 2016 victory," unpublished paper, March 8, 2018, 107–16, www.documentcloud.org/documents/4429952 -Fake-News-May-Have-Contributed-to-Trump-s-2016.html.

2. Aaron Blake, "A New Study Suggests Fake News Might Have Won Donald Trump the 2016 Election," *Washington Post,* April 3, 2018, www.washingtonpost.com/news/the-fix/wp/2018/04/03/a -new-study-suggests-fake-news-might-have-won-donald-trump-the-2016-election/?utm_term= .eef8fe055fe2.

3. Danielle Kurtzleben, "Did Fake News on Facebook Help Elect Trump? Here's What We Know," NPR, April 11, 2018, www.npr.org/2018/04/11/601323233/6-facts-we-know-about-fake-news-in-the -2016-election.

4. Blake, "A New Study."

5. Andrew Guess, Brendan Nyhan, and Jason Reifler, "Selective Exposure to Misinformation: Evidence from the Consumption of Fake News during the 2016 US Presidential Campaign," *European Research Council,* 2018, www.dartmouth.edu/~nyhan/fake-news-2016.pdf.

6. Christopher Klein, "'The War of the Worlds' Broadcast, 75 Years Ago," History Channel, www .history.com/news/the-war-of-the-worlds-broadcast-75-years-ago (accessed November 28, 2018).

7. Hal Gordon, "We Annihilated the World . . . ," *PunditWire,* October 27, 2010, punditwire.com /2010/10/27/we-annihilated-the-world/.

8. A. Brad Schwartz, "The Infamous 'War of the Worlds' Radio Broadcast Was a Magnificent Fluke," *Smithsonian,* May 6, 2015, www.smithsonianmag.com/history/infamous-war-worlds-radio -broadcast-was-magnificent-fluke-180955180/.

9. Schwartz, "The Infamous 'War of the Worlds.'"

10. Gordon, "We Annihilated the World."

11. Jefferson Pooley and Michael J. Socolow, "The Myth of the *War of the Worlds* Panic," *Slate,* October 28, 2013, www.slate.com/articles/arts/history/2013/10/orson_welles_war_of_the_worlds _panic_myth_the_infamous_radio_broadcast_did.html.

12. Jefferson D. Pooley and Michael J. Socolow, "Critical Communication History: Checking Up on the Invasion from Mars: Hadley Cantril, Paul Lazarsfeld, and the Making of a Misremembered Classic," *International Journal of Communication* 7 (2013): 29.

13. Klein, "'The War of the Worlds' Broadcast."

14. Jessica Johnson, "The Self-Radicalization of White Men: 'Fake News' and the Affective Networking of Paranoia." *Communication Culture & Critique* 11, no. 1 (2018): 100.

15. Žiga Turk, "Technology as Enabler of Fake News and a Potential Tool to Combat It" (Policy Department for Economic, Scientific and Quality of Life Policies, Ljubljana, Slovenia, May 2018), www.europarl.europa.eu/RegData/etudes/IDAN/2018/619008/IPOL_IDA(2018)619008_EN.pdf, p. 21 (accessed December 12, 2018).

16. Turk, "Technology as Enabler."

17. Turk, "Technology as Enabler."

18. Nathan Bomey, "Five Reasons Why 'Fake News' Likely Will Get Even Worse." *USA Today,* May 9, 2018, www.usatoday.com/story/opinion/2018/05/09/fake-news-donald-trump-journalism-video-audio-facebook-twitter-column/590006002/.

19. Katy Steinmetz, "How Your Brain Tricks You into Believing Fake News," *Time,* August 9, 2018, time.com/5362183/the-real-fake-news-crisis/.

CONNECTING PARTISAN SELECTIVE EXPOSURE AND FAKE NEWS

Jacob L. Nelson

Since 2016, the phrase "fake news" has become inescapable. Politicians world-wide now routinely use the term to dismiss critical news stories, which has led many academics to discourage its use altogether. Journalists, tech companies, and educators, however, still see fake news as a very real threat to both the public and the institutions upholding democratic society. As a result, news organizations like BuzzFeed and Slate and tech companies like Facebook and Google have taken steps to stifle fake news production and dissemination,[1] while educators throughout the country have begun trying to teach elementary- and middle-school students ways to tell fake news stories from real ones.[2]

Yet the extent to which online audiences are actually exposed to fake news remains unclear, as well as how that exposure compares with their exposure to real news. Has fake news consumption increased? Has it overshadowed real news consumption, or replaced it altogether? Although researchers have turned their focus to fake news and misinformation over the past few years, worries about its effects continue to outweigh knowledge about its scope. This chapter is one step toward bridging that gap.

What follows is an analysis of online audience data to explore what fake news consumption actually looked like leading up to the November 2016 election. I find that visitors to fake news sites comprised a small portion of the overall online news audience. I also find a significant, negative relationship between a news site being fake and the size of its audience, as well as the amount of time audiences were willing to engage with it. Furthermore, the fake news audience visited established, "real" news sites at a high rate that was strongly correlated with real news site popularity. Last, I find that visits to fake news sites originated from social network sites (SNSs) at a much higher rate than visits to real news sites, confirming the primary role social media play in spreading fake news content. That spread, however, appears to be much more limited than many suspected. This analysis stems from a study with Harsh Taneja published in *New Media & Society*.[3]

In light of these findings, I argue that the current "fake news" discourse overstates and simplifies its role in the news media landscape. In doing so, it echoes the discourse surrounding another oft-discussed topic within political communication—partisan selective exposure (that is, "filter bubbles"). Concerns surrounding both stem from the idea that, in an ever-expanding media environment, audiences turn to news sources that align with their beliefs and ignore sources that do not, and that the content from these news sources—whether they be one-sided or altogether false—shape the way audiences see the world around them. Yet recent studies have found that the partisan media audience (1) is small and (2) also consumes news from popular, centrist outlets.[4] I conclude that a similar phenomenon plays out when it comes to fake news.

To be sure, I do not dispute that US voters have grown more polarized politically or that they increasingly disagree on basic facts. These observations are an accurate description of the current political climate.[5] However, the discourse surrounding fake news suggests a simple formula wherein an increase in fake news production leads to widespread fake news consumption, resulting in an increase in political confusion. My findings dispute the second part of that equation, suggesting either that fake news plays a marginal role in the spread of political discord, or that its impact does not occur in the straightforward way in which it is currently discussed. In short, although the reach of fake news is far narrower than expected, its consequences remain difficult to measure.

A BRIEF HISTORY OF FAKE NEWS

The recent outbreak of fake news stories (that is, the "great fake news panic of 2016")[6] is a flare-up of an old phenomenon, not the start of a new one. Fake news has been around for as long as news itself, with frighteningly real consequences. Six centuries before stories appeared about Hillary Clinton selling weapons to

ISIS, a preacher in Italy spread anti-Semitic rumors that Jews had kidnapped and murdered a missing child, leading to arrests, tortures, and burnings at the stake. The printing press brought with it an increase in the availability of real news, along with the spread of stories about sea monsters, witches, and sinners who caused natural disasters.[7] As time went on, fake news became an ordinary part of the media ecosystem. In the eighteenth century, a peak of European fake news production, a London newspaper ended an article with the footnote, "Half of this article is true."[8]

When Europeans began settling in America, they brought fake news with them. In fact, misleading and manipulative reporting played a central role in American journalism long before the emergence of the objectivity that currently defines it. In de Tocqueville's study of early US democracy, he noted wearily that journalists distorted the truth to build "support of his own views."[9] For example, to discourage sympathy for Native Americans after the American Revolution, Benjamin Franklin got a Boston newspaper to publish a completely false news story about Native Americans working alongside the British to murder and scalp hundreds of children along the American frontier. Sensational, phony headlines were used throughout America's history not just to whip up anger for political purposes, but also to increase circulation: in 1835, the *New York Sun* garnered many new subscribers when it ran a series about the discovery of alien life on the moon.

So fake news is not new, but has it gotten worse? Many think so. As the *New York Times*'s president and CEO put it, "Fake news is not new . . . and yet what's happening now feels different."[10] Because news consumption increasingly occurs via SNSs, there is growing concern that news audiences no longer notice the sources of the headlines that they see in their newsfeeds, muddying the distinction between credible and sensational sources. This failure of news literacy to catch up with changing patterns of news consumption is used to explain why so many believe that the flood of pro-Trump fake news stories during 2016 helped win him the election.[11] Audiences clicked on and shared anti-Clinton articles that aligned with their political beliefs, without considering the credibility of the publisher.[12]

Political elites could be instrumental in distinguishing fact from fiction for less politically savvy citizens, but can just as easily make matters worse. When politicians pass fake news stories along on their own social media profiles, they give their followers the impression that these stories are credible and vouched for. For example, after the election, former Arkansas governor and Republican presidential nominee Mike Huckabee shared a link to a fictitious article about "liberal, Jewish Northwestern students who were trying to smear Trump and his supporters" to his two million Facebook followers.[13] The article was a manipulation of an actual incident where Northwestern University freshmen painted swastikas onto a chapel months before the election.[14] In another instance, former national security adviser Michael Flynn, as well as his son, tweeted out links to a fake news story that tied Hillary Clinton to a child sex ring,[15] leading a man to bring an assault rifle to the pizza parlor that was supposedly involved.[16] And since his inauguration, President Trump has made false claims about voter fraud and media companies he disapproves of, making him not only a potential beneficiary of fake news but also a seasoned practitioner of it. By making false claims or passing along fake news stories, political elites diminish the public's ability to fact-check the news at an especially precarious moment when the media environment is overflowing with contradictory content.

Russia appears to have noticed and capitalized on the current news media confusion. The country launched a sophisticated propaganda campaign in the lead-up to the US presidential election that included a team of people creating a network of websites and social media accounts to spread false, negative portrayals of Hillary Clinton.[17] Independent researchers as well as US intelligence agencies who investigated the Russian operation found that, by creating and spreading fake news stories, "Russians exploited American-made technology platforms to attack U.S. democracy" in an attempt to hack the election in Donald Trump's favor.[18] Though it is difficult to measure the impact of Russia's campaign, there is wide consensus that fake news as a whole sowed confusion among the electorate and perhaps even cost Hillary Clinton the White House.[19]

Those who support this conclusion blame Russia (as well as a small number of Americans who produced anti-Clinton fake news to capitalize on online ad revenue) for creating such influential fake news stories, but they also blame SNSs for providing the tool used to spread these stories to a wide and susceptible audience. A majority of US adults report getting news on social media platforms,[20] making them an obvious mechanism for fake news producers to cast a wide net with their content. By sharing fake news on SNSs, the argument goes, these publishers warped the Internet's most democratic asset—it's ability to lower the barrier for producing and disseminating media—into a tool for undercutting democracy itself: "The internet has broken down the traditional distinction between professional news-gathering and amateur rumor-mongering. On the internet . . . a fake news site designed to look like a real Colorado newspaper . . . can reach a wide audience as easily as real news organizations like the Denver Post, the New York Times, and Fox News."[21]

Yes, fake news sites *can* reach as wide an audience as established, credible news organizations. But do they? The heads of Facebook and Google appear to think so. Both companies recently cut off advertising revenue to fake news sites in an attempt to discourage their production. They have also partnered with seventeen news organizations to create a tool for debunking fake news stories in the lead-up to the French presidential election, which indicates that fears of fake news have extended outside the United States.[22] Meanwhile, Slate has created a web-browser app that allows users to flag fake news because "the scale at which it is now being produced and consumed is unprecedented."[23] Yet, at this point, few empirical analyses have confirmed or denied this conclusion. On the other hand, a good deal of research into a related area of political communication—partisan media, or "filter bubbles"—offers reason for skepticism when it comes to the reach of fakes news.

PARTISAN SELECTIVE EXPOSURE

In today's political climate, citizens are more polarized than ever.[24] In the United States, majorities of both the Democratic and Republican parties hold very unfavorable views of each other that stem from feelings of fear and anger.[25] Many suspect the root of this increasingly acrimonious partisanship is that, in a seemingly limitless news media environment, citizens have restricted their political news consumption to sources that align with their ideologies.[26]

This belief stems from the theory of *selective exposure,* a foundational concept in communication and media studies that states that people choose media that reinforce their existing attitudes and interests.[27] Within political communication, this phenomenon has been referred to as "partisan selective exposure," "filter bubbles," "echo chambers," and the "red/blue media divide." This theory offers an appealingly straightforward explanation of the mechanism by which citizens grow more polarized.

However, empirical studies of partisan selective exposure have been mixed. Though some have found evidence of "filter bubbles,"[28] others have concluded that audiences of all political identities congregate on more popular, ideologically centrist news media.[29] Instead of exclusively pursuing ideologically aligning news sources, online audiences tend to focus on what's popular. For example, they look for media that has been "liked" or "favorited," or has made a site's "most read" list.[30] On SNSs, popularity cues in the form of social endorsements reduce partisan selective exposure "to levels indistinguishable from chance,"[31] leading to crosscutting as well as like-minded political discussions.[32] Advocates of this line of reasoning argue that audiences equate popularity with quality,[33] and are thus likely to see the popularity of a news story as evidence of its importance and accuracy.[34]

There are also characteristics of the online media system that increase the likelihood of audiences being more exposed to more popular content. Though no one outside of Facebook and Google knows exactly what goes into the algorithms that determine their link placements, it is understood that content popularity plays an important role. As a result, a headline from a brand name in news media that already has millions of followers (for example, CNN) is likely to get pushed out to audiences more often and more forcefully than a headline from a niche partisan news site. Webster and Ksiazek call this phenomenon "the persistence of popularity" and argue that, because of it, "most niche media will be doomed to obscurity."[35]

This raises the question: If the "persistence of popularity" has prevented media audiences from self-segregating into ideological filter bubbles, might it have the same effect when it comes to fake news? After all, partisan media and fake news are alike in significant ways: both are likely be obscure brands compared to those producing more general, centrist news; and both are likely to only appeal to a subset of the total news audience. Even if a fake news story goes "viral," and is shared many times on SNSs, it is still likely to be shared by and with media audiences who will also come across news stories from brand-name, establishment sources, simply because those sources have the resources and built-in followings to more effectively push their content out to the public. In light of these similarities, I hypothesize that:

H1. Visitors to fake news sites will comprise a small portion of the overall news audience, and will also spend less time with fake news than they do with real news.

H2. The fake news audience will also consume news from established news brands.

Studies of the fake news audience, while limited at this point, have found that visitors to fake news sites come overwhelmingly from social media platforms like Facebook.[36] Therefore, I also hypothesize that:

H3. Visitors to fake news sites will originate from SNSs more often than visitors to real news sites.

DATA

My data come from comScore, a Web analytic company that reports monthly estimates of online audiences. The company's data have been used in past analyses of digital audience behavior. The data are collected from a panel of about one million people who load comScore tracking software on their desktop computers. That software tracks the URLs the user visits and the time spent looking at each address. comScore fuses these data with server-based counts of traffic that come from tagging websites. Each month, comScore uses weights to make projections about the online behavior of the total US online audience. In October 2016, comScore recorded a total Internet audience of about 232 million unique visitors. Of those, about 162 million visited online news sites, as classified by comScore.

Defining Fake News

For this analysis, I compared 30 fake news sites with 24 real news sites. The real news sites comprised a variety of established brands within the news media environment (for example, Yahoo-ABC News, CNN, *New York Times, Washington Post,* Fox News, and BuzzFeed). The fake news sites stemmed from a list compiled by OpenSources, a research team led by media professor Melissa Zimdars. This list is updated regularly, but included 941 sites during my analysis that were tagged with a wide variety of different genres of "fake," including "satire" and "clickbait." I included the 126 sites that OpenSources had tagged explicitly as "fake." Of those 126, only 30 attracted enough visits in October 2016 to meet comScore's 30-visitor-per-month requirement to be included in its reports. As a result, the total number of sites in the sample was 54.

Analysis

To address H1, I examined visitation (measured by unique visitors) and engagement (measured by average minutes per visitor) for real and fake news sites over time, in order to observe any changes in audience behavior in the year leading up to and immediately following the presidential election. To do this, I compared the monthly average of visitors to real news sites with the monthly average of visitors to fake news site between January 2016 and January 2017. I then compared the monthly average time spent with real news sites with the monthly average engagement time spent with fake news sites between January 2016 and January 2017.

Then, focusing exclusively on October 2016 data, I ran a series of Point-Biserial Correlation analyses to observe whether a news site being fake was significantly related to it audience size (measured by unique visitors), its audience engagement (measured by average minutes per visitor), and the frequency by which its visitors originate from Facebook (measured by the percentage of visits coming from Facebook). Point-Biserial Correlations are used when correlating a dichotomous variable with a continuous variable. In this instance, the dichotomous variable is whether or not a news site is fake, while the continuous variables are the audience size, engagement, and rate of visitors originating from Facebook. Point-Biserial Correlations follow the same assumptions as Pearson correlations and measure the how strongly variables are associated. Observing these correlations allowed me to more rigorously address H1 and H3.

Finally, I looked at cross-visitation patterns to see what percentage of visitors to fake news sites also visited real news sites in October 2016, in order to get at H2. Doing so allowed me to understand if the fake news audience exists in a "filter bubble" or if the audience has a more varied news diet.

RESULTS

As figure 4.1 reveals, the number of monthly visitors to an average real news site was more than twenty-five times larger than the number of monthly visitors to an average fake news site throughout 2016, including the months leading up to and immediately following the presidential election. The audience size for an average real news site was about 9 million unique visitors, while the audience size for an average fake news site was only about 350,000, meaning the average fake news site attracted only about 4 percent of the average real news site. Even when the real news audience dropped suddenly, immediately following the election, it still boasted millions more unique visitors than the fake news audience. What's more, the drop seems to have lasted only a month, as it grew nearly back to its November peak in January 2017. These results support H1.

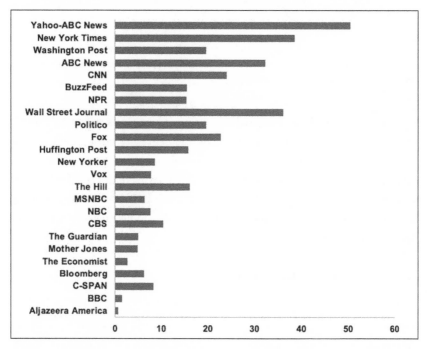

Figure 4.1. Audience size of real and fake news sites from January 2016 through January 2017 (as measured by unique visitors, in thousands).

Online audiences tended to also spend more time with real news than with fake news. As figure 4.2 shows, online audiences spent about nine minutes per month with an average real news site, while they only spent about half of that on average with an average fake news site. Note that engagement with real news increased following the election while engagement with fake news decreased.

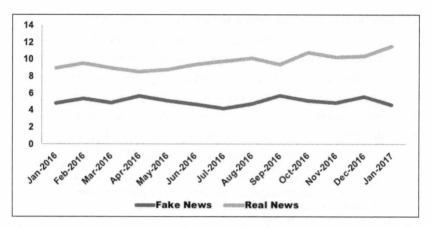

Figure 4.2. Engagement with real and fake news from January 2016 to January 2017 (as measured by average minutes per visitor).

I then performed Point-Biserial Correlation analyses to see if a news site being real or fake was significantly related to its audience size, engagement, and the source of its traffic. The results, as shown in table 4.1, reveal a strong, significant relationship between a news site being fake and it having both a smaller audience and lower levels of engagement, again corroborating H1. The results also reveal that visitors are significantly more likely to navigate to fake news sites from the SNS Facebook, supporting H3.

Table 4.1. Point-Biserial Correlation Results

	Unique visitors	Average minutes per visitor	% of visits from Facebook
Fake news	-0.5445* (-4.689)	-0.376**	0.6184*** (5.675)
df	52	52	52
N	54	54	54

Note: t-values in parentheses; * p<0.05, ** p<0.01, *** p<0.001.

Finally, I examined the rate at which the fake news audience also visits real news sites. As figure 4.3 shows, there appears to be quite a bit of overlap between real and fake news audiences. On average, 40 percent of the visitors to fake news sites in the sample also visited Yahoo-ABC, *New York Times, Wall Street Journal,* and ABC News. What's more, the percentage of the fake news audience that visited real news sites was very strongly correlated (.9) with the overall popularity of the real news site. So, although a small portion of the fake news audience visited the least popular real news sites in the sample—Al Jazeera (0.7 percent) and BBC (1.5 percent)—about half of the fake news audience visited the most popular sites in the sample—*New York Times* (40 percent) and Yahoo-ABC News (50 percent). This suggests that, rather than confined to an echo chamber, the fake news audience instead exposes itself to news content that a vast majority of the online audience also consumes. This supports H2.

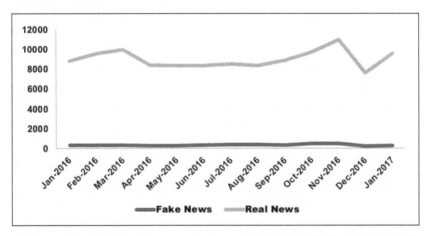

Figure 4.3. Percentage of visitors to fake news sites who also visited real news sites in October 2016. [Real news sites ranked in ascending order by unique visitors per month.]

DISCUSSION

The research director at Reuters Institute for the Study of Journalism recently observed that, when it comes to fake news, "We do not really know what is going on: how much is there, produced by whom, who uses it, why, and how much does it influence them?"[37] Many academics have heeded this call, and the results have been a tremendous outpouring of recent scholarship exploring these important questions. This essay is one more contribution intended to address them as well.

In doing so, it has found that the fake news audience is tiny compared to the real news audience, and has been that way since at least the beginning of 2016 up until and immediately following the US 2016 presidential election. The data analysis also revealed that a site's audience size and engagement are significantly and negatively related to it being a source of fake news. These results echo Allcott and Gentzkow's fake news analysis, which concluded that, "even the most widely circulated fake news stories were seen by only a small fraction of Americans." And, similar to prior studies of political news audiences behavior, the news audience is unlikely to segregate into echo chambers. Instead, the fake news audience visits popular, more centrist real news sites at a high rate that is strongly correlated with real news site popularity. Taken together, these findings indicate that the discourse surrounding fake news has overstated the size and isolation of its audience.

However, just because news audiences look at both real and fake news does not mean that real news corrects the misperceptions perpetuated by fake news. Exposure to political news is one thing, interpretation another. In fact, corrections frequently fail to change false or unsubstantiated beliefs, and might actually strengthen them, a result Nyhan and Reifler call "the backfire effect."[38] One limitation of this study is that it could not assess the way audiences reacted to the fake news they were exposed to. Yet, the fact that the fake news audience did not decrease in the past year, despite a large portion of it being exposed to real news, suggests this audience might not realize these fake news outlets are spreading lies. Instead, this audience may visit real news sites just to see "how the rest of the world 'falsely' understands current events."[39] This interpretation suggests that fake news does not change minds; it just confirms beliefs. If this is indeed the case, it means that real news in its current form will not bring citizens back to reality, even if it drowns fake news out or replaces it altogether.

So what's the solution? For now, there is a lot of experimentation, but there are few concrete answers. The two ideas that have attracted perhaps the most enthusiasm are investing more in local news and pushing newsrooms to be more transparent about their work. Many assume that local news is seen as more trustworthy and less partisan than national news, because it caters to a smaller, more geographically confined audience. It's easier to dislike the reporter you've never met in person than the one you run into at community events, or so the argument goes. And many also believe that journalists should "share their work," meaning they should be explicit about how they sourced their reporting, chose their quotes, and honed their narratives. Doing so will demonstrate to audiences that these decisions are not made lightly; nor are they made to "dupe" the public into going against their ideological leanings.

These ideas are valuable regardless of whether they serve as an antidote to fake news. Even if a percentage of the public never learns to trust the work of professional journalists acting in good faith to accurately report the news, there is something to be said for those journalists questioning how they can be reporting those stories in a way that leaves fewer, less obvious opportunities for doubt. And their pursuit speaks to a silver lining of the fake news crisis: that journalism as an institution is increasingly willing to question the norms and practices it had previously taken for granted.

NOTES

1. Shan Wang, "Slate's Chrome extension helps identify fake news on Facebook—and lets readers flag it themselves," last modified December 13, 2016, www.niemanlab.org/2016/12/slates-chrome-extension-helps-identify-fake-news-on-facebook-and-let-readers-flag-it-themselves/ (accessed February 13, 2018); Laura Hazard Owen, "Clamping down on viral fake news, Facebook partners with sites like Snopes and adds new user reporting," last modified December 15, 2016, www.niemanlab.org/2016/12/clamping-down-on-viral-fake-news-facebook-partners-with-sites-like-snopes-and-adds-new-user-reporting/ (accessed February 13, 2018); Ken Doctor, "Newsonomics: Fake-news fury forces Google and Facebook to change policy," last modified November 15, 2016, www.niemanlab.org/2016/11/newsonomics-fake-news-fury-forces-google-and-facebook-to-change-policy/ (accessed February 13, 2018); Ben Smith, "How tech and media can fight fake news," last modified November 17, 2016, www.cjr.org/first_person/ben_smith_fake_news_buzzfeed_facebook.php (accessed February 13, 2018).

2. Carolyn Thompson, "Teachers are now showing students how to spot fake news," last modified February 13, 2017, nypost.com/2017/02/13/teachers-are-now-showing-students-how-to-spot-fake-news/ (accessed February 13, 2018); Jerry Large, "Librarians take up arms against fake news," last modified February 5, 2017, www.seattletimes.com/seattle-news/librarians-take-up-arms-against-fake-news/ (accessed February 13, 2018).

3. Jacob L. Nelson and Harsh Taneja, "The Small, Disloyal Fake News Audience: The Role of Audience Availability in Fake News Consumption," *New Media & Society,* 2018, doi.org/10.1177/1461444818758715.

4. Matthew Gentzkow and Jesse M. Shapiro, "Ideological Segregation Online and Offline." *Quarterly Journal of Economics* 126, no. 4 (2011): 1799–1839, doi: 10.1093/qje/qjr044; Brian E. Weeks, Thomas B. Ksiazek, and R. Lance Holbert, "Partisan Enclaves or Shared Media Experiences? A Network Approach to Understanding Citizens' Political News Environments," *Journal of Broadcasting & Electronic Media* 60, no. 2 (2016): 248–68.

5. Amy Mitchell, Jeffrey Gottfried, Jocelyn Kiley, and Katerina Eva Matsa, "Political Polarization & Media Habits," Pew Research Journalism Project, 2014, www.journalism.org/2014/10/21/political-polarization-media-habits/.

6. David Uberti, "The real history of fake news," last modified December 16, 2016, www.cjr.org/special_report/fake_news_history.php (accessed February 15, 2018).

7. Jacob Soll, "The Long and Brutal History of Fake News," last modified December 18, 2016, www.politico.com/magazine/story/2016/12/fake-news-history-long-violent-214535 (accessed February 15, 2018).

8. Robert Darnton, "The True History of Fake News," last modified February 13, 2017, www .nybooks.com/daily/2017/02/13/the-true-history-of-fake-news/ (accessed February 15, 2018).

9. Alexis de Tocqueville, *Democracy in America,* ed. Eduardo Nolla, trans. James T. Schleifer (Indianapolis: Liberty Fund, 2012).

10. Mark Thompson, "Mark Thompson Delivers Speech on Fake News," last modified December 12, 2016, www.nytco.com/mark-thompson-delivers-speech-on-fake-news/ (accessed February 15, 2018).

11. Caitlin Dewey, "Facebook fake-news writer: 'I think Donald Trump is in the White House because of me,'" last modified November 17, 2016, www.washingtonpost.com/news/the-intersect /wp/2016/11/17/facebook-fake-news-writer-i-think-donald-trump-is-in-the-white-house-because -of-me/?utm_term=.da2d23c4f0ab (accessed February 15, 2018).

12. Dave Davies, "Fake News Expert on How False Stories Spread and Why People Believe Them," last modified December 16, 2016, www.npr.org/2016/12/14/505547295/fake-news-expert-on-how-false -stories-spread-and-why-people-believe-them (accessed February 17, 2018).

13. Brian Flood, "Mike Huckabee Apologizes for Sharing Fake News about 'Liberal, Jewish' Students," last modified November 18, 2016, www.thewrap.com/mike-huckabee-facebook-fake-news -liberal-jewish-students-apology (accessed February 14, 2018).

14. Jason Silverstein, "Northwestern University freshmen allegedly spray-paint slurs, swastika and 'Trump' in campus chapel," last modified March 13, 2016, www.nydailynews.com/news/national /northwestern-freshmen-paint-slurs-trump-chapel-article-1.2563021 (accessed February 16, 2018).

15. Aaron Blake, "Michael Flynn's tweet wasn't actually about #PizzaGate, but his son is now defending the baseless conspiracy theory," last modified December 5, 2016, www.washingtonpost .com/news/the-fix/wp/2016/12/05/did-michael-flynn-really-tweet-something-about-pizzagate-not -exactly/?utm_term=.b2b157b72f4d (accessed February 15, 2018).

16. Anthony Ha, "WTF Is Fake News?" last modified February 5, 2017, techcrunch.com/2017 /02/05/wtf-is-fake-news (accessed February 14, 2018).

17. Craig Timberg, "Russian propaganda effort helped spread 'fake news' during election, experts say." *Washington Post,* November 24, 2016. www.washingtonpost.com/business/economy/russian -propaganda-effort-helped-spread-fake-news-during-election-experts-say/2016/11/24/793903b6–8a 40–4ca9-b712–716af66098fe_story.html?utm_term=.eebfde8a22f8.

18. Brian Bennett, "U.S. intelligence report says Putin targeted presidential election to 'harm' Hillary Clinton's chances," last modified January 6 2017, www.latimes.com/nation/la-na-trump-russia -20170106-story.html (accessed February 15, 2018).

19. Max Read, "Donald Trump Won Because of Facebook," last modified November 9, 2016, nymag.com/selectall/2016/11/donald-trump-won-because-of-facebook.html (accessed February 15, 2018); Hannah Jane Parkinson, "Click and elect: how fake news helped Donald Trump win a real election," November 14, 2016, www.theguardian.com/commentisfree/2016/nov/14/fake-news-donald -trump-election-alt-right-social-media-tech-companies.

20. Jeffrey Gottfried and Elisa Shearer, "News Use Across Social Media Platforms 2016," Pew Research Center, www.journalism.org/2016/05/26/news-use-across-social-media-platforms-2016/.

21. Timothy B. Lee, "Facebook's fake news problem, explained," last modified November 16, 2016, www.vox.com/new-money/2016/11/16/13637310/facebook-fake-news-explained (accessed February 15, 2018).

22. Lulu Chang, "Google Is Fighting Fake News in France with a New Project Called Crosscheck," last modified February 7, 2017, www.digitaltrends.com/web/google-fake-news-crosscheck/ (accessed February 17, 2018).

23. Will Oremus. "Only You Can Stop the Spread of Fake News," last modified Dec. 13, 2016, www .slate.com/articles/technology/technology/2016/12/introducing_this_is_fake_slate_s_tool_for _stopping_fake_news_on_facebook.html (accessed February 16, 2018).

24. Philip Bump, "Political polarization is getting worse. Everywhere," *Washington Post,* April 9, 2016, www.washingtonpost.com/news/the-fix/wp/2016/04/09/polarization-is-getting-worse-in-every -part-of-politics/?utm_term=.233cc3242d91.

25. Carroll Doherty, Jocelyn Kiley, and Bridget Jameson, "Partisanship and Political Animosity in 2016," Pew Research Center, assets.pewresearch.org/wp-content/uploads/sites/5/2016/06/06-22 -16-Partisanship-and-animosity-release.pdf.

26. Susanna Dilliplane, "All the News You Want to Hear: The Impact of Partisan News Expo- sure on Political Participation," *Public Opinion Quarterly* 75, no. 2 (2011): 287–316, doi:10.1093/poq /nfr006; Natalie J. Stroud, "Polarization and Partisan Selective Exposure," *Journal of Communication* 60, no. 3 (2010): 556–76; Matthew Levendusky, *How Partisan Media Polarize America* (Chicago: University of Chicago Press, 2013); David A. Jones, Kathleen Ferraiolo, and Jennifer Byrne, "Selective media exposure and partisan differences about Sarah Palin's candidacy," *Politics & Policy* 39, no. 2 (2011): 195.

27. Dolf Zillmann and Jennings Bryant, eds., *Selective Exposure to Communication* (Hillsdale, NJ: Lawrence Erlbaum Associates, 1985); Joseph T. Klapper, *The Effects of Mass Communication* (Glencoe, IL: Free Press, 1960); P. F. Lazarsfeld and E. Katz, *Personal Influence: The Part Played by People in the Flow of Mass Communications* (Glencoe, IL: Free Press, 1955).

28. Seth Flaxman, Sharad Goel, and Justin M. Rao, "Filter Bubbles, Echo Chambers, and Online News Consumption," *Public Opinion Quarterly* 80 (2016): 298–320, doi:10.1093/poq/nfw006.

29. Jacob L. Nelson and James G. Webster, "The Myth of Partisan Selective Exposure: A Portrait of the Online Political News Audience," *Social Media + Society* 3, no. 3 (2017): 52, doi: 10.1177/2056305117729314.

30. Silvia Knobloch-Westerwick, Nikhil Sharma, Derek L. Hansen, and Scott Alter, "Impact of Popularity Indications on Readers' Selective Exposure to Online News," *Journal of Broadcasting & Electronic Media* 49, no. 3 (2005): 296–313; JungAe Yang, "Effects of Popularity-Based News Recom- mendations ('Most-Viewed') on Users' Exposure to Online News," *Media Psychology* 19, no. 2 (2015): 243–71, doi:10.1080/15213269.2015.1006333.

31. Solomon Messing and Sean J. Westwood, "Selective Exposure in the Age of Social Media," *Communication Research* 41, no. 3 (2014): 1042–63, doi:10.1177/0093650212466406.

32. Kyle A. Heatherly, Yanqin Lu, and Jae Kook Lee, "Filtering out the other side? Cross-cutting and like-minded discussions on social networking sites," *New Media & Society,* 2016, doi:10.1177/1461444816634677.

33. J. G. Webster, *The Marketplace of Attention: How Audiences Take Shape in a Digital Age* (Cambridge, MA: MIT Press, 2014); J. G. Webster and T. B. Ksiazek, "The Dynamics of Audience Fragmentation: Public Attention in an Age of Digital Media," *Journal of Communication* 62, no. 1 (2012): 39–56, doi:10.1111/j.1460–2466.2011.01616.

34. Diana C. Mutz and Lori Young, "Communication and Public Opinion," *Public Opinion Quarterly* 75, no. 5 (2011): 1018–44, doi:10.1093/poq/nfr052; S. Asch, "Effects of group pressure upon the modification and distortion of judgment," *Journal of Social Psychology* 12 (1951): 433–65.

35. Webster and Ksiazek, "Dynamics of Audience Fragmentation," 52.

36. Hunt Allcott and Matthew Gentzkow, "Social Media and Fake News in the 2016 Election," *Journal of Economic Perspectives* 31, no. 2 (Spring 2017): 211–36, web.stanford.edu/~gentzkow/research /fakenews.pdf.

37. Rasmus Kleis Nielsen, "Fake news—an optimistic take," rasmuskleisnielsen.net, last modified January 17, 2017, rasmuskleisnielsen.net/2017/01/17/fake-news-an-optimistic-take/ (accessed February 13, 2018).

38. Brendan Nyhan and Jason Reifler, "When Corrections Fail: The Persistence of Political Misperceptions," *Political Behavior* 32, no. 2 (2010): 303–30. doi:10.1007/s11109–010–9112–2.

39. Jacob L. Nelson, "Is Fake News a Fake Problem?" last modified January 31, 2017, www.cjr.org /analysis/fake-news-facebook-audience-drudge-breitbart-study.php (accessed February 10, 2018).

CAN MEDIA LITERACY REDUCE BIASES IN BELIEFS ABOUT SUSCEPTIBILITY TO FAKE NEWS?

A SURVEY EXPERIMENT

Tryfon Boukouvidis, Pamela Labbe, and Michael Henderson

R ecent years have seen a rise in so-called fake news, that is, fabricated information masquerading as news reporting of actual facts and circulated online, particularly through social media. This phenomenon has generated substantial public and scholarly attention since the 2016 US presidential election. The question of how fake news affects democratic governance has been a chief concern, with good reason. Most normative theories of democracy require a citizenry equipped with at least a modicum of accurate information about candidates, government, and policies. Because so much of public affairs unfold at a distance from the experiences of our day-to-day lives, we rely largely on media as sources for this kind of information.

From this perspective, the rise of fake news poses a powerful threat to democratic governance by injecting misinformation in the guise of news reports. Although there is some debate about the potential for fake news to distort the outcome of any particular election, widespread concern remains about the susceptibility of voters to believe misinformation cloaked as news reporting.[1] Additionally, there is widespread scholarly agreement that misperceptions matter for opinions about policies and candidates.[2] Worse still, exposure to political information does not stop shaping the public's attitudes even when the information is later discredited, suggesting that fact-checking and other forms of correction may prove insufficient to reverse these effects.[3] Looking beyond isolated political issues, fake news may have even more pernicious effects by degrading trust in media generally.[4]

A consequence of protections for freedoms of speech and press in the United States is that the onus for assessing the credibility of news falls upon the media consumer. Even as new fact-checking organizations emerge (as well as fact-checking enterprises within existing news organizations), news consumers must make the effort to access these sources or to verify the accuracy of reports in other ways. A central question, then, is whether media consumers are savvy enough to recognize fake news when exposed to it. Americans certainly believe they are well equipped to do so. Recent survey evidence from the Pew Research Center indicates that 39 percent are "very confident" in their ability to recognize news that is made up; another 45 percent are "somewhat confident."[5] Only 15 percent are either "not very confident" or "not at all confident."

There are at least two reasons for skepticism about this high degree of self-confidence. First, individuals' self-assessments of their abilities are frequently subject to an overconfidence effect—that is, their subjective assessments far exceed their actual performance. Second, individuals' beliefs about who is susceptible to media effects tend to suffer a third-person effect—that is, people assume others are far more likely to be swayed by what they encounter in media than they are themselves. In the context of fake news, a third-person effect implies that most Americans have grave doubts about their fellow citizens' ability to handle the obligation of citizenship to make political decisions rooted in accurate information. Such doubts would not bode well for general faith in the democratic system of governance.

To asses these perils—and explore the potential for information about media literacy and methods to identify fake news to mitigate them—we conducted an online survey measuring confidence in ability to recognize false news stories as well as behaviors that reflect media literacy. We embedded a question-order experiment within the survey, allowing us to measure the effect of exposure to information about how to identify fake news (and, thus, exposure to how frequently or infrequently individuals use these means) on self-assessments of ability to identify fake news as well as on assessments of others' abilities. For the latter we measure individuals' confidence in Americans generally, in co-partisans, and in individuals who identify with the opposite political party. We find that confidence in one's own ability to recognize fake news is poorly correlated with behaviors that would facilitate such recognition. We demonstrate as well that exposure to information about media literacy can reduce overconfidence in one's ability to recognize fake news and reduce the partisan gap in the third-person effect.

THE THREAT OF FAKE NEWS

The academic study of fake news is in its infancy, invigorated by the prominence of the term in public discussion of the 2016 US presidential contest. During that campaign, digital media—particularly social media platforms—witnessed the spread of misinformation in the form of factually incorrect articles masked as news stories. Research has yet to confirm the effect of this misinformation on the outcome of the election. On the one hand, fake news was widely disseminated during the 2016 election. Allcott and Gentzkow, after analyzing 156 fake news stories that appeared in the months prior to the election, estimated the articles had been shared nearly 38 million times.[6] On the other hand, exposure was largely concentrated among individuals least likely to be persuaded by it, that is, who already opposed the candidate criticized in the stories.[7] Whatever the ultimate determination on the question of the 2016 election, fake news continues to capture scholarly and public attention largely due to concern about two broader sets of consequences.

First, there is scholarly agreement that factual beliefs matter for political opinions. Misperceptions about whether the US military found weapons of mass destruction in Iraq were highly correlated with support for the war there.[8] Beliefs that the Affordable Care Act established "death panels" or beliefs that the bill did not include popular policies such as preserving coverage for preexisting conditions depressed support for the legislation.[9] Previous work has shown that misinformation about the share of the federal budget spent on welfare programs can substantially shift opinions on spending, and information about local school districts' spending can move opinions on education finance. Inaccurate beliefs about the risks of vaccines reduce intentions to receive vaccination.[10] There are high-profile instances of severe responses to fake news—such as an individual showing up at a Washington, DC, area restaurant with a firearm in response to misinformation claiming it was a site for a traffic sex trafficking involving political leaders. However, fake news poses a broader threat to democracy by distorting citizens' preferences from what they would be if accurately informed.

Second, the existence of fake news poses another set of consequences for democratic governance in how our society chooses to deal with this threat. Increasingly there are calls for more regulation of media to curb the threat of misinformation online, but there are also calls for greater sophistication among the consumers of media—that is, for media literacy campaigns. In the former, the government or media companies would play a larger role in addressing the threats posed by fake news. In the latter, the onus would be on consumers and any organizations working to enhance critical consumption of online media. The prospects of success—that is, the ability of digital news consumers to become media literate and assess not only the veracity of purported news, but also their own potential susceptibility to misinformation—remains unknown.

THE OVERCONFIDENCE EFFECT

Research in psychology and economics has long demonstrated that people are prone to overconfidence across a variety of domains.[11] We tend to believe that we are better at predicting future events, better at learning, better at teaching, better at driving, and better at just about anything than we actually are when behavior or performance is measured objectively.[12] Our judgments of our capabilities tend to be poorly calibrated; that is, our subjective assessments of performance fail to line up with empirically measured performance.

Furthermore, these biases in judgment have negative consequences for behavior. Overestimation of one's abilities tends to induce errors. In other words, people who express higher levels of confidence in their abilities are more likely to engage in riskier behaviors and make mistakes than those who express less confidence. Much of the research on the effects of overconfidence has been done in the realms of financial investment and consumer behavior.[13] Yet, little is known about how the problem of overconfidence may apply to media consumption. If the same pattern holds for media consumption, then Americans are more in danger of being misled by fake news than they realize.

THE THIRD-PERSON EFFECT

Even if Americans properly calibrate their judgments about their own ability to recognize attempts to misinform them, a second problem remains regarding their trust in the ability of their fellow citizens to do the same. Democracy requires a certain amount of faith in the citizenry as a whole to handle the responsibilities of democratic citizenship, including making political decisions rooted in factually accurate perceptions of the world. Even when citizens disagree with the particular decisions made, the system requires a shared acceptance of the legitimacy of those decisions.

Yet, just as individuals often overestimate their own abilities, they also tend to judge the abilities of others as worse than their own. In the study of media, this is known as the third-person effect.[14] The third-person effect suggests people believe media are less likely to affect them than their peers.[15] The effect is rooted in a psychological desire for self-enhancement through perceptions of comparative superiority.[16]

The phenomenon has political consequences. Americans who think of themselves as smarter than the next person tend to believe vulnerable others need protection from media influence.[17] Prior research links gaps in third-person perception, which is the difference in perceived media influence on others versus oneself, to pro-censorship attitudes toward media perceived as potentially harmful.[18]

If Americans are confident in their own ability to identify fake news while simultaneously remaining incredulous of their neighbors' capacity to inoculate themselves from misinformation, then the rise of fake news may embolden efforts to restrict the means of mass communication. This threat is particularly poignant given the common association between instances of fake news (or accusations of fake news) and political topics. This political context raises a question about how partisanship shapes the third-person effect.

The third-person effect is more prevalent as the social distance between individuals or groups increases.[19] We tend to see people who are demographically, geographically, or politically similar to us as more socially proximate and those who are different from ourselves on these dimensions as socially distant.[20] As a result, we assume the former are more likely to respond in the same way we do to communications than are others who seem different from us.

Partisanship is itself a powerful social identity.[21] It not only shapes how we process information but also how we perceive each other. Increasingly, partisans in the United States have more negative attitudes of the opposing party and associate individuals identifying it with more negative traits. Indeed, partisanship causes a political and social divide based on in-group favoritism and out-group animosity that stands even stronger than American racial differences.[22] It is likely then that Americans do not simply have little faith in their fellow citizens to resist fake news, but are especially doubtful of the ability of individuals identifying with the opposing party to do so. This poses an acute problem for American democracy. If a generic third-person effect prompts individuals to support government intervention in media, then a partisan third-person effect may lead to politically biased censorship of news—real or fake. The recent work of Jang and Kim, showing that individuals identifying with each major party are more dubious of the other party's ability to resist fake news, highlights this danger.[23] One potential implication is that the overlap of partisanship with perceived susceptibility to fake news and policy preferences for dealing with this threat can lead to polarization in attitudes toward censorship, in which each side calls for intervention in media perceived as supporting the other side. This risk heightens the importance of knowing whether an alternate approach emphasizing media literacy promotion over regulation can reduce both overconfidence and the third-person effect.

MEDIA LITERACY

Media literacy is receiving attention as a potential aid for individuals navigating an increasingly treacherous landscape of mass communication.[24] Media literacy involves efforts to inform an audience about aspects of the media with the intention of reducing media's potentially harmful effects.[25] Instruction in media literacy aims at increasing skills, building knowledge and encouraging critical thinking.[26] The purpose is to provide consumers of media with more control over how media affect them. Proponents of media literacy instruction simultaneously claim that media effects, triggered by mass media's direct and indirect influence, can be harmful to individuals, and that interventions can be constructed that help people avoid the media's potentially negative effects. In short, media literacy's core assumption is that, when people are effectively taught the necessary skills to access, evaluate, analyze, and produce media, they can better understand the roles and responsibilities of media in civic life.[27]

The body of literature testing media literacy is limited but growing. Current research suggests that certain interventions can help insulate individuals from normatively problematic media effects.[28] One such experiment, for example, demonstrates that individuals exposed to a short media literacy presentation are less likely to perceive accurate news as biased.[29]

Yet, little empirical evidence exists about the effect of media literacy on perceptions of ability to identify fake news. At the same time, calls for greater media literacy in assessing the accuracy of purported news are on the rise. Many common interventions to spot fake news exist, including checking whether the story cites records or data, looking up the quotes in the story, and verifying factual information and whether the data in the story is correct as statistics are often misrepresented.[30] Additionally, fact-checking organizations, such as FactCheck. org, check whether story sources back up the reporter's claim. The Center for Media Literacy advises readers to examine whether news stories with questionable arguments and data also appear in trusted news sources.[31] Questions about the extent to which Americans engage in these behaviors or take advantage of these fact-checking resources and about how these activities relate to beliefs about one's ability to distinguish between real news and misinformation remain open.

RESEARCH QUESTIONS

We will examine four research questions. First, do Americans overestimate their ability to recognize fake news? Following the psychological theory about the overconfidence effect, we expect that individuals poorly calibrate their ability to identify fake news. In other words, individuals tend to overestimate their ability to identify fake news relative to the kinds of actions and behaviors they engage in to consume news. As a result, ratings of one's ability to identify fake news will not reflect higher levels of media literacy.

Second, does instruction in media literacy reduce overconfidence? If, as we expect, individuals overestimate their ability to recognize fake news relative to the kinds of behaviors they actually use when reading news online, then we expect that highlighting these behaviors (and, thus, their infrequency of use) to individuals will reduce the tendency to overestimate ability. Because individuals overestimate their ability relative to their behaviors, when they are asked to report on the frequency with which they engage in behaviors to help identify fake news, they will recalibrate their confidence to do so. In other words, showing confident individuals the kinds of actions they do not do (or do not do regularly) that would help them identify fake news will lead them to lower their confidence in their ability to identify it.

Third, is there a partisan gap in perceptions of susceptibility to fake news? Although individuals generally think other people are more susceptible to media effects than they are themselves, we expect this third-person effect will be stronger when assessing members of an opposing political party than when assessing members of their own political party.

Finally, does instruction in media literacy reduce the partisan gap in perceptions of susceptibility? We expect that exposure to information about media literacy that describes ways of identifying fake news online will reduce the partisan gap in the third-person effect. This expectation parallels our expectation regarding the impact of information about media literacy on perceptions of one's own abilities to recognize fake news. That is, individuals will reassess their confidence in their co-partisans once exposed to information about actual behaviors that would help identify fake news. This effect is imbalanced across parties because individuals are already likely to have minimal levels of confidence in their opposing party's ability to identify fake news, leaving little room for further decline.

METHODOLOGY

To understand confidence in ability to recognize made-up news stories, we fielded a survey containing questions about confidence and a battery of items measuring self-reported media consumption behaviors. The survey company YouGov administered the survey online to a representative sample of the US population. The sample consists of one thousand US adults.[32]

The question asking about participants' confidence in themselves resembles the following item from the Pew Research Center: "As you may have heard, there have recently been some instances of so called 'fake news stories' circulating widely online. How confident are you in your own ability to recognize news that is made up? Are you very confident, somewhat confident, not very confident, or not at all confident?"

Additionally, participants were asked about their confidence in others to identify fake news, but they were randomly assigned to one of three versions of the question. One group was asked: "How confident are you in the ability of Americans generally to recognize news that is made up?" A second group was asked: "How confident are you in the ability of Democrats to recognize news that is made up?" A third group was asked: "How confident are you in the ability of Republicans to recognize news that is made up?" Comparing responses across these three conditions allows us to see how the magnitude of the third-person effect varies by the correspondence or dissimilarity between the partisanship of the respondent and the partisanship of the group in question relative to a comparison with a generic "American" as the baseline.

The survey also included a media behavior battery with five items. Research shows that fake news articles tend to differ from actual news articles on a number of predictable dimensions related to style and content.[33] In selecting items for inclusion in the survey, we follow public recommendations for media consumption based on these patterns—specifically, media literacy initiatives at Stony Brook University and Louisiana State University. Additionally, we include use of online fact-checking services as they are increasingly common.[34] The battery reads:

> Below, there are five methods that are recommended to help recognize news stories that are made up. When reading a news story, how often do you:
>
> 1. Check whether the news story cites records or data?
>
> 2. Check the internet address of the site on which the story appears to make sure it's not an altered version of a common web address (for example, abc.go.com versus abc.com.co)?
>
> 3. Check the quotes in the story (for example, copying and pasting a quote into an internet search to see if it is also published elsewhere)?
>
> 4. Check the images in a story (for example, by using Google Images to see whether the image has been used in other stories or on other sites)?
>
> 5. Visit fact-checking websites, such as FactCheck.org or PolitiFact. com, to verify the information in the story?

The items were presented in grid format with each appearing in a separate row. Response options (in columns) included: "Never," "Almost never," "Sometimes," "Fairly often," and "Very often."

Finally, to test the effect of providing information about media consumption behaviors that help individuals recognize fake news, we included a question-order experiment. Participants were randomly assigned either to answer the confidence questions before the behavior questions or vice versa. Participants in the latter group, thus, were first forced to think about media literacy and how their behavior measures up to these suggested behaviors before being asked about their confidence. Therefore, their responses reveal whether instruction in media literacy can mitigate overconfidence effects and third-person effects.

DO AMERICANS OVERESTIMATE THEIR ABILITY TO
RECOGNIZE FAKE NEWS?

We begin by examining the relationship between confidence in one's ability to identify fake news and actual behaviors people could use to identify such stories online. Considering only the participants who answered the confidence questions prior to the media literacy questions, Americans are quite confident in their ability to recognize made-up news: 31 percent say they are very confident, and 49 percent say they are somewhat confident. Just 17 percent say they are not very confident in their ability to recognize news that is made up, and only 4 percent say they are not at all confident. Although most Americans believe they can identify fake news, relatively few use the means included in this survey to do so. Table 5.1 shows the self-reported frequencies for the five media literacy items. In no case does a majority of participants indicate they engage in the behavior fairly often or very often. The final row of the table reports the Kendall's tau coefficient for the relationship between each item and the measure of confidence in one's ability to identify fake news. Kendall's tau coefficient is a common measure for the strength of correlation between two ordinal variables, with values closest to one indicating a stronger positive relationship and values closer to zero indicating a weaker relationship. With all values falling below 0.30, the confidence measure is weakly correlated with behavior in each case here. In fact, the coefficient exceeds 0.25 for only one item: check whether the news story cites records or data.

Table 5.1. Self-Reported Frequency of Behaviors

	Never	Almost never	Sometimes	Fairly often	Very often	Tau-b
Check for records and data?	18	13	27	24	18	0.28
Check URL?	22	14	28	20	16	0.22
Check quotes?	29	18	32	12	9	0.20
Check images?	32	23	30	10	6	0.18
Use fact-checking sites?	28	15	33	15	10	0.22

Note: Values of the first five columns are percentages in each response category. Percentages may not sum to 100 due to rounding. Tau-b coefficients are for correlation with self-confidence measure.

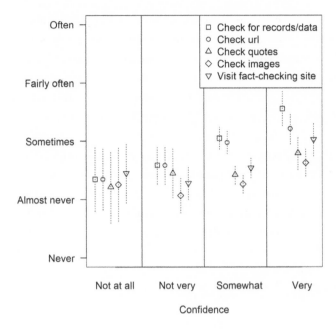

Figure 5.1. Frequency of behavior by level of confidence in own ability to identify fake news. Markers indicate the mean response on a one ("Never") to five ("Often") point scale for each of five behavior items broken out by reported confidence in ability to identify fake news (horizontal axis). Dashed lines indicate 95 percent confidence intervals around mean response. Results are only for participants who were asked the confidence question prior to the behavior questions.

Figure 5.1 displays these relationships visually, showing the average response on a scale from 1 ("never") to 5 ("very often") for each behavior item by response to the confidence item. Lower values on the left side of the figure (for those who answer "not at all confident") and higher values on the right side (for those who answer "very confident") indicate a positive association whereby individuals who are more confident in their own ability to identify fake news also engage in these behaviors more frequently. Yet, in only two cases—checking whether the news story cites records or data and checking the internet address of the site on which the story appears to make sure it's not an altered version of a common web address—do individuals who are "somewhat confident" or "very confident" engage in media literate behaviors more frequently than those who are "not very confident" or "not at all confident."

Perhaps more importantly, the figure shows just how rarely Americans check the purported news stories they encounter online. There is only one instance for which the average frequency of behavior among those who are "very confident" in their own ability to identify fake news exceeds "sometimes": checking whether the news story cites records or data. For all other levels of confidence and behaviors, respondents' average frequency is "sometimes" or less.

DOES INSTRUCTION IN MEDIA LITERACY REDUCE OVERCONFIDENCE?

The results so far indicate people likely overstate their ability to recognize fake news. They are confident in their own ability, but they do not tend to engage in the kind of critical approaches that would actually help them identify news that is made up. Can this overconfidence be corrected?

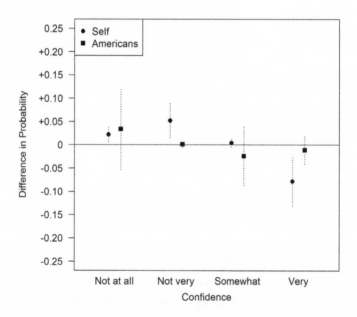

Figure 5.2. Effect of information about identifying fake news on confidence. Markers show the estimated effect of prior exposure to the media literacy battery on the probability (vertical axis) of responses to the questions about confidence in one's own ability to identify fake news and the ability of other Americans to identify fake news. Markers above the horizontal line indicate the response shown on the horizontal axis is more likely after exposure to the media literacy battery. Markers below the horizontal line indicate the response is less likely. Dashed lines indicate 95 percent confidence intervals around mean response.

Our question-order experiment indicates that people will reduce their estimate of their own ability to better reflect their actual behaviors if they are first instructed about what kinds of behaviors are helpful for identifying fake news. Figure 5.2 shows the treatment effect of exposure to the media literacy items before the confidence item on the probability of answering with each response option to the latter. Points above the dashed line indicate that individuals who saw the media literacy items first are more likely to select the particular response shown on the horizontal axis than individuals who saw the confidence item first. Likewise, points below the dashed line indicate they are less likely to select the response option.

Individuals exposed to information about how to check the veracity of purported news stories online are more likely to say they are "not very confident" (+0.02) or "not at all confident" (+0.05) in their own ability to identify fake news. They are also less likely to say they are "very confident" (-0.08). Although the effects are relatively small, they nevertheless show that instruction in how people could actually evaluate the accuracy of online news stories reduces the tendency to overestimate their own abilities to do so.

DOES INSTRUCTION IN MEDIA LITERACY REDUCE THE PARTISAN GAP IN PERCEPTIONS OF SUSCEPTIBILITY?

Table 5.2 shows the responses among partisans to the questions measuring confidence in one's own ability to identify fake news, confidence in other Americans' ability to do so, confidence in individuals who share the respondent's own party identification, and confidence in individuals who identify with the opposing party. The first two columns reveal the standard third-person effect: individuals tend to think others are more susceptible to fake news than themselves. The last two columns, however, shed new light on the third-person effect. When it comes to evaluating co-partisans there is little evidence of a third-person effect at all: 85 percent of partisans are "somewhat confident" or "very confident" in their own ability to identify fake news, and 79 percent are "somewhat confident" or "very confident" in their fellow partisans. In contrast, there is a wide gap between how partisans view themselves (or their co-partisans) and how they view individuals who identify with the opposite party. Whereas only 3 percent are "not at all confident" in themselves, nearly half are "not at all confident" in the opposite party's ability to identify fake news. In short, consistent with recent work from

Jang and Kim, Americans tend to think that only the other side of the political aisle is susceptible to the threat of deception from fake news.[35]

Table 5.2. Confidence in Ability to Identify Fake News (among Partisans)

	Self	Americans	Co-partisans	Opposing partisans
Very	37	6	30	5
Somewhat	48	27	49	18
Not very	12	38	15	29
Not at all	3	28	7	48

Note: Values are percentages in each response category. Percentages may not sum to 100 due to rounding.

EFFECT OF MEDIA LITERACY ON THE PARTISAN GAP IN CONFIDENCE

Whereas previous research explores the effect of a third-person effect on attitudes toward media literacy interventions versus media regulation, our analysis examines the effect of a media literacy intervention on third-person effects. Figure 5.3 shows the effects of exposure to the media literacy items on confidence in one's own ability, the ability of other Americans, the ability of co-partisans, and the ability of opposing partisans to identify fake news. Once again, exposure to methods for identifying fake news has a negative effect on partisans' confidence in themselves just as for the entire sample above. Partisans exposed to these behaviors are significantly less likely to say they are "very confident" in their own ability to recognize fake news.

Interestingly, this information does not have a similar effect on evaluations of co-partisans. There is no evidence that confidence in co-partisans' ability to identify fake news differs by exposure to information about how to assess the accuracy of news stories online. However, exposure to this information does reduce the partisan gap in perceptions of susceptibility to fake news—not by reducing confidence in co-partisans, but by increasing confidence in partisans from the opposite side. Partisans exposed to means of identifying fake news are less likely to say they are "not at all confident" that individuals in the opposing party can identify fake news (-0.11) and more likely to say they are "somewhat confident" (+0.06).

This last result is unexpected. Although the explanation remains unclear, one possibility is that exposure to the media literacy battery primes accuracy motivations relative to partisan motivations in assessing abilities to identify fake news. As a consequence, partisans may be less inclined to underestimate the ability of opposing partisans.

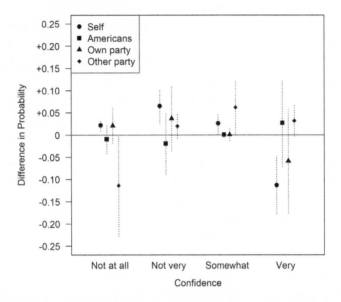

Figure 5.3. Effect of information about identifying fake news on confidence, partisans only. Markers show the estimated effect of prior exposure to the media literacy battery on the probability (vertical axis) of responses to the questions about confidence in one's own ability to identify fake news, the ability of other Americans to identify fake news, and the ability of partisan groups to identify fake news. Markers above the horizontal line indicate the response shown on the horizontal axis is more likely after exposure to the media literacy battery. Markers below the horizontal line indicate the response is less likely. Estimates in this figure are for partisans only (that is, individuals who either identify with or lean toward one of the two major American political parties). Dashed lines indicate 95 percent confidence intervals around mean response.

DISCUSSION

The results of this study demonstrate that individuals tend to overestimate their ability to identify fake news relative to the kinds of actions they take to do so. This is an instance of the overconfidence effect and, as such, suggests that Americans are more susceptible to misinformation than they suspect. Perceptions about capacity to identify fake news also exhibit a third-person effect whereby individuals assess others' abilities more poorly than their own. Furthermore, the third-person effect is, in part, a reflection of partisanship—we assess the ability of individuals in the opposing party as much worse than our own ability (and worse than generically identified Americans), and we assess the ability of our co-partisans about as well as ourselves.

Informing people about how to actually go about identifying fake news—and reminding them of how rarely they engage in these behaviors—tends to decrease self-reported confidence. This information also reduces the partisan third-person effect. However, this latter effect follows an unexpected pattern—not by reducing confidence in one's co-partisans (as it does for confidence in one's own abilities), but rather by boosting confidence in opposing partisans' abilities. The results provide an extension to discussion of how third-person effects can drive preferences for how to deal with the threat of fake news online. The work of Jang and Kim, for example, raises the possibility that a partisan-tilted third-person effect can enhance calls for regulation, particularly of media seen as supporting the opposing side—a deeply problematic normative concern in a democracy.[36] The results presented here offer some salvo. Media literacy—over and above any effect it may have on the ability to identify fake news—reduces the partisan third-person effect.

Together, these two effects suggest that instruction in media literacy can have positive outcomes for democratic citizenship. It can reduce overconfidence, which is prone to error. It can also reduce skepticism about one's fellow citizens, especially citizens on the other side of the partisan aisle, to successfully navigate the media landscape.

NOTES

1. Alice Marwick and Rebecca Lewis, *Media Manipulation and Disinformation Online* (New York: Data and Society Research Institute, 2017).

2. James H. Kuklinski, Paul J. Quirk, Jennifer Jerit, David Schwieder, and Robert F. Rich, "Misinformation and the Currency of Democratic Citizenship," *Journal of Politics* 62, no. 3 (2000): 790–816; Martin Gilens, "Political Ignorance and Collective Policy Preferences," *American Political Science Review* 95, no. 2 (2001): 379–96; John Sides, "Stories or Science? Facts, Frames, and Policy Attitudes," *American Politics Research* 44, no. 3 (2016): 387–414; Beth E. Schueler and Martin R. West, "Sticker Shock: How Information Affects Citizen Support For Public School Funding," *Public Opinion Quarterly* 80, no. 1 (2015): 90–113; Briony Swire, Adam J. Berinsky, Stephan Lewandowsky, and Ullrich K. H. Ecker, "Processing Political Misinformation: Comprehending the Trump Phenomenon," *Royal Society Open Science*, 4 (2017): 16082; Brendan Nyhan, Ethan Porter, Jason Reifler, and Thomas Wood, "Taking Corrections Literally But Not Seriously? The Effects of Information on Factual Beliefs and Candidate Favorability," June 29, 2017), dx.doi.org/10.2139/ssrn.2995128.

3. Emily Thorson, "Belief Echoes: The Persistent Effects of Corrected Misinformation," *Political Communication* 33, no. 3 (2015): 460–80.

4. Andrew Guess, Brendan Nyhan, and Jason Reifler, *"You're fake news!" Findings from the Poynter Media Trust Survey* (St. Petersburg, FL: Poynter Institute, 2017).

5. Michael Barthel, Amy Mitchell, and Jesse Holcomb, "Many Americans Believe Fake News Is Sowing Confusion," *Pew Research Center,* December 2016.

6. Hunt Allcott and Matthew Gentzkow, "Social Media and Fake News in the 2016 Election," *Journal of Economic Perspectives* 31, no. 2 (2017): 211–36.

7. Andrew Guess, Brendan Nyhan, and Jason Reifler, "Selective Exposure to Misinformation: Evidence from the Consumption of Fake News during the 2016 U.S. Presidential Campaign," 2018, www.dartmouth.edu/~nyhan/fake-news-2016.pdf.

8. Brendan Nyhan and Jason Reifler, "When Corrections Fail: The Persistence of Political Misperceptions," *Political Behavior* 32, no. 2 (2010): 303–30.

9. Adam J. Berinsky, "Rumors and health care reform: Experiments in political misinformation," *British Journal of Political Science* 47, no. 2 (2017): 241–62; Conor M. Dowling, Michael Henderson, and Michael G. Miller, "Knowledge Persists, Opinions Drift: Learning and Opinion Change in a Three-Wave Panel Experiment," *American Politics Research,* March 7, 2019.

10. Kuklinski et al., "Misinformation and the Currency of Democratic Citizenship"; Schueler and West, "Sticker Shock: How Information Affects Citizen Support For Public School Funding"; Brendan Nyhan and Jason Reifler, "Does Correcting Myths about the Flu Vaccine Work? An Experimental Evaluation of the Effects of Corrective Information," *Vaccine* 33, no. 3 (2015): 459–64.

11. Howard Raiffa and Marc Alpert, "A Progress Report on the Training of Probability Assessors," in *Judgement Under Uncertainty: Heuristics and Biases,* ed. Daniel Kahneman, Paul Slovic, and Amos Tversky (Cambridge, UK: Cambridge University Press, 1982), 294–305; Terrance Odean, "Volume, Volatility, Price, and Profit When All Traders Are Above Average," *Journal of Finance* 53, no. 6 (1998): 1887–1934; David Hirshleifer and Guo Ying Luo, "On the Survival of Overconfident Traders in a Competitive Securities Market," *Journal of Financial Markets* 4, no. 1 (2001): 73–84; Don A. Moore and Paul J. Healy, "The Trouble with Overconfidence." *Psychological Review* 115, no. 2 (2008): 502–17.

12. Dominic D. P. Johnson and James H. Fowler, "Evaluation of Overconfidence," *Nature* 477 (2015): 317–20.

13. Alen Nosić and Martin Weber, "How Riskily Do I Invest? The Role of Risk Attitudes, Risk Perceptions, and Overconfidence," *Decision Analysis* 7, no. 3 (2010): 282–301; Marie H. Broihanne, Maxime Merli, and Patrick Roger, "Overconfidence, Risk Perception and the Risk-Taking Behavior of Finance Professionals," *Finance Research Letters* 11 (2014): 64–73; Kamran Razmdoost, Radu Dimitriu, and Emma K. Macdonald, "The Effect of Overconfidence and Underconfidence on Consumer Value," *Psychology & Marketing* 32, no. 4 (2015): 392–407.

14. Phillips W. Davison, "The Third-Person Effect in Communication," *Public Opinion Quarterly* 47, no 1 (1983): 1–15.

15. Stanley J. Baran and Dennis K. Davis, *Mass Communication Theory: Foundations, Ferment, and Future* (Stamford, CT: Cengage Learning, 2015).

16. Julie L. Andsager and Allen H. White, *Self Versus Others: Media, Messages, and the Third-person Effect* (Mahwah, NJ: Lawrence Erlbaum Associates, Inc., 2015).

17. Davison, "The Third-Person Effect in Communication."

18. Hernando Roja, Dhavan V. Shah, and Ronald J. Faber, "For the Good of Others: Censorship and the Third-Person Effect," *International Journal of Public Opinion Research* 8, no. 2 (1996): 163–86; Seong Choul Hong, "Do Cultural Values Matter? A Cross-Cultural Study of the Third-Person Effect and Support for the Regulation of Violent Video Games," *Journal of Cross-Cultural Psychology* 46, no. 7 (2015): 964–76; Mo S. Jang and Joon K. Kim, "Full Length Article: Third Person Effects of Fake News: Fake News Regulation and Media Literacy Interventions," *Computers in Human Behavior* 80 (2018): 295–302.

19. Davison, "The Third-Person Effect in Communication."

20. Andsager and White, *Self Versus Others.*

21. Donald Green, Bradley Palmquist, and Eric Schickler, *Partisan Hearts and Minds* (New Haven, CT: Yale University Press, 2002).

22. Shanto Iyengar and Sean J. Westwood, "Fear and Loathing across Party Lines: New Evidence on Group Polarization," *American Journal of Political Science* 59, no. 3 (2014): 690–707.

23. S. Mo Jang and Joon K. Kim, "Third Person Effects of Fake News: Fake News Regulation and Media Literacy Interventions," *Computers in Human Behavior* 80 (2018): 295–302.

24. Smita C. Banerjee and Robert Kubey, "Boom or Boomerang: A Critical Review of Evidence Documenting Media Literacy Efficacy," in Angharad N. Valdivia and Erica Scharrer, eds., *The International Encyclopedia of Media Studies: Media Effects/Media Psychology* (Hoboken, NJ: John Wiley and Sons, 2013).

25. Se-Hoon Jeong, Hyunyi Cho, and Yoori Hwang, "Media Literacy Interventions: A Meta-Analytic Review," *Journal of Communication* 62, no. 3 (2012): 454–72.

26. James W. Potter, "The State of Media Literacy," *Journal of Broadcasting & Electronic Media* 54, no. 4 (2010): 675–96.

27. Patricia Aufderheide, "Aspen Media Literacy Conference Report—Part II" (Queenstown, MD: Aspen Institute, 1993).

28. Potter, "The State of Media Literacy."

29. Emily K. Vraga, Melissa Tully, and Hernando Rojas, "Media Literacy Training Reduces Perception of Bias," *Newspaper Research Journal* 30, no. 4 (2009): 68–81.

30. Judith Burns, "Fake News: Universities Offer Tips on How to Spot It," *BBC,* November 9, 2017; Amy Wilson-Chapman, "Six Tips for How to Spot (and Stop) Fake News." *International Consortium of Investigative Journalists,* October 17, 2017.

31. Tricia Tongco, "Here's What You Can Do to Stop Fake News, According to an Expert," *ATTN,* December 2, 2016.

32. YouGov recruits respondents to opt in to its online panel and participate in multiple surveys for rewards. When fielding a particular survey, YouGov uses statistical weighting and matching to assemble a final sample for the study that represents the demographic composition of the US adult population. YouGov surveys are widely accepted in academic publications, and their methodology has been recognized by the Pew Research Center as one of the best approaches to online nonprobabil-

ity surveys. See Courtney Kennedy, Andrew Mercer, Scott Keeter, Nick Hatley, Kyley McGeeney, and Alejandra Gimenez, "Evaluating Online Nonprobability Surveys," *Pew Research Center,* May 2, 2016.

33. Benjamin D. Horne and Sibel Adali, "This Just in: Fake News Packs a Lot in Title, Uses Simpler, Repetitive Content in Text Body, More Similar to Satire Than Real News," published at the Second International Workshop on News and Public Opinion at ISWSM, 2017.

34. Petter Bae Brandtzaeg and Asbjørn Følstad, "Trust and Distrust in Online Fact-Checking Services," *Communications of the ACM* 60, no. 9 (2017): 65–71.

35. Jang and Kim, "Third Person Effects of Fake News."

36. Jang and Kim, "Third Person Effects of Fake News."

MILEY, CNN, AND THE *ONION*

WHEN FAKE NEWS BECOMES REALER THAN REAL

Dan Berkowitz and David Asa Schwartz

When singer-actress Miley Cyrus emerged twerking from a giant teddy bear while dressed in a rather small teddy bear suit at the 2013 MTV Video Music Awards, she quickly caught the nation's attention. Her performance set a record for peak Twitter tweets at 306,100 per minute—much more than the 98,300 peak tweets of the previous VMA awards show. Cyrus became the number-one most-searched person at Google for 2013, and her twerking performance led to Google's number-one "What is?" question.[1] With all this visibility, Oxford Dictionaries Online[2] added the term, defined as: "dance to popular music in a sexually provocative manner involving thrusting hip movements and a low, squatting stance."

This event became so sensationalized that CNN.com topped its website with the story of Miley's twerking, placing it above all other world and national news. That, in turn, led to a fake column on the satirical news website, the *Onion*, with the CNN.com editor supposedly explaining why this was the top story of the morning for monetary reasons. The media snowball kept on rolling, as commentary sprung out arguing that the *Onion*'s fake column about the Cyrus scandal had become "hyperreal," more real than the real content of CNN.com. Surprisingly, this hubbub triggered collective memory of yet another piece from the *Onion News Network,* a spoof video from 2008 featuring so-called "entertainment scientists" who predicted that, at her current performance pace, "Miley Cyrus will be depleted by 2013." In essence, this hyperreal non-real was used by a variety of media sources to mock-verify assertions by the current satire of CNN.com and lend it greater authority.

"Fifth Estate" media, largely comprised of bloggers and columnists, have the ability—through satire—to hold the Fourth Estate accountable, engaging in boundary work that attempts to relocate journalists back to the central mission of their professional realm.[3] "Fake-news organizations," in their various forms, have become part of that growing Fifth Estate.

CONTEXT OF THE STUDY

To better understand the context of our analysis, it will be helpful to first present a brief sketch of Miley Cyrus and her career. A short history of the *Onion* follows, with these two elements combining to explain the general scenario of the VMA Awards performance.

Miley Cyrus, the daughter of country singer Billy Ray Cyrus, began her singing and acting career at a young age.[4] Her rise to fame began in 2006 while in her teens with a lead role on the Disney Channel television series *Hannah Montana*. A year later, she debuted a hit music album. Her acting and singing career continued, and by 2013, she had developed a controversial persona emerging from provocative music videos connected to her album *Bangerz*. This image of Cyrus carried over to her VMA appearance, which incorporated visual images from her videos, including dancing bears, twerking, and a frequently extended tongue.

The *Onion* is a satirical news agency founded in 1988 in Madison, Wisconsin. It began strictly as a print publication, launched its website in 1996, and the online broadcast Onion News Network (ONN) in 2007. In 2013 it ceased publication of its print edition but continues to publish written and broadcast content online at theonion.com.

In 2008 ONN ran the story "Sources Warn Miley Cyrus Will be Depleted by 2013."[5] The story included a farcical graphic that predicted what could happen to Cyrus, including "Is she too wild?" and "Public meltdown." In August 2013, Cyrus created a media firestorm after twerking with pop singer Robin Thicke at MTV's VMAs. The Parents Television Council and media outlets across the globe described the performance as "disgusting."[6]

CNN.com made Cyrus's performance its top website news story for much of the next day. The *Onion* responded with the parody article "Let Me Explain Why Miley Cyrus' VMA Performance Was Our Top Story This Morning."[7] It was written "first person" by a parody version of CNN.com managing editor Meredith Artley, with many online readers believing the real Artley wrote the parody article. She denied her involvement with the *Onion*'s column, issuing a light-hearted Twitter post: "To clarify, I did not write this . . . But I accept all compliments and deny all accusations. Tx for the page views."

BACKGROUND AND CONCEPTUAL FOUNDATION

On August 26, 2013—the day after Cyrus's appearance on MTV's VMAs—CNN.com prominently featured an item comparing her performance to a previously outrageous appearance by Lady Gaga, who had worn a dress made of meat while covered in fake blood. The CNN item explained:

> While Gaga came equipped with multiple costume- and wig-changes on her side, Cyrus took over the stage with gigantic, dancing bears and more twerking than viewers at home probably knew what to do with.
>
> The 20-year-old pop star stepped out onto the stage a ball of energy, wearing a fuzzy gray leotard, as her hit single, "We Can't Stop," played. An animated and uninhibited performer, Cyrus' dance moves were a clear departure from her "Hannah Montana" days. (Meaning, they involved a crotch grab or two.)

The article went on to highlight "6 memorable moments from the VMAs," raising questions about why "The Worldwide Leader in News" would feel compelled to display such material so prominently on the CNN.com website against a backdrop of global turmoil. Cyrus's performance allowed CNN.com to wade into coverage of entertainment news. Comparing Cyrus to Lady Gaga, meanwhile, was a clear case of memory work on the part of CNN, even though Cyrus and Gaga had little in common beyond being famous artists: Gaga's performance was notable for its design; Cyrus's performance was notable for its sexual overtones. This was not lost on the *Onion*, which offered a faux-opinion commentary piece the same day, titled "Let Me Explain Why Miley Cyrus' VMA Performance Was Our Top Story This Morning." The explanation was simple: an effort to increase web traffic and boost advertising income:

> There was nothing, and I mean *nothing*, about that story that related to the important news of the day, the chronicling of significant human events, or

the idea that journalism itself can be a force for positive change in the world. . . . In fact, putting that story front and center was actually doing, if anything, a disservice to the public. And come to think of it, probably a disservice to the hundreds of thousands of people dying in Syria, those suffering from the current unrest in Egypt, or, hell, even people who just wanted to read about the 50th anniversary of Martin Luther King's "I Have A Dream" speech.

This satirical example demonstrates the Fifth Estate's role in fake news within a hyperreal context. Although many studies have explored aspects of fake news on *Saturday Night Live* (SNL), the *Daily Show* (TDS) and the *Colbert Report* (TCR), relatively little has been studied regarding the *Onion*. Fake news succeeds because it parodies traits of real news, including broadcast set pieces and mimicking the tone of "real" hosts found on cable channels such as CNN and Fox News.[8] It would be a conceptual error, though, to assume that what has been learned about production and reception of SNL, TDS, and TCR can directly be applied to understanding the *Onion*. There are two key conceptual differences between the *Onion* and the others.

First, SNL, TDS, and TCR are largely about their hosts and their presentation of fake news. In contrast, the presentation of the *Onion* is nearly anonymous: print news items do not carry a byline, and video news reporters are unnamed, unseen, or unfamiliar. Fake news exists in different forms. The *Onion*'s "Onion News Network" (ONN) has even hired traditional news anchors to read its copy, including one later hired away from ONN by CNN.[9]

Second, social commentary on SNL, TDS, and TCR is often steeped in strong exaggeration that signals its comedic intent. As part of the experience, the hosts laugh, grin, and even crack up during their news presentations, making it clear to their audience that their content was intended to appear as fake from the onset. In contrast, the *Onion* avoids the slapstick and clowning, turning instead to the "hyperreal" where both text presentations and on-screen delivery are relatively realistic.[10] Virginia Heffernan, a blogger for the *New York Times,* described the *Onion*'s video spoofs as "A near-perfect facsimile of a deadly serious cable broadcast."[11]

Conceptual Foundation

Although in recent years fake news has enjoyed popularity through venues such as SNL, TDS, and TCR, fake news owns a far richer history.[12] Historians have found fake news, satire, and parody from the eighth century. Fake news as we conceptually understand it today got its start in the late nineteenth century, a time of rapid growth for newspapers that was aided by emerging technologies.[13] With journalism again in a period of technological revolution, boundaries between "fake news" and "real news" have shifted in both academic and journalistic circles. Fake news is hyperreal because it blurs lines between nonfiction and fiction, which challenges journalistic boundary work when journalistic practices overlap with fake news. The tension has grown from how journalists use fake and real news to challenge the boundaries of what news is and how news is created and with what purpose and effects.

Fake news bears resemblance to real news thematically. General topics and issues may be the same, such as politics and the economy. Aesthetically, fake news broadcasts such as the *Daily Show* and the *Onion Week in Review* possess the feel of real news programs. But fake news is not bound by the same ethical codes as real news.[14] Free from the ethical codes accepted by traditional journalists, purveyors of fake news are free to parody, mock, criticize, and fabricate. Fake news does not exist independently of real news. Instead, is exists as a critique of real news, a farcical watchdog that lampoons both journalists and the subjects they cover.[15]

In addition to their role as watchdog, fake news programs engage young news consumers, a part of the population that was once considered apolitical.[16] Success of programs such as the *Colbert Report,* which provide news to previously disengaged consumers, has complicated journalism because "fake" news is driving "real" information to media consumers. Also, those who deliver fake news, such as Jon Stewart, are in some instances more trusted than the journalists who deliver real news because consumers perceive Stewart as one who holds "real" journalists accountable.[17]

The relationship between fake news and media consumers has been addressed by scholars. Less studied is the relationship between fake news and traditional news organizations. The *New York Times* in 2010 compared Stewart with legendary broadcast journalist Edward R. Murrow.[18] This acceptance of Stewart by the *New York Times* and other traditional and newer journalism outlets, such as blogs, stretched the negotiated membership boundaries of journalism.[19]

Boundary work allows journalists to decide who is in the group, who is not, ethical expectations, and matters of standards and practice.[20] These boundaries can shift over time as culture and society shift. Traditional news organizations may depict newer forms of media as being outside professional norms, such as when multiple traditional organizations questioned the methods of WikiLeaks.[21] Journalists share common understandings of society. Because of this, traditional journalists draw and redraw professional, ethical, and ideological boundaries.[22] Journalists, for instance, performed boundary work by publicly discussing the mentality of pack journalism.[23]

Traditional journalists create their own professional boundaries, often portraying themselves as officers of the public good.[24] Journalists adopt codes of ethics and admonish those who fail to live up to them. Those codes, though, are becoming increasingly difficult to identify, which leaves the door open for fake news to enter the boundaries of journalism as defined by those who practice it,[25] such as the case with the *New York Times* and Stewart in the role of Murrow. The term "fake news" is more of a label than a definition. Stewart and Colbert parody the news but also create it when they conduct original interviews or appear on current-affairs shows on traditional cable news networks such as CNN and Fox News Channel. The line between "fake news" and "real news" is further blurred by publications such as the *Onion*, which creates fake news stories based on real events while also providing serious content on such cultural issues as sexuality and film.

Within hyperreality, the line between nonfiction and fiction vanishes and what can be considered "authentic" is delegitimized.[26] Hyperreality "calls into question the claims of representation, both cultural and political."[27] Recent studies in hyperreality grew from Eco[28] and Baudrillard,[29] who wrote that in the postmodern era reality and simulation operate simultaneously along a single track, without difference. They exist together on a "roller-coaster continuum," a track in which reality bleeds into imagination to produce a new representation of an idea.[30]

In March 2014, for instance, President Barack Obama appeared on the fictional online talk show *Between Two Ferns*. *Ferns* takes on the appearance and form of a cable-access interview show, but the host is a comedian who purposely bumbles his way through segments. Obama engaged in comedic banter played straight with the host but also was given time to promote the Affordable Care Act. Some journalists criticized the president for jeopardizing the dignity of the office by appearing on a fake news show, but the president said the move allowed him to reach a wider audience.[31]

The hyperreal also occurred in 2008 when two aspiring filmmakers created a fictional political pundit named Martin Eisenstadt, who commented on real and fictional political events. Unable to distinguish simulation from reality, numerous news organizations reported one of Eisenstadt's reports as fact.[32] In 2009 *Washington Monthly* ran an editorial piece praising an upcoming book "written" from Eisenstadt's fictional perspective with the acknowledgment that Eisenstadt was a fake. *Washington Monthly* wrote that the Eisenstadt memoir was "the best fake news memoir of the campaign season."[33] Then in 2012 one of the United States' most historic cultural magazines, the *New Yorker,* acquired a fake news website.[34] This further blurred the line between real news and fake news. The *New Yorker* links to a fake news website, "The Borowitz Report," from its homepage with no indication that the site is a parody until after readers click on the page.

If hyperreality lives in the fake, it follows that "real" news operates in the realm of truth. Truth, of course, can be subjective. Journalists make choices about what information to share, not share, and how to present that information.[35] Two key differences between "real" news and "fake" news help segregate the tracks. The first is producer intent. A "real" news reporter, perhaps unaware she is making decisions that will affect audience perception and reveal her biases, operates under the umbrella of journalistic authority and at the very least believes she is reporting the truth.[36] A "fake" news reporter, such as one who works for the *Onion,* is aware that she is producing parody. The second difference is audience perception. Audiences hold separate expectations between what they expect from "real" news outlets and "fake" news outlets. When a "real" news organization reveals bias or makes an error, audiences feel outrage. When a "fake" news organization takes sides, it is part of the joke.[37] Becker's findings "suggest that viewers draw a measurable and pronounced dividing line between political comedy programs and hard news content."[38]

In hyperreality, simulation swallows reality. Fake news can become more "real" than real news.[39] Hyperreality of journalism reaches even more intense levels when fake news actually predicts future events, such as when the *Onion* reported Miley Cyrus's 2013 journalism meltdown in 2008 and fictional pundit Eisenstadt hinted in 2009 at a future political scandal involving New York politician Anthony Weiner.[40]

Hyperrealism can be intentional. Fake news organizations practice boundary work by creating content with social goals such as creating public dialog.[41] ONN purposively designed its set and journalistic tone to mimic traditional broadcast journalism.[42] Said ONN's director: "our goal from the start was to make it look like TV."

Fake news, in its hyperrealism, offers social critique in ways that "real news" cannot,[43] and in that respect becomes more real than real. It has acquired an epistemic authority, the legitimate power to define bounded domains of reality.[44] Whereas mainstream journalism likes to declare itself the watchdog estate, "fake news" puts "real news" into the position of needing to be watched, natural results of parody and satire. Hyper-realization allows fake news to address issues of "great civic importance."[45]

Mainstream journalists use collective memory to reestablish journalistic authority when "fake news" becomes real. Collective memory can help build journalistic authority.[46] From collective memory springs media memory. Media memory is the journalistic practice of using the media to narrate a collective past.[47] Media memory also enables mainstream journalists to practice boundary work, defining what is and is not journalism.[48] When ONN's fake news story accurately predicted the exact year of a Miley Cyrus media meltdown, mainstream journalism acknowledged the fake news story. It practiced boundary work first by welcoming ONN into the realm of "real" news, then by dismissing ONN through regular reminders to viewers that ONN was a "fake" organization.

When mainstream news outlets such as MSN.com (Microsoft), the *Orlando Sentinel,* and Gawker Media reported on ONN's fake report, it clarified how hyperrealized fake news has become the Fifth Estate, a network of alternative news sources realized through new technologies and alternative journalistic forms, most notably humor, parody, and mimicry.[49] The academic term "Fifth Estate" has been claimed by such disciplines as journalism, labor studies, criminal studies, and organizational theory, among others. In journalism studies the term divides between electronic media, radio broadcasting, watchdog journalism (WikiLeaks, for example), gatekeeping theory, and of course fake news. The organic nature of blogs, which rely on voluntary interactions rather than structural power, extend blogs into a Fifth Estate role of watching over the Fourth Estate.[50] This conceptualization of the Fifth Estate should be explicated to also include fake news because of its less formal structure and the organic means through which it attracts audiences. This paper conceptualizes the Fifth Estate as a hybrid of hyperrealized fake news and watchdog journalism as a challenge to the professional boundaries of traditional journalism.

This leads to four research questions:

RQ1: How did the fake news Fifth Estate engage with other elements of the Fifth Estate (columnists, bloggers) to relocate CNN (and mainstream journalism in general) back within conventional Fourth Estate boundaries?

RQ2: How did the notion of hyperreal news shape the authority of the Fifth Estate in the boundary work with CNN.com's VMA coverage?

RQ3: How did memory of the *Onion*'s 2008 prediction about the depletion of the Miley Cyrus resource reinforce the authority of its fake CNN editor's column?

RQ4: What does this case add to the understanding of professional boundary repair in an age of a rising Fifth Estate?

METHOD

This study was accomplished through qualitative textual analysis focusing on common themes related to the conceptual framework.[51] Data came from Google News searches and a Google News category using the terms "Miley Cyrus" and "the Onion." These search terms were useful for the study of boundary work and the role of memory for enhancing fake news authority.

In all, these searches yielded 29 news items, blogs, and opinion pieces. Of these, 18 were about CNN.com, the *Onion,* and coverage of the VMA broadcast. An additional 11 items related to the 2008 ONN report about depleting Miley Cyrus. Items were considered from the day that the CNN.com story about Cyrus first appeared on August 26, 2013, through late September and early October, when a few follow-up stories appeared. At that point, the stories ceased to appear and no additional items were collected.

A spreadsheet was built to catalog all the items, which were numbered consecutively to facilitate coordination between the researchers. Both researchers read each item and took notes related to central themes that followed from the conceptual framework. This was done for each of the two main issues. These key themes were then connected to examples that illustrated them.

THE HYPERREAL FIFTH ESTATE GETS DOWN TO BUSINESS

The dialog among blogs and columnists developed through three main themes. First, the discussion addressed the nature of the boundary skirmish. Second, these opinion writers pondered implications for the media as social institution. Third, boundary lines were drawn and redrawn, suggesting which organizations belonged within the boundary of "good journalism."

Early in the conversation among members of this "Fifth Estate," three main concerns were identified through a brief piece from the news organization *Epoch Times:*[52] (1) the potential monetary gain in the form of "more clicks"; (2) the notion that nothing was important about the story, so that it did not merit the high visibility it received; and (3) that, ultimately, the VMA story represented a public disservice by a mainstream news organization whose mission was supposedly to serve the public. By pointing to these issues, members of the Fifth Estate were assuming their boundary work, with an effort to bring the mainstream media—particularly CNN.com—back within the Fourth Estate boundary expectations. One of the big questions left dangling asked, "How did this happen?" Two answers surfaced, one pointing at the expectations of a media audience seeking entertainment, one stemming from the basics of maintaining a media business in a highly competitive digital environment.

For example, a commentary piece by writer Allen Clifton on *ForwardPro gressives.com* brought blame squarely on the audience: "a point I've been talking about for years—quality journalism is dying and we're the ones killing it."[53] Clifton argued that stories like what CNN.com had run about Cyrus's twerking were simply a research to audience demands:

> Now I know what some of you are saying, "Well, I don't read trash stories. I want good news reporting and quality journalism." Well, *if* that is true, you're sadly becoming the exception rather than the rule. But you mean to tell me you've *never* clicked on one of the *many* stories I see on media sites about "Man Exposes Himself at Taco Stand" or "Butt Implants Are Newest Rage for Men" (yes, this was actually a headline today at the Huffington Post).[54]

By casting the situation this way, *ForwardProgressives* painted a clear line about the boundaries for quality news organizations and the temptation for some to cross the boundary line for the sake of profit: "See, consumers are the reason why the media sucks so badly these days," Clifton concluded. As a bottom line, he argued that *CNN.com* should not be singled out as going beyond the boundary, because that news organization had simply given the audience what it desired.

This argument was furthered by the news blog site, *LA Observed,* where writer Kevin Roderick ruminated, "This may be the best skewer you have ever read of the web strategy that more and more media outlets use."[55] Part of the online media old guard, *Salon,* pondered "how and how much cable news ought to be covering Miley Cyrus."[56] In doing so, the *Salon* writer attempted to place both CNN and MSNBC outside the "good journalism" boundary. CNN's Anderson Cooper, for example, opined on air for more than three minutes about the Miley Cyrus flap (while nonetheless showing more clips of the VMA awards program); MSNBC's Mika Brzezinski offered her take on Cyrus's health condition. Explained *Salon* writer Daniel D'Addario, with a twist of irony about how Cooper drew attention to the situation while simultaneously urging his audience to ignore it: "'It's all so yawningly formulaic,' said Cooper, just before showing a clip of a four-year-old Cyrus performance in which the singer was said to have pole-danced. Cooper instructed his audience not to pay attention to the VMAs; he, indeed, said he hadn't watched the show at all. But the Cyrus story is such guaranteed gold that it's worth weighing in on—if only to tell others not to bother being outraged."[57]

Celebrity news website MStarz—an outsider to the institution of journalism—also played up how the hyperreal column in the *Onion* played a Fifth Estate role: "While the entire Internet was buzzing about Miley Cyrus' VMA performance yesterday, we still expect a little more from our journalistic bastions than we do Twitter, Tumblr and BuzzFeed. That's why it is so surprising that CNN.com ran a twerking recap as their top story (aka the most important thing IN THE WORLD today), a move that got the news organization openly shamed by *The Onion.*"[58]

British political/cultural/current affairs magazine and online website *New Statesman* took advantage of the situation to accomplish a bit of boundary work with one of its competitors, the *Independent.* That publication, it turned out, initially took the *Onion* column as real-real, rather than hyperreal, first publishing that "Meredith Artley, Managing Editor of CNN.com, wrote in *The Onion* to explain why CNN put Miley as their top story."[59] Once the error had been pointed out via Twitter, the *Independent* quickly recast its remark: "A piece in *The Onion* even joked why CNN put Miley as their top story." To twist the proverbial knife a little deeper, the *New Statesman* piece commented on how the *Independent* had in the past mocked other news outlets for making the exact same kind of mistake.

In a few cases, Fourth Estate organizations took advantage of the situation to do Fifth Estate–like boundary work. *U.S. News* writer Robert Schlesinger wrote an opinion piece wherein he first distanced himself from actually paying attention to the VMA program and then stepping in for the kill: "Being firmly entrenched in middle age and something of a crank, I didn't watch the MTV's Video Music Awards. . . . And yet I know all about Miley Cyrus' lewd gyrations with singer Robin Thicke. Why is that? Because I have CNN on at my desk all day long, so I got to watch the controversial Miley Cyrus clip yesterday, all day long."[60]

The *Onion*'s fake column, Schlesinger concluded, "has the virtue of being funny (and, really, not funny) because it's spot-on true." As much as this Fourth Estate boundary work capitalized on the veracity of hyperreal fake news, another wanna-be member of the Fourth Estate—the entertainment news publication, *Variety*—donned its Fourth Estate robes to defend the status quo of its boundaries. Editor-in-chief Andrew Wallenstein argued that the *Onion* "oversimplifies the realities of the digital-news biz," and therefore was wrong about the situation.[61] In a somewhat apologetic tone for the media mainstream, *Variety* offered a boundary-stretching take on those "realities," one that oddly took advantage of similarities between the words "Cyrus" and "Syria": "But were the Onion a real news organization, it might understand a more complicated truth behind the uneasy coexistence of Cyrus and Syria in modern digital newsrooms: It's difficult to subsist on substantive journalism without some help from more crowd-pleasing content."[62]

Chalking up the CNN decision to play up Cyrus's VMA performance to, essentially, the cost of doing business in a digital media era, journalists themselves sometimes find themselves "'twerking' uncomfortably close to the groin of their employer's financial goals."[63] From this pragmatic perspective, the piece argued that successful news organizations must strike a balance between audience-driving content and the content that audiences need to know. Continuing with the effort to redraw journalistic boundaries, Wallenstein explained: "But that's where those who cherish the Syria coverage need to understand that Cyrus doesn't detract from Syria; it actually bears the weight of traffic demands that Syria shouldn't be expected to meet. Thus Cyrus is helping shoulder the cost of more substantial coverage that Syria can't possibly meet on its own."

Still forgetting that the *Onion* is a fake news organization, Wallenstein kept moving the argument farther ahead due to the hyperreal nature of the CNN parody, likening news of the Cyrus ilk to the function of a circus barker: "Syria can even benefit from a little Cyrus time; there's something to be said for any kind of content triggering a mass influx of users, which increases the chance they will move on to other content on the site. Come for Cyrus, stay for Syria."[64]

Dangling *Variety's* unreal explanation of the hyperreal *Onion* column, though, caught some pushback from the paper's attempt to claim turf within mainstream journalism's boundaries. Peter Bella, a writer on the *Chicago Tribune's* blog site *Chicago Now* responded the next day with a takeoff of *Variety's* piece, "Why the Onion Is Wrong About CNN and Miley Cyrus." The similarly titled "Variety is wrong about The Onion and Miley Cyrus" made a blunt attempt to relocate *Variety* outside the boundaries of the journalistic mainstream with the battle cry, "the editors and so-called reporters at Variety have too much time on their hands and no sense of humor."[65] Claiming that *Variety* subsists on content from "entertainment public relations weasels and ferrets," Bella condoned its more-or-less unauthorized effort at boundary work: "Variety goes even deeper into the miasma when they attempt to explain quality journalism. That is laughable. The Onion should do a humor hit piece of the alleged 'quality journalism' Variety claims they produce. Maybe because they are in Hollywood they can get away with calling their drek "journalism.""[66]

The real reason that *Variety* ran its take on quality journalism, he claimed, was to undertake its own boundary work to keep mainstream journalism outside the boundaries of entertainment journalism: "The only reason *Variety* ran this piece was to assuage the weasels and ferrets retained by entertainers and studios."[67]

Closure to the CNN/Cyrus flap came a month or two later. *USA Today*, in early October, turned to head *Onion* writer Seth Reiss to shore up the *Onion's* Fifth Estate standing: "The Cyrus/CNN story—a real-time take on the news of the moment that rapidly became an Internet meme—encapsulates the *Onion's* aggressive shift from weekly humor newspaper to 24/7 digital satirist, all the while clinging tightly to its image as the righteous spitball thrower of the American media."[68]

The previous week, news blog *PandoDaily* went to Cyrus herself through some outtakes published by the not-quite-Fourth Estate magazine *Rolling Stone*. *PandoDaily* reporter Hamish McKenzie reconnected back to the *Onion's* column to express the kind of "media outrage" such as what came in response to the CNN coverage of the VMA program. Cyrus opined: "I think it's all marketing. If a website is like, 'We love Miley's performance!,' I don't think people are gonna click on it. 'Miley's cute performance with teddy bears!'—no one is gonna click on that."[69]

In all, this discussion began with the premise that the *Onion*'s fake column by CNN.com editor Meredith Artley—and the controversy surrounding it—represented Fifth Estate boundary work to readjust the appropriate roles for mainstream news organizations. In CNN.com's case, it had featured salacious click-bait about Cyrus's VMA twerking performance while temporarily downplaying national and world news of the day. The *Onion*'s column had touched a tender spot in mainstream journalism's flesh that really deployed a critique of CNN's decision as synecdoche for the economic imperatives facing mainstream journalism as a whole, with its hyperreal presentation lending authority and credibility to its Fifth Estate critique.

THE *ONION* TIMES TWO: FAKE MEMORY AS REAL AUTHORITY

Mainstream news organizations and Fifth Estate bloggers also granted real authority to the *Onion* based on its previous success in predicting true elements of future news. In doing so, mainstream organizations and bloggers presented fake news organizations in two ways. First, mainstream news organizations presented the *Onion* as more than a novelty act that just happened to accurately predict the coming of "real" news. Via the accuracy of the *Onion*'s 2008 Cyrus article, mainstream news organizations and Fifth Estate bloggers bestowed authority upon the *Onion* that those same mainstream organizations and bloggers then used as a device to employ media memory in its representation of Cyrus's VMA performance.

Additionally, mainstream news organizations described the *Onion* with amazement and admiration. In these instances, mainstream tone focused more on the audacity of Cyrus's performance and less on the reputation and representation of the *Onion*. In both types of description—memory device and amazement—mainstream news organizations deployed media memory to sell their Cyrus narratives.

The *Onion*'s original 2008 article gave Fifth Estate bloggers the connector they needed to invoke other instances of "shocking" celebrity actions. This memory work was evident in numerous pieces, including one in *Neon Tommy*, a popular blog run by students at the University of Southern California's Annenberg

School for Communication and Journalism. In the post, *Neon Tommy* assumed its readers were familiar with the *Onion*. Nowhere did it describe the *Onion* as a fake news organization.

The blog wrote that the *Onion* was "spot on" in its 2008 segment. Then the author invoked the names of troubled celebrities in an attempt to put Cyrus's actions into context: "She [Cyrus] is turning into a Britney Spears or a Lindsay Lohan because it seems as she is just off her rocker. She could end up in a situation like Amanda Bynes, where she starts lashing out at anyone and everyone and makes remarks towards them that just don't make sense."[70]

Neon Tommy provided no context for Spears, Lohan, and Bynes. Their names alone *were* the context. In reality, the three celebrities noted by *Neon Tommy* had little in common with Cyrus. Spears struggled with personal problems and was hospitalized.[71] Lohan and Bynes have each faced legal troubles.[72] Cyrus, as of this analysis, has not dealt with any of the issues faced by the three celebrities invoked by *Neon Tommy*. But the blog nonetheless used the *Onion*'s 2008 article as the vessel for introducing Spears, Lohan, and Bynes into the narrative. The *Onion*'s validated fake news gave it authority that was then used by *Neon Tommy* to provide context that may or may not have been accurate.

The *Neon Tommy* sample echoed a post in the *Memphis Flyer*, which acknowledged its lack of understanding of Cyrus's career, but it still invoked the names of other celebrities to contextualize Cyrus's actions: "I do not know if Miley Cyrus is just the latest in the entertainment media's production line of soon-to-be-burnt-out, drug-addled young music/screen stars, a la Lohan, Spears, Bynes, [Justin] Bieber, [Amy] Winehouse, etc., or whether she is skillfully, soberly, and purposefully being outrageous to enhance her career, a la Lady Gaga and Madonna before her."[73]

The *Memphis Flyer* went on to write that the *Onion* in 2008 "got the Miley Cyrus story exactly right." The *Onion* story was the impetus behind the post. Without the *Onion*'s 2008 predictive article, the *Memphis Flyer* would not have been able to compose its post that employed media memory even more extensively. *Neon Tommy* stopped at Spears, Lohan, and Bynes, but the *Memphis Flyer* introduced Winehouse, a pop singer who died from drug overdose, to contextualize Cyrus. It also invoked the memories of Lady Gaga and Madonna to consider whether Cyrus might not be a tragic celebrity at all, but instead a shrewd businesswoman.

Neon Tommy and the *Memphis Flyer* are obscure next to *Gawker.com,* a mammoth Fifth Estate journalistic watchdog organization with hundreds of millions of page views.[74] Gawker, too, used the *Onion's* predictive article to generate new content. Gawker declared "at least we'll always have *The Onion*" in its August 2013 post about the *Onion's* 2008 article predicting Cyrus's media meltdown.[75] The article opened with a bit of memory work, hyperlinking to a website that described the *Onion's* editorial history. By establishing in the lead the *Onion's* history of fudging its corporate timeline, Gawker was able to also establish, via humor, that the *Onion's* ability to bend time had precedent: "there is good reason to believe *The Onion* may actually be from the future. How else would one explain its eerie ability to accurately predict future events? Case in point: Miley Cyrus."[76] Gawker went on to use a mystical term, writing that the *Onion* "prophesied" Cyrus's VMA performance five years before it happened. It concluded by paraphrasing the original article from the *Onion,* sharing with readers access to the information which led to Gawker's post.

Memory work was also performed by *Huffington Post.* Similar to *Neon Tommy, Huffington Post* provided no context for its readers for what the *Onion* was. *Huffington Post* allowed the *Onion* as a standalone entity to create its own authority through meaning. For some readers that might have meant "humorous parody news organization." For other readers unfamiliar with the *Onion* it might have meant "news organization."

Also invoking mystical terminology to establish the *Onion's* authority, *Huffington Post* even used a variation on *Gawker's* term, "eerie": "As always, *The Onion* was able to see what was happening and accurately call out the situation long ago. . . . Check out the eerily prescient video."[77]

Because of its 2008 article on Cyrus, the *Onion* was described by mainstream media as a prophet. It was called prescient and eerie. It was praised for its mere existence and was built into a journalistic authority figure that then allowed members of the Fifth Estate to institute media memory that, ironically, may have portrayed Cyrus inaccurately. The fake news organization got it right, which afforded legitimate news organizations the ability to get it wrong. Mainstream coverage of the *Onion's* 2008 Cyrus "prophecy" created a hyperreal situation in which the most accurate news organization was the one dealing in fabrication and parody.

In all, the *Onion* gained journalistic authority through the memory work of *Gawker, Huffington Post, Neon Tommy,* and the *Memphis Flyer.* Each added authority to the *Onion* in its own way: *Gawker* cited the *Onion*'s history and predictive capabilities; *Huffington Post* praised the *Onion* for its accuracy; *Neon Tommy* used the *Onion*'s 2008 Cyrus article as the foundation of its contemporary Cyrus coverage; and the *Memphis Flyer,* which also used the *Onion* as foundational work, highlighted the *Onion*'s accuracy while giving readers no indication that the *Onion* was a fake news organization.

CONCLUSION

Bloggers, columnists, and even fake news organizations have come to serve as a Fifth Estate watching over the mainstream journalism institution. This Fifth Estate engages in boundary work attempting to bring journalists back to the practices of their professional realm.

In recent years, fake news purveyors have gained traction as part of the new Fifth Estate. Although broadcast satirists such as Jon Stewart, Stephen Colbert, and SNL's "Weekend Update" cast members have taken on that role, the hyperreal nature of the *Onion* and *Onion News Network* has gained some extra credibility by following journalism forms of mainstream media while also offering a satirical view that avoids the obvious gestures of their joker-in-arms comrades. That was certainly the case when the *Onion*'s fake column supposedly by CNN.com editor Meredith Artley drew widespread attention to the appropriate boundaries for mainstream media organizations. This authority was shored up ironically through memory of *ONN*'s report about the depletion of the Miley Cyrus resource by 2013, the year the VMA program was broadcast.

Through textual analysis of blogs and columns, we explored four research questions. The first question asked how fake news—the *Onion* in particular—interacted with other elements of the Fifth Estate to bring CNN.com back to within its professional boundaries. In this situation, bloggers over and over again began by accepting the *Onion*'s critique as accurate and then focused on why CNN.com chose to highlight Cyrus's twerking performance in terms of Fourth Estate norms. Part of the blame was placed on the audience and its interests; other blame pointed to the necessities of doing business in a digital media environment. Lurking below the surface of this critique was the synecdoche of CNN.com representing a larger swath of the struggling media institution.

A second question asked about the effect of the *Onion*'s hyperreal approach to satire. By avoiding the mixture of clowning and critique found with other fake news sources, the *Onion* avoided ambiguity in its message that added authority, and even believability. A third question asked about the effect of the *Onion News Network*'s 2008 prediction of a five-year depletion of the Miley resource. This provided a tongue-in-cheek double authority for the CNN.com column that reaffirmed the accuracy of the *Onion*'s vision of society. A final question asked about what this case study can add to the understanding of professional boundary work. What stands out most clearly is how the growing Fifth Estate has begun taking on a vital role in watching the watchers as the mainstream media continue to strike a balance between making a profit in a new media economy and providing news that serves society.

We have clarified the distinction between two related concepts: boundary work and paradigm repair. In its traditional application, the notion of paradigm repair has implied an effort to re-instill confidence in a paradigm about the unwritten rules for professional practice. Paradigm repair, then, is a process adopted by those who base their work on a paradigm incorporating aspects such as truth, objectivity, confidentiality, honesty as well as a set of practices designed to assure those aspirations are attained. Boundary work, in contrast, can be undertaken by both those within the Fourth Estate who adjust and adapt to changes and pressures in the media environment, as well as those outside the Fourth Estate who attempt to stake out an area of journalistic turf where they can also play a valuable role, whether for their own gain or for the betterment of society.

NOTES

This essay was originally published as "Miley, CNN and The Onion: When fake news becomes realer than real" in *Journalism Practice* 10, no. 1 (2016): 1–17.

1. "What Did the World Search for in 2013?" Google.com, December 17, 2013, www.google.com/trends/topcharts?date=2013.

2. Siraj Datoo, "Oxford Dictionary Adds 'twerk,' 'derp,' 'selfie,' 'phablet,' and More Voguish Vocabulary," *Quartz*, August 28, 2013, qz.com/119200/oxford-dictionary-adds-twerk-derp-selfie-phablet-and-more-voguish-vocabulary/.

3. Adam Cohen, "The Media That Need Citizens: The First Amendment and the Fifth Estate," *Southern California Law Review* 85, no. 1 (2011–12): 1–84; Stephen D. Cooper, *Watching the Watchdog: Bloggers as the Fifth Estate* (Phoenix, AZ: Marquette Books, 2006).

4. "Miley Cyrus," Wikipedia, November 30, 2014, en.wikipedia.org/wiki/Miley_Cyrus.

5. "Sources Warn Miley Cyrus Will Be Depleted by 2013," *The Onion*, July 1, 2008, www.youtube.com/watch?v=HOgj2etJs3Y.

6. Lucy Buckland, "Miley Cyrus VMA Show was 'Disgusting Sexual Exploitation' Say Leading Parents Group," *Mirror,* August 27, 2013, www.mirror.co.uk/3am/celebrity-news/miley-cyrus-sexual-exploitation-vma-2228134.

7. "Let Me Explain Why Miley Cyrus' VMA Performance Was Our Top Story This Morning," *The Onion,* August 26, 2013, www.theonion.com/articles/let-me-explain-why-miley-cyrus-vma-performance-was,33632/.

8. Sandra L .Borden and Chad Tew, "The Role of Journalist and the Performance of Journalism: Ethical Lessons From "Fake" News (Seriously)," *Journal of Mass Media Ethics* 22, no. 4 (2007): 300–314.

9. Johnny Sharp, "Tomorrow's Nonsense Today," *The Guardian,* April 4, 2008, www.theguardian.com/technology/2008/apr/05/internet.television.

10. Don J. Waisanen, "Crafting Hyperreal Spaces for Comic Insights: *The Onion News Network's* Ironic Iconicity," *Communication Quarterly* 59, no. 5 (2011): 508–28.

11. Virginia Heffernan, "Broadcast Spoofs." *New York Times,* April 20, 2008, www.nytimes.com/2008/04/20/magazine/20wwln-medium-t.html?pagewanted=all&_r=0.

12. Kevin G. Barnhurst, "The New 'Media Affect' and the Crisis of Representation for Political Communication," *International Journal of Press/Politics* 16, no. 4 (2011): 573–93.

13. Robert Love, "Before Jon Stewart—Fake News Is Back, but Our Tolerance for It Isn't What It Was Before Journalism Donned the Mantle of Authority," *Columbia Journalism Review,* March 1, 2007, www.cjr.org/feature/before_jon_stewart.php?page=all.

14. Borden and Tew, "The Role of Journalist."

15. Jeffrey P. Jones and Geoffrey Baym, "A Dialogue on Satire News and the Crisis of Truth in Postmodern Political Television," *Journal of Communication Inquiry* 34, no. 3 (2010): 278–94.

16. Priscilla M. Meddaugh, "Bakhtin, Colbert, and the Center of Discourse: Is There No 'Truthiness' in Humor?" *Critical Studies in Media Communication* 27, no. 4 (2010): 376–90.

17. Chad Painter and Louis Hodges, "Mocking the News: How *The Daily Show With Jon Stewart* Holds Traditional Broadcast News Accountable," *Journal of Mass Media Ethics* 25, no. 4 (2010): 257–74.

18. Dan Berkowitz and Robert E. Gutsche Jr., "Drawing Lines in the Journalistic Sand: Jon Stewart, Edward R. Murrow, and Memory of News Gone By," *Journalism & Mass Communication Quarterly* 89, no. 4 (2012): 643–56.

19. Berkowitz and Gutsche, "Drawing Lines in the Journalistic Sand."

20. Thomas F. Gieryn, *Cultural Boundaries of Science: Credibility on the Line* (Chicago: University of Chicago Press, 1999).

21. Mark Coddington, "Defending a Paradigm by Patrolling a Boundary: Two Global Newspapers' Approach to WikiLeaks," *Journalism & Mass Communication Quarterly* 89, no. 3 (2012): 377–96.

22. Matt Carlson and Daniel A. Berkowitz, "Twilight of the Television Idols: Collective Memory, Network News and the Death of Walter Cronkite," *Memory Studies* 5, no. 4 (2012): 410–24.

23. Russell Frank, "'These Crowded Circumstances': When Pack Journalists Bash Pack Journalism." *Journalism* 4, no. 4 (2003): 441–58.

24. Matt Carlson, "War Journalism and the 'KIA Journalist': The Cases of David Bloom and Michael Kelly," *Critical Studies in Media Communication* 23, no. 2 (2006): 91–111.

25. Geoffrey Baym, "The Daily Show: Discursive Integration and the Reinvention of Political Journalism," *Political Communication* 22, no. 3 (2005): 259–76.

26. Bonnie Brennen and Erika dela Cerna, "Journalism in Second Life," *Journalism Studies* 11, no. 4 (2010): 546–54.

27. John Storey, *Cultural Theory and Popular Culture: A Reader* (Essex, UK: Pearson Education, 2012), 196.

28. Umberto Eco, *Faith in Fakes: Travels in Hyperreality* (London: Mandarin Paperbacks, 1973), 7.

29. Jean Baudrillard, *Simulacra and Simulation* (Ann Arbor: University of Michigan Press, 1994), 1–42.

30. Storey, *Cultural Theory*, 193.

31. Ted Johnson, "President Obama Defends Doing Funny or Die's 'Between Two Ferns.'" *Variety*, March 22, 2014, variety.com/2014/biz/news/president-obama-defends-doing-funny-or-dies-between -two-ferns-1201140586/.

32. Richard Perez-Pena, "A Senior Fellow at the Institute of Nonexistence," *New York Times*, November 12, 2008, www.nytimes.com/2008/11/13/arts/television/13hoax.html?_r=0.

33. Joshua Green, "True Lies," *Washington Monthly*, December 2009, www.washingtonmonthly .com/features/2009/0911.green.html.

34. Andy Borowitz, "SHOCKER: *The New Yorker* Acquires the Borowitz Report," *New Yorker*, February 27, 2014, www.newyorker.com/online/blogs/borowitzreport/2012/07/shocker-the-new -yorker-acquires-the-borowitz-report.html.

35. Mark Deuze, "What Is Journalism? Professional Identity and Ideology of Journalists Recon-sidered," *Journalism* 6, no. 4 (2005): 442–64.

36. Matt Carlson, "Rethinking Journalistic Authority: Walter Cronkite and Ritual in Television News," *Journalism Studies* 13, no. 4 (2012): 483–98.

37. Amy B. Becker, Michael A. Xenos, and Don J. Waisanen, "Sizing Up The Daily Show: Audi-ence Perceptions of Political Comedy Programming," *Atlantic Journal of Communication* 18, no. 3 (2010): 144–57.

38. Becker, Xenos, and Waisanen, "Sizing Up The Daily Show," 155.

39. Robert T. Tally, "I Am the Mainstream Media (and So Can You!)," in *The Stewart/Colbert Effect: Essays On the Real Impacts of Fake News*, ed. Amarnath Amarasingam, 149–63 (Jefferson, NC: McFarland, 2011).

40. Terry Keefe, "A Satirical Pundit Foreshadowed Anthony Weiner's Woes in 2009 Book," *Huff-ington Post*, June 17, 2011, www.huffingtonpost.com/terry-keefe/a-satirical-pundit-recoll_b_878961 .html.

41. Waisanen, "Crafting Hyperreal Spaces."

42. Jemima Kiss, "@Future of Journalism: *The Onion News Network* and the High Art of Satire," *Guardian*, September 9, 2008, www.theguardian.com/media/pda/2008/sep/09/futureofjournalism theonion?gusrc=rss&feed=media.

43. Tally, "I Am the Mainstream Media."

44. Gieryn, *Cultural Boundaries*, 1.

45. Ian Reilly, "Satirical Fake News and/as American Political Discourse," *Journal of American Culture* 35, no. 3 (2012): 258–75.

46. Dan Berkowitz, "Telling the Unknown Through the Familiar: Collective Memory as Journalistic Device in a Changing Media Environment," in *On Media Memory: Collective Memory In a New Media Age,* ed. Motty Neiger, Oren Meyers, Eyal Zandberg, and Andrew Hoskins, 201–12 (New York: Palgrave Macmillan, 2011).

47. Motti Neiger, Oren Meyers, O. Eyal Zandberg, and Andrew Hoskins, eds., *On Media Memory: Collective Memory In a New Media Age.* (New York: Palgrave Macmillan, 2011).

48. Carlson, *War Journalism.*

49. William H. Dutton, "The Fifth Estate Emerging Through the Network of Networks," *Prometheus* 27, no. 1 (2009): 1–15.

50. Carlson, *War Journalism.*

51. Thomas Lindlof and Bryan C. Taylor, *Qualitative Communication Research Methods* (Thousand Oaks, CA: SAGE Publications, 2010).

52. Jack Phillips, "*The Onion*'s CNN Article Draws Response from Network's Meredith Artley Over Miley Cyrus," *Epoch Times,* August 26, 2013, www.theepochtimes.com/n3/264928-the-onions -cnn-article-draws-response-from-networks-meredith-artley-over-miley-cyrus/.

53. Allen Clifton, "*The Onion* Obliterates CNN's Obsessive Miley Cyrus Coverage, Exposes Bigger Issues," *Forward Progressives,* August 26, 2013, www.forwardprogressives.com/the-onion-obliterates -cnns-obsessive-miley-cyrus-coverage-exposes-bigger-issues/.

54. Clifton, "*The Onion* Obliterates CNN's Obsessive Miley Cyrus Coverage."

55. Kevin Roderick, "*The Onion* Skewers a Familiar Name Over CNN's Miley Cyrus," *LA Observed,* August 26, 2013, www.laobserved.com/archive/2013/08/the_onion_skewers_a_famil.php.

56. Daniel D'Addario, "After *The Onion* Goes After CNN's Miley Cyrus Coverage, Anderson Cooper Spotlights Twerking," *Salon,* August 27, 2013, www.salon.com/2013/08/27/after_the_onion_goes_after _cnns_miley_cyrus_coverage_anderson_cooper_spotlights_twerking/.

57. D'Addario, "After *The Onion* Goes After CNN's Miley Cyrus Coverage."

58. Alex Galbraith, "Miley Cyrus VMAs: *The Onion* Blasts CNN Over Running Twerking Recap as Story," *MStarz.com,* August 27, 2013, www.mstarz.com/articles/18419/20130827/miley-cyrus-vmas -the-onion-blasts-cnn-over-running-twerking-recap-as-top-story.htm.

59. Media Mole, "The Independent Falls for The Onion's Miley Cyrus Spoof," *New Statesman,* August 27, 2013, www.newstatesman.com/media-mole/2013/08/independent-falls-onions-miley -cyrus-spoof.

60. Robert Schlesinger, "*The Onion* Explains CNN and Miley Cyrus," *U.S. News & World Report,* August 27, 2013, www.usnews.com/opinion/blogs/robert-schlesinger/2013/08/27/the-onion-on-cnns -miley-cyrus-vma-obsession.

61. Andrew Wallenstein, "Why *The Onion* Is Wrong About CNN and Miley Cyrus." *Variety,* August 28, 2013, variety.com/2013/digital/news/why-the-onion-is-wrong-about-cnn-and-miley -cyrus-1200589821/.

62. Wallenstein, "Why *The Onion* Is Wrong."

63. Wallenstein, "Why *The Onion* Is Wrong."

64. Wallenstein, "Why *The Onion* Is Wrong."

65. Peter Bella, "*Variety* Is Wrong about *The Onion* and Miley Cyrus," *Chicago Now,* February 18, 2014, www.chicagonow.com/interesting-chicago/2013/08/variety-is-wrong-about-the-onion-and -miley-cyrus/.

66. Bella, "*Variety* Is Wrong."

67. Bella, "*Variety* Is Wrong."

68. Roger Yu, "'Onion' Digital Strategy Is No Laughing Matter." *USA Today,* October 4, 2013, www.usatoday.com/story/money/business/2013/10/03/onion-turns-25/2910381/.

69. Hamish McKenzie, "Miley Cyrus: Millennial Media Critic (Clickbait Edition)," *Pando.com,* September 27, 2013, pando.com/2013/09/27/miley-cyrus-millennial-media-critic-clickbait-edition/.

70. Vanessa Gomez, "Miley Cyrus Will Hit Rock Bottom Soon," *Neon Tommy,* September 22, 2013, www.neontommy.com/news/2013/09/miley-cyrus-will-hit-rock-bottom-soon.

71. Michelle Singer, "Timeline: Britney's Meltdown," *CBSNews.com,* February 20, 2007, www .cbsnews.com/news/timeline-britneys-meltdown/.

72. Kelley L. Carter, "Lindsay Lohan's Legal Troubles: A Timeline," *MTV.com,* July 6, 2010, www .mtv.com/news/articles/1643089/lindsay-lohans-legal-troubles-timeline.jhtml; Gil Kaufman, "Amanda Bynes: A Timeline of Her Troubles," *MTV.com,* August 12, 2013, www.mtv.com/news/articles/1712157 /amanda-bynes-troubles.jhtml.

73. Bruce Vanwyngarden, "*The Onion* Was Right About Miley Cyrus," *Memphis Flyer,* August 27, 2013, www.memphisflyer.com/TheBruceVBlog/archives/2013/08/27/the-onion-was-right-about -miley-cyrus.

74. Jeff Bercovici, "The Playboy Interview: A Candid Conversation with Gawker's Nick Denton," *Playboy,* March 7, 2014, playboysfw.kinja.com/the-playboy-interview-a-candid-conversation-with -gawke-1527302145.

75. Neetzan Zimmerman, "This *Onion* Piece From 2008 Accurately Predicted Miley Cyrus in 2013," *Gawker,* August 26, 2013, gawker.com/this-onion-piece-from-2008-accurately-predicted-miley -c-1201768477.

76. Zimmerman, "This *Onion* Piece From 2008."

77. Ross Luippold, "*The Onion* Predicted Miley Cyrus VMA Backlash in 2008," *Huffington Post,* August 26, 2013, www.huffingtonpost.com/2013/08/26/the-onion-predicted-miley-cyrus-backlash -2008_n_3817462.html.

FIGHTING FALSITY

FAKE NEWS, FACEBOOK, AND THE FIRST AMENDMENT

Joel Timmer

ollowing the victory of Donald Trump in the 2016 presidential election, Facebook found itself "in the eye of a postelection storm . . . embroiled in accusations that it helped spread misinformation and fake news stories that influenced how the American electorate voted."[1] These fake news stories, often "masterfully manipulated to look like credible journalistic reports,"[2] became widespread on Facebook in the months leading up to the election. For example, one such story which falsely claimed that "Pope Francis had endorsed Mr. Trump for president . . . was shared nearly a million times" on Facebook. The widespread reach of misinformation like this, combined with Trump's "unexpected victory," has led people to question "whether Facebook had influenced the electorate."[3]

The term "fake news" in this context describes false stories about political candidates or issues that are spread through social media sites such as Facebook.[4] While the problems associated with fake news are not confined to Facebook,[5] Facebook has played the largest role in the dissemination of false news. We may never know if the fake news stories circulating during the 2016 presidential campaign altered the outcome of the election. The possibility exists, however, that fake news stories may have swayed people's votes. Thus, misinformation may have played a significant role in the 2016 presidential election results.

One of the biggest problems with fake news is that it "can distort the electoral process."[6] Fake news stories "might trick voters into voting for the 'wrong' candidate or voting the 'wrong' way on a ballot measure," with "wrong" meaning voters vote differently from how they would have had they not been exposed to fake news stories.[7] An important reason then for stopping or curtailing the spread of fake news stories is to help voters make better informed decisions about how to vote. The question thus arises: what legal steps, if any, can be taken to prohibit or restrict the flow of fake news in political campaigns? I will first examine fake news and its widespread reach in the months leading up to the 2016 presidential election. Second, I will examine the First Amendment protections provided to both political speech and to false speech, which leads to the conclusion that the government is unlikely to be able to craft a law targeting fake news that would survive First Amendment scrutiny. Instead, courts are likely to suggest that the way to fight fake news is to expose its falsity with the truth. Candidates who themselves are the subject of defamatory statements in fake news stories may be able to pursue defamation claims against the providers of fake news stories, although this is unlikely to be effective in addressing the potential harm fake news stories might have in an election.

Next I will consider whether the fact that the speech at issue occurs online on a social media site alters the analysis regarding the level of First Amendment protection provided to it. Also considered is whether Facebook or its users who help spread fake news stories might be held legally accountable. The conclusion here is that, due to the broad immunity provisions of the Communications Decency Act, Facebook and its users cannot be held legally responsible for the spread of fake news or for the harms it might cause. Next I will examine efforts being taken by Facebook to stem the flow of fake news on its site, efforts which themselves are the subject of legal protections provided by the Communications Decency Act. The article concludes that, given the significant protections provided to false political speech under the First Amendment and the justifications for that protection, allowing Facebook to take action to address the problem is preferable to significant government action.

FAKE NEWS AND FACEBOOK

Fake news stories may be created with the purpose of affecting the public's views and possibly votes on a political candidate or issue. They might also be created simply for the advertising revenues that can be earned when Facebook users click on the links to the stories and are taken to third-party sites containing ads.[8] Fake news, however, is nothing new: "Publications like the *National Enquirer* . . . have long bent the truth, often shamelessly."[9] In the context of election campaigns, fake news exists in an environment where "[i]gnoring the facts has long been a staple of political speech. Every day, politicians overstate some statistic, distort their opponents' positions, or simply tell out-and-out whoppers."[10] Fake news, then, can be found alongside "everyday exaggerations, hard-charging opinion and political hyperbole" in political campaigns, which can make it "seem normal."[11] While fake news has been around for a long time, what is new about it "is the speed at which it can be disseminated"[12] to a large audience.

Worldwide, Facebook has 1.79 billion users.[13] In the United States, Facebook is "used by more than 200 million people . . . each month, out of a total population of 320 million,"[14] and it "reaches approximately 67% of U.S. adults."[15] Facebook users spend an average of over fifty minutes a day on the site.[16] About 44 percent of US adults say they get news from Facebook. In fact, digital sources of news were widely used in 2016: "[a]bout 65% of U.S. adults [said] . . . they learned about the election in a past week from digital sources. About 48% said they did so from news sites or apps and 44% from social networking sites."[17]

This large user base gives fake news stories on Facebook great potential to reach a large number of people. According to a BuzzFeed News study, "In the final three months of the US presidential campaign, the top-performing fake election news stories on Facebook generated more engagement than the top stories from major news outlets such as the *New York Times, Washington Post, Huffington Post,* NBC News, and others." During that time period, the "20 top-performing false election stories from hoax sites and hyperpartisan blogs generated 8,711,000 shares, reactions, and comments on Facebook," more than the "20 best-performing election stories from 19 major news websites[, which] generated a total of 7,367,000 shares, reactions, and comments on Facebook." An examination of the subjects of these widely viewed and distributed fake news stories does little to allay concerns that fake news might have had an impact on the outcome of the election. "Of the 20 top-performing false election stories identified in the analysis, all but three were overtly pro–Donald Trump or anti–Hillary Clinton. Two of the biggest false hits were a story claiming Clinton sold weapons to ISIS and a hoax claiming the pope endorsed Trump." The sources of these top twenty fake news stories were identified as "[e]ither fake news websites that only publish hoaxes or . . . hyperpartisan websites that present themselves as publishing real news." All but one of the top "false viral election stories from hyperpartisan sites came from right-wing publishers." One example of a "remarkably successful" hyperpartisan right-wing site is *Ending the Fed,* which "was responsible for four of the top 10 false election stories identified in the analysis: Pope Francis endorsing Donald Trump, Hilary Clinton selling weapons to ISIS, Hillary Clinton being disqualified from holding federal office, and the FBI director receiving millions from the Clinton Foundation." These four stories "[r]eceived more Facebook engagement than stories from the *Washington Post* and *New York Times.* For example, the top four election stories from the *Post* generated roughly 2,774,000 Facebook engagements—nearly 180,000 fewer than" the "roughly 2,953,000 Facebook engagements" generated by *Ending the Fed's* top four false posts in the three months leading up to the election.[18]

Other fake news sources may not have had such a partisan purpose in publishing their stories. BuzzFeed's analysis revealed that "many of the pro-Trump fake news sites—over 100 of them—were being operated as for-profit click-farms by Macedonian teenagers,"[19] who were apparently "motivated by the advertising dollars they could accrue if their stories went viral."[20] As it turns out, fake news site owners "[c]an make thousands of dollars per month through internet ads"[21] when Facebook users click on links that take them to third-party fake news story sites. One Los Angeles–based fake news site brought in "between $10,000 and $30,000 a month," while a "computer science student in the former Soviet republic of Georgia [said] that creating a new website and filling it with both real stories and fake news that flattered Trump was a 'gold mine.'"[22]

For its part, Facebook's chairman and chief executive Mark Zuckerberg said that Facebook affecting the election was "a pretty crazy idea."[23] Another Facebook executive said the company did not believe fake news on the site "had directly caused people to vote for a particular candidate, given that 'the magnitude of fake news across Facebook is one fraction of a percent of the content across the network.'"[24] Others, however, aren't so certain. A former employee in Facebook's advertising sales department, Antonio Garcia Martinez, labeled Zuckerberg's view as hypocritical: "It's crazy that Zuckerberg says there's no way Facebook can influence the election when there's a whole sales force in Washington DC that does nothing but convince advertisers that they can," said García Martínez.[25] According to Garcia Martinez, Facebook's sales people "literally go and tell political advertisers, '[l]ook, Facebook is the most influential platform in the world. We will win you an election.'"[26] In fact, he added, "[w]e used to joke that we could sell the whole election to the highest bidder."[27]

FIRST AMENDMENT PROTECTION FOR FAKE POLITICAL NEWS

There are a number of potential problems with regulating fake news. For one, giving the government the authority to determine "what is true or false in campaign speech opens the door to partisan abuse."[28] Thus, any law regulating false speech in political campaigns raises "the possibility that these laws will be the subject of manipulation by government authorities who want to favor one side or the other in an election."[29] Similarly, such a law could allow "courts and/or other regulatory bodies to be used as political weapons."[30] In addition, it is possible that the government might make mistakes in determining certain stories to be false "and ironically lead voters to make wrong decisions."[31] Finally, restricting political speech—even false political speech—may violate the First Amendment.[32]

The US Supreme Court "often makes a point to say that it affords political speech the highest level of Constitutional protection."[33] In fact, the "discussion of political affairs lies at the heart of the First Amendment."[34] Illustrating that point is the following quotation from the Supreme Court's opinion in *Buckley v. Valeo*:

> Discussion of public issues and debate on the qualifications of candidates are integral to the operation of the system of government established by our Constitution. The First Amendment affords the broadest protection to such political expression in order "to assure [the] unfettered interchange of ideas for the bringing about of political and social changes desired by the people." ... "[T]here is practically universal agreement that a major purpose of [the First] Amendment was to protect the free discussion of governmental affairs, ... of course including discussions of candidates. ..." This no more than reflects our "profound national commitment to the principle that debate on public issues should be uninhibited, robust, and wide-open." ... "[I]t can hardly be doubted that the constitutional guarantee has its fullest and most urgent application precisely to the conduct of campaigns for political office."[35]

This protection can even extend to false speech, and speech which is untrue. In fact, the "First Amendment is a value-free provision whose protection is not dependent on 'the truth, popularity, or social utility of the ideas and beliefs which are offered.'"[36] As the Supreme Court once observed:

In the realm of religious faith, and in that of political belief, sharp differences arise. In both fields the tenets of one man may seem the rankest error to his neighbor. To persuade others to his own point of view, the pleader, as we know, at times, resorts to exaggeration, to vilification of men who have been, or are, prominent in church or state, and even to false statement. But the people of this nation have ordained in the light of history, that, in spite of the probability of excesses and abuses, these liberties are, in the long view, essential to enlightened opinion and right conduct on the part of the citizens of a democracy.[37]

Accordingly, "erroneous statement is inevitable in free debate, and . . . it must be protected if the freedoms of expression are to have the 'breathing space' that they 'need . . . to survive.'"[38] As Supreme Court Justice Oliver Wendell Holmes famously observed, "The ultimate good desired is better reached by free trade in ideas. . . . the best test of truth is the power of the thought to get itself accepted in the competition of the market. . . . That at any rate is the theory of our Constitution."[39] In crafting the First Amendment, the founding fathers "did not trust any government to separate the true from the false for us."[40] As a result, "[i]n the free marketplace of ideas, true ideas are supposed to compete with false ones until the truth wins."[41]

In 2012, the Supreme Court provided an opinion that may be its strongest statement yet on the necessity and value of protecting false speech generally, not just in the political context. At issue in *United States v. Alvarez* was the constitutionality of the Stolen Valor Act of 2005.[42] Xavier Alvarez, who was found guilty of violating the act for falsely claiming that he had been awarded the Congressional Medal of Honor, contended that the act, which also made it a crime to falsely claim receipt of military decorations or medals, violated his First Amendment rights.[43] Reluctant to deny First Amendment protection to speech based solely on its falsity, the Supreme Court observed:

[T]here are broad areas in which any attempt by the state to penalize purportedly false speech would present a grave and unacceptable danger of suppressing truthful speech. Laws restricting false statements about philosophy, religion, history, the social sciences, the arts, and other matters of public concern would present such a threat. The point is not that there is no such thing as truth or falsity in these areas or that the truth is always impossible to ascertain, but rather that it is perilous to permit the state to be the arbiter of truth.[44]

The government in *Alvarez* pointed to several prior statements of the court to support its position that false speech, including that targeted by the act, should not be protected by the First Amendment. Representative of those statements is this one: "False statements of fact are particularly valueless [because] they interfere with the truth-seeking function of the marketplace of ideas."[45] The court responded that the quotations cited by the government in support of its position "all derive from cases discussing defamation, fraud, or some other legally cognizable harm associated with a false statement."[46] The court acknowledged that "there are instances in which the falsity of speech bears upon whether it is protected,"[47] but even then, the falsity of the speech at issue is only a relevant factor, not a determinative one.[48] The court observed, "few statutes, if any, simply prohibit without limitation the telling of a lie, even a lie about one particular matter. Instead, in virtually all these instances limitations of context, requirements of proof of injury, and the like, narrow the statute to a subset of lies where specific harm is more likely to occur."[49]

The court rejected the position that false statements are not protected by the First Amendment[50] or that "false speech should be in a general category that is presumptively unprotected."[51] Accordingly, the court refused to create "any general exception to the First Amendment for false statements."[52] In doing so, the court identified some dangers of laws against false speech:

Allowing the state to proscribe false statements in these areas also opens the door for the state to use its power for political ends. Statements about history illustrate this point. If some false statements about historical events may be banned, how certain must it be that a statement is false before the ban may be upheld? And who should make that calculation? While our cases prohibiting view-point discrimination would fetter the state's power to some degree, the potential for abuse of power in these areas is simply too great.[53]

The Supreme Court's decision in *United States v. Alvarez* will almost certainly be one that courts look to in the future when faced with First Amendment challenges to laws targeting false speech in the context of election campaigns (or otherwise).[54] It is clear from that decision that the falsity of the speech alone would not be sufficient to deny protection to that speech. As one scholar observed, "Although the Court's decision in *Alvarez* is badly fractured, there seems unanimous skepticism of laws targeting false speech about issues of public concern and through which the state potentially could use its sanctioning power for political ends. Especially dangerous are criminal laws punishing false speech that could lead to selective criminal prosecution."[55]

A major problem, then, if the government were to seek to enact a law targeting fake news stories in the context of political campaigns, is that the "Court considers broad, content-based restrictions on false statements in political messages to be generally impermissible."[56] While the government might seek to argue for the creation of a new exception to First Amendment protection for this speech, the court has stated that "the First Amendment stands against any 'freewheeling authority to declare new categories of speech outside the scope of the First Amendment.'"[57] Nevertheless, the court has acknowledged that there may be "[s]ome categories of speech that have been historically unprotected . . . but have not yet been specifically identified or discussed . . . in our case law."[58] Before the court would create a new exception, though, it must first "be presented with 'persuasive evidence that a novel restriction on content is part of a long (if heretofore unrecognized) tradition of proscription.'"[59] This is not the case with false speech in the context of an election campaign, as "the First Amendment 'has its fullest and most urgent application' to speech uttered during a campaign for political office."[60]

Thus, a law that targeted false political speech would be "subject to strict scrutiny, which requires the government to prove that the restriction furthers a compelling interest and is narrowly tailored to achieve that interest."[61] The government could likely establish that such a law serves a compelling government interest. The Supreme Court has recognized that the government "has a compelling interest in preserving the integrity of its election process."[62] Further, this interest "carries special weight during election campaigns when false statements, if credited, may have serious adverse consequences for the public at large."[63] Consequently, the court has held that the government "has a compelling interest in protecting voters from confusion and undue influence."[64]

While the government can establish that such a law serves a compelling interest, this is not the "end [of] the matter" as the "First Amendment requires that the Government's chosen restriction on the speech at issue be 'actually nec-essary' to achieve its interest."[65] This showing also requires that "the restriction must be the 'least restrictive means among available, effective alternatives'"[66] to achieve that interest. Among the potential alternatives of combating the harms associated with fake news is counter-speech, speech directed at exposing and counteracting the false speech. Consequently, the government would need to show that counter-speech would be less effective than the restriction in serving the government interest. In *Alvarez*, for example, the government's case failed in part because it could not show "why counterspeech would not suffice to achieve its interest," leaving the court to believe that "the dynamics of free speech, of counterspeech, of refutation, [could] overcome the lie."[67]

Justice Breyer in his *Alvarez* concurrence acknowledged the difficulty in craft-ing a law against fake news in political campaigns: "I recognize that in some contexts, particularly political contexts, such a narrowing [as that required by the strict scrutiny test] will not always be easy to achieve."[68] Further, there is little case law on restrictions on false speech in political campaigns to provide the gov-ernment guidance on this point. Breyer did point to two cases that "upheld the constitutionality of roughly comparable but narrowly tailored statutes in political contexts,"[69] but then appeared to cast some doubt on the holdings in those cases. He first declined to "express any view on the validity of those cases,"[70] then noted his agreement with the plurality "that in this area more accurate information will normally counteract the lie."[71]

The fact that the cases Breyer cited were decided before *Alvarez*, combined with the strong protection that *Alvarez* provides for laws aimed at false speech, provides additional reason to doubt the applicability of those cases to any fu-ture challenges to laws aimed at false speech in the political context. In fact, the holding in one of those cases is in direct opposition to that in *Alvarez*. In *Treasurer of Committee to Elect Lostracco v. Fox*, the Michigan Court of Appeals was faced with a challenge to a law that made it a "misdemeanor for a candidate for public office to give the impression in campaign advertisements that he is the incumbent when in fact he is not."[72] In making its decision, the court cited *Vanasco v. Schwartz* for the principle that "the knowingly false statement and the false statement made with the reckless disregard of the truth do not enjoy constitutional protection."[73] Based on this, the *Fox* court concluded "[k]nowing misrepresentations are not constitutionally protected free speech" and found that the candidate's First Amendment rights were not infringed by the application of the law at issue in the case.[74] The basis for the holding in this case then is in opposition to what the court held in *Alvarez*, where it explicitly rejected the notion that false statements are outside the protection of the First Amendment.[75]

Pre-*Alvarez* case law then provides little guidance on how a court might rule on a law aimed at fake news in an election campaign. Further, both the *Alvarez* plurality and concurrence expressed the view that counter-speech is the preferred method for dealing with false speech.[76] Based on this, it appears any law attempting to restrict or prohibit fake news in a political campaign will face an uphill battle when challenged in the courts. Nevertheless, a few observations can be offered on how the government might try to narrow the applicability of a law restricting fake news stories in a political campaign to better its chances of surviving strict scrutiny. It should first be noted, however, that even with such narrowing, the constitutional validity of such a law is far from assured. The First Amendment and the Supreme Court's holding in *Alvarez* put significant obstacles—perhaps insurmountable ones—in the way of any government law attempting to restrict or prohibit false political speech.

The prime difficulties for the government in crafting a law against fake news in political campaigns that can withstand strict scrutiny are to show that the means chosen are both necessary to achieve the government's interest and the least restrictive way of doing so. One way of narrowing the reach of such a restriction would be to require that it "be possible to actually prove the statements were false," so that the statute "would apply only to statements of fact, not opinions or ideas." This narrowing might also be achieved by limiting the restriction's applicability "to statements that are 'material or have a recognizable effect on a candidate's electoral prospects.'" There are two narrowing components here. One, the false statements must be material; "[m]inor misstatements should not be actionable if the [statement itself] is substantially accurate." Two, false statements "should also not be actionable if no reasonable voter would change or base her vote on the false statement."[77]

This standard would exclude minor misstatements of fact as well as those that had little or no chance of negatively affecting a candidate's prospects. However, limiting a restriction in this way "may be too hard a test for the courts to implement."[78] Where does one draw the line between minor and material misstatements of fact? How does one show that a voter would change his or her vote because of a false statement? How does one establish that a single fake news story is responsible for a person voting the way he or she did, rather than it being attributable to the cumulative impact of all the news stories and other information—both accurate and false—a voter is exposed to in the days and weeks leading up to an election? Is it sufficient that a single voter's vote was changed by a fake news story, or must it be shown that enough votes were affected by the falsity to change the outcome of the election? Again, how would one show these things to a court's satisfaction?[79]

One additional protection for fake news stories that would likely be required to be contained in such a law would be for the burden of proving the falsity of the stories on the government, rather than requiring the speaker (or source) to prove the story's truth, as is generally the case with defamation laws. The Supreme Court's opinion in *New York Times v. Sullivan* provides the justification for such a requirement:

> A rule compelling the critic of official conduct to guarantee the truth of all his factual assertions—and to do so on pain of libel judgments virtually unlimited in amount leads to a comparable "self-censorship." Allowance of the defense of truth, with the burden of proving it on the defendant, does not mean that only false speech will be deterred. Even courts accepting this defense as an adequate safeguard have recognized the difficulties of adducing legal proofs that the alleged libel was true in all its factual particulars. Under such a rule, would-be critics of official conduct may be deterred from voicing their criticism, even though it is believed to be true and even though it is in fact true, because of doubt whether it can be proved in court or fear of the expense of having to do so. They tend to make only statements which "steer far wider of the unlawful zone." The rule thus dampens the vigor and limits the variety of public debate. It is inconsistent with the First and Fourteenth Amendments.[80]

Another aspect of defamation law that would likely be necessary to incorporate in such a law is that its applicability be limited to only those stories that were published with "actual malice," in that the speaker or author of the story knew it was false or acted with reckless disregard for the story's falsity when publishing the story. This is a standard found in defamation law that the Supreme Court has required for public officials who wish to take legal action against those who make false statements about them which can harm the official's reputation. The actual malice requirement was instituted as a recognition of "a profound national commitment to the principle that debate on public issues should be uninhibited, robust, and wide-open, and that it may well include vehement, caustic, and sometimes unpleasantly sharp attacks on government and public officials."[81] Thus, "even though falsehoods have little value in and of themselves, they are 'nevertheless inevitable in free debate.'"[82] The court was concerned that a lesser standard, such as negligence, that allowed public officials to recover "for false factual assertions [about them] would have an undoubted 'chilling' effect on speech relating to public figures that does have constitutional value."[83] The actual malice requirement reduces the likelihood of a chilling effect on speech with constitutional value by making it harder for officials to prevail in defamation actions simply because a false, harmful statement was made about them. Instead, the speaker must have made the statement knowing it was false or with reckless disregard for whether the statement was false. As the *Alvarez* plurality observed, "The requirements of a knowing falsehood or reckless disregard for the truth as the condition for recovery in certain defamation cases exists to allow more speech, not less."[84]

Given the First Amendment protections provided to political speech, false speech, and false political speech, even incorporating limitations like those just discussed into a law aimed at fake news in election campaigns is unlikely to result in the law surviving strict scrutiny. Defamation law does, however, provide an existing cause of action for candidates who are the targets of fake news stories to pursue legal action against the source of a fake news story, as well as against certain parties who publish or distribute the story. In general, "[d]efamation statutes focus upon statements of a kind that harm the reputation of another or deter third parties from association or dealing with the victim."[85] To make out a claim for defamation, a plaintiff must generally establish that a false statement was made to a third party about the plaintiff and that the statement was of such a nature that it harmed, or would tend to harm, the plaintiff's reputation.[86] This is the standard that typically applies to private individuals asserting a defamation claim.[87] For reasons just discussed, public officials, including candidates for public office, typically need to prove an additional requirement: actual malice, meaning that "the statement was made 'with knowledge that it was false or with reckless disregard of whether it was false or not.'"[88]

While existing defamation laws provide candidates with a potential action against the sources of fake news stories about themselves, reliance on defamation statutes alone is unlikely to be an effective means of combatting fake news and its harms. Defamation laws typically allow the subject of the defamatory statement to bring an action in order to punish the speaker.[89] Victims of allegedly defamatory statements are often reluctant to bring defamation actions for a number of reasons. For one, it can take significant resources to pursue a defamation claim.[90] For another, victims of such statements might fear that bringing a defamation action will only bring more attention to the statement, compounding the initial harm that might have been done. It can also take a significant amount of time to get a court decision on a defamation claim.[91] Fake news stories likely to do the most harm to a candidate may often occur close to an election, with a lawsuit based on the statements not likely to be decided until well after the election has occurred. Finally, the candidate can only pursue defamation claims against fake news stories that are about the candidate himself or herself. Fake news stories that are not actually about a candidate but that still may harm that candidate's prospects—for example, a story that the Pope endorsed Trump, which might have adversely affected Hillary Clinton's prospects—are not stories that the candidate could properly pursue via a defamation action.[92] Accordingly, defamation actions would do little, if anything, to ameliorate the harm caused to the election itself by a fake news story.

PROTECTION FOR ONLINE SPEECH

Does the fact that fake news is often disseminated online through Facebook and other online sites affect its protection under the First Amendment? The answer to this is no, as speech on the Internet enjoys "the same level of constitutional protection as traditional forms of speech."[93] In coming to this conclusion in 1997 in *Reno v. ACLU,* the Supreme Court observed that, "[t]hrough the use of chat rooms, any person with a phone line can become a town crier with a voice that resonates farther than it could from any soapbox," and that, "[t]hrough the use of Web pages, mail exploders, and newsgroups, the same individual can become a pamphleteer."[94] While the Supreme Court has not yet had occasion to address whether speech on social media sites like Facebook is similarly protected, the court's observations in *Reno* about the communication possibilities provided by the Internet would seem to apply with equal, if not more, force to Facebook. In addition, "various lower courts have confronted this question" and concluded that "posting comments on Facebook constitutes speech."[95] Because of this protection afforded speech on the Internet, including on social media, all of the First Amendment issues raised by a law targeting fake news in political campaigns apply with equal force to speech on Facebook and other social media sites.

The protections granted to false political speech by the First Amendment make it unlikely the government would be able to craft a law targeting fake news in the context of an election campaign that can survive First Amendment scrutiny. Defamation appears to be a candidate's sole legal remedy against harmful fake news stories about him or her. Under traditional defamation law, not only can the source of a defamatory statement be held liable, but parties that repeat or republish the statement can often be held liable as well.[96] In 2016, fake news stories appeared on Facebook, then were often spread to larger audiences through the actions of Facebook users who shared, commented on, or liked the stories, all of which can cause the stories to appear in other users' news feeds.[97] Because of this, Facebook and its users could be considered to be repeating or republishing fake news stories. Might targeting defamation actions at Facebook and/ or its users help to deter Facebook from allowing these stories to be posted or to remain on its site once there, or to deter Facebook users from acting to make the stories available to others? The answer to this is provided by section 230 of the Communications Decency Act of 1996 ("CDA").[98]

Section 230 of the Communications Decency Act provides immunity to sites such as Facebook—referred to as "interactive computer service provider" under the law—for liability arising out of content posted on the site by the site's users.[99] This includes liability for defamation.[100] With this immunity, Congress sought, in part, "to provide a legal framework for the Internet to flourish in [the area of] political discourse"[101] and to avoid a law that would restrict the Internet's growth.[102] Congress was concerned that interactive service providers might be burdened by lawsuits for speech posted on their sites by third parties, and feared "the potential for chilled online speech" that could result from a law making service providers liable in such situations.[103] Thus, section 230 of the Communications Decency Act of 1996[104] states, "[n]o provider or user of an interactive computer service shall be treated as the publisher or speaker of any information provided by another information content provider."[105] This provision has generally been interpreted by courts as providing "broad immunity when plaintiffs have attempted to hold an online entity liable for web site content posted by a third party in defamation and other types of civil claims."[106] This immunity includes social media sites like Facebook, which have been held to qualify as interactive computer services under the law.[107] It does not include the actual authors of defamatory content, however, who may still be held liable.[108]

Zeran v. America Online, Inc., was one of the first cases to rule on the protection provided to interactive computer service providers under section 230. In that case, Zeran sought to have America Online ("AOL") held liable for allegedly defamatory statements about him posted on the service by a third party, claiming specifically that "AOL unreasonably delayed in removing defamatory messages posted by an unidentified third party, refused to post retractions of those messages, and failed to screen for similar postings thereafter." The court observed that Zeran was seeking to impose liability on AOL for acting in the role of a publisher.[109] The basis for Zeran's argument was the fact that traditionally, under defamation law, "[p]ublishers can be held liable for defamatory statements contained in their works even absent proof that they had specific knowledge of the statement's inclusion."[110] The court noted that Congress changed this traditional rule, however, with section 230, making "a policy choice . . . not to deter harmful online speech . . . [by] imposing tort liability on companies that serve as intermediaries for other parties' potentially injurious messages."[111] A contrary rule—in which interactive service providers were liable for the communications posted on their services by others—would force providers like AOL "to police the huge volume of electronic traffic [which] would certainly chill the growth of the then-expanding Internet and other technological advancements."[112] Thus, section 230 "creates a federal immunity to any cause of action that would make service providers liable for information originating with a third-party user of the service."[113]

Facebook itself then cannot be held liable for defamatory fake news stories posted on its site by its users. However, Facebook only provides the platform where these stories can potentially reach a large audience. One way that these stories can reach a large audience is when other users see these stories and interact with them, which can then make the stories available to other Facebook users. For example, a user could share, like, or comment on a story, which can result in the story showing up in other users' Facebook news feeds, along with the first user's specific interaction with the story. In other contexts, a party who repeats a defamatory statement originally made by another can be held liable for defamation, in addition to the original speaker.[114] Can Facebook users—and those of other interactive computer services—be held liable for sharing fake news stories which are defamatory? Under the immunity provisions of section 230, Facebook users are provided the same protection as Facebook itself. Thus, the law not only exempts Facebook and other social media sites for defamatory fake news stories posted on the sites by others; it also protects users of those sites who repost or otherwise assist in the spread of that content.[115]

Courts have not had as many occasions to consider the protections afforded to users of interactive computer services by section 230 as they have those provided to the services themselves.[116] One of the first published cases to consider this was *Barrett v. Rosenthal*.[117] Rosenthal was sued for defamation for posting emails written by a third party on Usenet newsgroups. Those emails allegedly contained defamatory statements about the plaintiffs.[118] The court observed that Rosenthal, as "an individual who had no supervisory role in the operation of the Internet site where allegedly defamatory material appeared . . . was clearly not a provider of an 'interactive computer service' [as defined by] the CDA."[119] The court noted that section 230 had "been widely and consistently interpreted to confer broad immunity against defamation liability for those who use the Internet to publish information that originated from another source."[120] Concluding that "section 230(c)(1) immunizes individual 'users' of interactive computer services," the court held that Rosenthal could not be held liable for distributing defamatory statements made by another.[121]

This immunity attaches even if information service providers or users know that the stories they are republishing are false or defamatory, and presumably even if such knowledge satisfies the actual malice standard. Traditionally under defamation law, publishing or distributing a statement made by another with the knowledge that the statement is defamatory can be sufficient to hold that party liable for the defamation in addition to the original speaker.[122] Section 230 changes this. In both *Zeran* and *Rosenthal,* the defendants were notified prior to the suit being brought that the statements at issue were defamatory, but this had no effect on either court's analysis.[123] The relevant consideration was whether the defendants qualified as either an interactive computer service provider or user under the statute. Once it was determined that they did, they were immune from liability, regardless of whether they had knowledge or notice of the defamatory nature of the statements. There are practical reasons for the law to be crafted this way, at least as it concerns service providers:

> Subjecting service providers to notice liability would defeat "the dual purposes" of section 230, by encouraging providers to restrict speech and abstain from self-regulation. A provider would be at risk for liability each time it received notice of a potentially defamatory statement in any Internet message, requiring an investigation of the circumstances, a legal judgment about the defamatory character of the information, and an editorial decision on whether to continue the publication."[124]

As the court further observed, "Defamation law is complex, requiring consideration of multiple factors. These include whether the statement at issue is true or false, factual or figurative, privileged or unprivileged, whether the matter is of public or private concern, and whether the plaintiff is a public or private figure."[125] Investigating whether a posting is defamatory or not "is thus a daunting and expensive challenge."[126] While such an investigation "might be feasible for the traditional print publisher, the sheer number of postings on interactive computer services would create an impossible burden in the Internet context."[127] Additionally, imposing liability when service providers have notice of defamatory content on their services could deter them from screening and investigating content posted by users, as such screening "would only lead to notice of potentially defamatory material more frequently and thereby create a stronger basis for liability. Instead of subjecting themselves to further possible lawsuits, service providers would likely eschew any attempts at self-regulation."[128]

Furthermore, notice-based liability would give those displeased with certain speech appearing on social media sites a significant weapon to combat that speech. As the court observed in *Zeran,* "Whenever one was displeased with the speech of another party conducted over an interactive computer service, the offended party could simply 'notify' the relevant service provider, claiming the information to be legally defamatory."[129] This would obligate the provider to investigate the defamatory statement to determine whether the statement should be removed from the service or be allowed to remain. This could result in service providers being faced with "ceaseless choices of suppressing controversial speech or sustaining prohibitive liability."[130] The achievement of Congress's objectives with section 230 could be significantly hindered as a result, as "[t]he specter of potential litigation, with its attendant cost and effort, would likely result in shutting down many websites."[131]

The justification for providing this immunity to users is not as clear as it is for service providers. The *Rosenthal* court expressed the view that defamation liability for users for information originally provided by another "would tend to chill online speech." Users may not be threatened with defamation liability as frequently as service providers, but "their lack of comparable financial and legal resources makes that threat no less intimidating." On the other hand, users "do not face the massive volume of third-party postings that providers encounter," making "[s]elf-regulation . . . a far less challenging enterprise for them."[132]

At the same time, the *Rosenthal* court suggested that "[u]sers are more likely than service providers to actively engage in malicious propagation of defamatory or other offensive material."[133] This led the court to identify some "disturbing implications" that might come from providing users with immunity from defamation suits when they "intentionally redistribute defamatory statements on the Internet."[134] In his concurring opinion, Justice Moreno argued that the immunity should "not apply if the 'user' is in a conspiracy" with the original source of the defamatory statement.[135] For example, two parties could conspire to defame someone, with one party, set up to be "judgment proof," providing the defamatory content, and the other, a user of a service provider's site, engaged in actively disseminating the defamatory statements. In this situation, the latter party—the user, as the one whose actions can give the statements a wide reach—would be protected by section 230's immunity.[136] Moreno did not believe the user should be immune from liability for defamation in such circumstances.[137]

There need not be an actual conspiracy for the harm that Moreno foresaw to occur. Even absent a conspiracy between a user and an information content provider, a Facebook user could see a fake news story on Facebook that benefited his or her preferred candidate at the expense of the candidate's opponent, know that the story was false and defamatory about the opponent, take action to spread the story to other Facebook users, and yet be immune from any liability for the harm this might cause under section 230. With section 230, "plaintiffs who contend they were defamed in an Internet posting may only seek recovery from the original source of the statement," no matter the role or culpability of a user who acts to spread the reach of such a statement. As the *Rosenthal* majority observed, "Any further expansion of liability must await congressional action."[138]

With the immunity provided by section 230, Congress sought to ensure that interactive computer service providers "continued to promote the free exchange of ideas and messages, rather than restrict postings because of the fear of lawsuits."[139] Congress also had another goal with section 230, which was "to encourage service providers to self-regulate the dissemination of offensive material over their services."[140] Before the enactment of section 230, providers engaging in self-regulation of content posted by others on their sites would be placed "in the traditional role of publisher, which would have exposed them to strict liability" for content posted on their services by those third parties.[141] Concerned that the prospect of such liability would "deter service providers from blocking and screening offensive material," Congress provided immunity for this by "forbid[ding] the imposition of publisher liability on a service provider for the exercise of its editorial and self-regulatory functions."[142] Thus, section 230 also provides: "No provider or user of an interactive computer service shall be held liable on account of—(A) any action voluntarily taken in good faith to restrict access to or availability of material that the provider or user considers to be obscene, lewd, lascivious, filthy, excessively violent, harassing, or otherwise objectionable, whether or not such material is constitutionally protected."[143] This provision explicitly shields service providers from civil liability for removing materials from their sites that are "obscene, lewd, lascivious, filthy, excessively violent, harassing, or otherwise objectionable."[144] Fake news—or false statements—is not one of the types of material listed in the statute. The question then is whether fake news qualifies under the statute as content that is "otherwise objectionable."

In *E360Insight, LLC v. Comcast, Corp.*,[145] e360 was an Internet marketing company that would, for a fee, send email solicitations and advertisements to millions of email users, which the court observed would lead many to call the company "a spammer." To prevent these unwanted and unsolicited messages from reaching its subscribers, Comcast began blocking all emails from e360 to its subscribers, which was the basis for e360 bringing suit in this case. Ruling that section 230(C)(2)(B) protected Comcast's use of filters to block e360's marketing messages sent to Comcast subscribers, the court determined that "unsolicited and bulk e-mails (whether you call them spam or mass marketing mailings) are the sort of communications an entity like Comcast could deem to be objection-able."[146] In doing so, the court observed that "section 203(c)(2) only requires that the provider subjectively deems the blocked material objectionable."[147] Consistent with this view is that of another court, which noted that section 230(c)(2) "does not require that the material actually be objectionable; rather, it affords protection for blocking material 'that the provider or user considers to be' objectionable."[148] Based on these rulings, a service provider such as Facebook has considerable leeway to classify fake news stories as objectionable.

Section 230(c)(2) further requires that the actions taken by an information service provider to restrict objectionable materials be "taken in good faith."[149] Courts have engaged in little analysis of what is required for a service provider's actions to be considered to be in good faith; those that have provide little reason to believe that the good-faith requirement places any significant restriction on service provider efforts to self-regulation of objectionable content on their services. One court to consider the issue observed that "good faith" means the action was taken "with an absence of malice."[150] Another court stated that good faith requires that "the provider must actually believe that the material is objectionable for the reasons it gives."[151] Yet another court observed, "To raise an issue of an absence of good faith, an allegation of conduct outside the scope of the traditional publisher's function would be required."[152] This court said further:

> [T]he good samaritan provision [for the blocking and screening of offensive material] . . . was inserted not to diminish the broad general immunity provided by § 230(c)(1), but to assure that it *not* be diminished by the exercise of traditional publisher functions. If the conduct falls within the scope of the traditional publisher's functions, it cannot constitute, within the context of § 230(c)(2)(A), bad faith. This principle, although not articulated in the cases we have [reviewed], is implicit in them.[153]

Section 230(c)(2)(A) then provides a service provider with immunity arising from lawsuits arising from "its exercise of a publisher's traditional editorial functions" in regard to content provided by the service's users that the provider considers to be "objectionable."[154] This immunity helps further Congress's goal of encouraging service providers to engage in "self-regulation to eliminate access to obscene or otherwise offensive materials . . . without fear of liability."[155] Courts analyzing this provision have concluded that this immunity applies so long as the service provider's activities go "no further than the traditional editorial functions of a publisher."[156] These "traditional editorial functions" include activities such as deciding "whether to publish, withdraw, postpone or alter content provided by others."[157] Courts have generally interpreted these protected functions broadly.

Deleting inaccurate information from a site has been held to fall within the "editorial functions" protected by section 230.[158] Even a failure to delete information after being informed of its defamatory nature has been found to be a protected editorial function. In *Schneider v. Amazon.com*, an author, Schneider, complained to Amazon about allegedly defamatory comments made about him in some reviews of Schneider's books by Amazon users. Amazon acknowledged that some of the postings violated its guidelines and agreed to remove them within a couple of days. However, it failed to do so.[159] Referring to a case in which a service provider's deletion of inaccurate information was held to be protected under section 230 as an editorial function, the court observed that, "if actual editing does not create liability, the mere right to edit can hardly do so."[160] The court went on to observe that the immunity provided by Congress "as an incentive to Internet service providers to self-police the Internet for obscenity and other offensive material [applied] even where the self-policing is unsuccessful or not even attempted."[161] Accordingly, the court held that the "failure to remove the posting" was "an exercise of editorial discretion," and thus an activity protected by section 230.[162]

The Third Circuit followed the same approach in *Green v. America Online*.[163] Green notified AOL of allegedly defamatory statements made about him by another user in a chat room hosted by AOL, then attempted to have AOL held liable for its failure to take any action on the comments. The statements also allegedly violated AOL's own guidelines.[164] The court observed that Green was attempting "to hold AOL liable for decisions relating to the monitoring, screening, and deletion of content from its network—actions quintessentially related to a publisher's role."[165] These actions, the court found, were protected by section 230.[166] In coming to this conclusion, the court observed, "Section 230(c)(2) does not *require* AOL to restrict speech; rather it allows AOL to establish standards of decency without risking liability for doing so."[167]

"Selective editing and commenting" have also been held to be activities falling "within the scope of the traditional publisher's function."[168] In *Batzel v. Smith*,

Smith sent an email to the operator of the Museum Security Network website, which focused on stolen artwork. The email detailed Smith's claim that Batzel was a descendant of a high-ranking Nazi official who was in possession of numerous pieces of artwork stolen by Nazis during World War II. The operator of the website posted Smith's message, with some minor wording changes, accompanied by a "moderator's message" that "the FBI has been informed" about Smith's allegation.[169] Batzel learned of the posting several months later and filed suit for defamation.[170]

The court determined that to fall outside the category of protected editorial functions and lose section 230 immunity requires "something more substantial than merely editing portions of an e-mail and selecting material for publication." Indeed, the court held that section 230's immunity allows service providers "to choose among proffered material and to edit the material published while retaining its basic form and message" without risking liability for doing so. As a justification, the court observed, "If efforts to review and omit third-party defamatory, obscene or inappropriate material make a computer service provider or user liable for posted speech, then website operators and Internet service providers are likely to abandon efforts to eliminate such material from their site."[171]

As these cases establish, section 230(c)(2) provides broad immunity for service providers who seek to remove defamatory or other actionable content from their sites, and even for those who fail to do so when notified of the defamatory character of content provided by users of their sites. This immunity from tort liability applies where the provider takes "an active, even aggressive role in making available content prepared by others," as well as when a service provider's "self-policing is unsuccessful or not even attempted."[172] Given the scope of service-provider activities protected by this provision, section 230 would seem to give Facebook significant protection for any efforts it undertook to remove or limit fake news on its site.

FACEBOOK EFFORTS TO LIMIT FAKE NEWS

Facebook does not view itself as a media company or as being in the content distribution business. Facebook itself does not write the news stories its users read and share. Rather, Facebook views itself as "an open technology platform that relies on media publishers and its users to share accurate information."[173] As such, Facebook regards itself as a nonpartisan information source,[174] "a neutral place where people can freely post, read and view content" and where "people can share all opinions." While Facebook sees itself as "a technology company" rather than a media company, it has come to recognize that it has "a greater responsibility than just building technology that information flows through." Indeed, in late 2016, Mark Zuckerberg stated, "We have a responsibility to make sure Facebook has the greatest positive impact on the world."[175]

Facebook does not want to be in the role of an editor[176] or "an arbiter of truth."[177] Facebook's head of media partnerships, Patrick Walker, has stated, "We believe it's essential that Facebook stay out of the business of deciding what issues the world should read about. That's what editors do." Nevertheless, Facebook has acknowledged that it is "more than just a distributor of news." Said Zuckerberg, "[w]e're a new kind of platform for public discourse—and that means we have a new kind of responsibility to enable people to have the most meaningful conversations, and to build a space where people can be informed."[178] To this end, Facebook has begun a series of experiments to limit the appearance and spread of fake news on its site, an act which points to Facebook's recognition that "it has a deepening responsibility for what is on its site."[179]

One of Facebook's initial efforts to combat fake news involves making it easier for Facebook users to report fake news stories appearing on the site. Facebook is also partnering "with outside fact-checking organizations to help it indicate when articles are false,"[180] who will have the ability to "label stories in the News Feed as fake."[181] Facebook will also be "changing some advertising practices to stop purveyors of fake news from profiting from it." These early efforts are targeted only at "fake news content; [Facebook] does not plan to flag opinion posts or other content that could not be easily classified," nor will its efforts "affect satirical sites like The Onion, which often jabs at political subjects through tongue-in-cheek humor."[182] With these experiments, Facebook is striving to ensure that it does not "mistakenly block 'accurate content.'"[183] It also wants to avoid exposure to censorship claims against it.[184]

One change Facebook is making is allowing users "to flag content that may be fake." Currently, Facebook users can report posts in their news feeds that they don't like, with the ability to select from different options for why they dislike the story, such as "I don't think it should be on Facebook." With the new experiment, "users will have the option to flag a post as fake news as well as to message the friend who originally shared the piece to tell him or her the article is false."[185] Articles that are flagged by enough users as fake can be directed to third-party fact-checkers, all of whom are signatories of Poynter's International Fact Checking Code of Principles.[186] These include ABC News, the Associated Press, FactCheck.org, PolitiFact, and Snopes, which will then fact-check the article. If the article is false, the fact-checkers "can mark it as a 'disputed' piece, a designation that will be seen on Facebook."[187] Facebook researchers will not only review stories flagged by Facebook users, but "will also review website domains . . . that appear to be faked or spoofed (like washingtonpost.co)" and send these domains to third-party fact-checkers.[188]

Articles designated as "disputed" by Facebook's fact-checkers will appear lower in users' news feeds. Users can still share these disputed articles with others, but if they do, "they will receive a pop-up reminding them that the accuracy of the piece is in question." Facebook will also analyze patterns of the reading and sharing of news articles by its users, which may allow it to take additional steps to limit the spread of fake news. For example, Facebook will identify articles that many users read but do not then share, which could indicate that an "article was misleading or of poor quality." These articles will also "be ranked lower on people's feeds."[189] In addition, Facebook will use "algorithms that detect whether a story that appears fake is going viral, to determine if it should label the story as fake and bury it in people's feeds."[190]

Based on its finding that "a lot of fake news is financially motivated,"[191] Facebook also "plans to impede the economics of spreading fake articles across the network."[192] Fake news providers often make money when people click on links to their articles, some of which are made to look like they're from well-known news organizations. Once users click on these links, they are taken to third-party websites, which often consist largely of ads.[193] Facebook will examine the links to stories to see if the third-party websites are "mostly filled with advertising content—a dead giveaway for spam sites—or to see whether a link masquerades as a different site, like a fake version of *The New York Times*." If either of these is the case, the sites will "not be eligible to display Facebook advertising on their pages." Articles identified by fact-checkers as disputed will also be ineligible "to be inserted into Facebook ads, a tactic viral spammers have used to spread fake news quickly and gain more clicks on their websites."[194]

These steps all seem to fit squarely within the CDA's immunity for the blocking and screening of objectionable material by interactive computer service providers. Facebook has considerable leeway to classify fake news as "objectionable" under the statute. The company's actions involve its deciding how and where fake news stories will appear on its site, including marking some of these stories as "disputed." These actions seem to fall within "a publisher's traditional editorial functions—such as deciding whether to publish, withdraw, postpone or alter content"[195] as well as "[s]elective editing and commenting"[196] and deleting inaccurate information—all of which have been held to fall within section 230's protection. Will this be effective? Time will tell. For its part, Facebook has labeled these steps as "experiments."[197] Presumably Facebook will review the results of its efforts and make adjustments where its efforts don't seem as effective as they could be.

Observers have already pointed out a number of concerns or issues with Facebook's proposals. One concern is over the ability of any Facebook user to report a story as fake or a hoax with a simple click. While this may help address the problem, "the potential for abuse is immediately obvious. People can flood the system with fake reports of fake news, either to punish websites and news organizations they dislike or to subvert the fake-news-flagging process itself."[198] In addition, the new system will only flag "articles hosted by external sites. "That means that videos, memes, or photos will be unaffected—even if they contain the very same false information or hoaxes." It has been reported though that Facebook will "reassess this once they have tested the system with news articles[,]"[199] indicating an openness by Facebook to adjusting the system as it gains experience with it.

The fact-checking process itself is also complicated and fraught with issues. Fact-checkers are typically trying to verify claims made by politicians, rather than by news stories. Labeling a "story as reliable or not reliable, rather than an individual claim . . . [is] going to require some adjustment by the fact-checkers."[200] Furthermore, making conclusions about whether a story is true or false can be difficult: "truth and falsehood are rarely black and white, at least in the mouths of politicians. More often than not, the devil is in the details—or in the context."[201] Finally, there is reason to believe that the findings of the fact-checkers may not be accepted by all: "Conservatives [have expressed] extreme skepticism [that] the fact-checking would be applied equally to both sides of the political spectrum."[202]

In early 2017, about a month after announcing these initiatives, Facebook unveiled the Facebook Journalism Project, the goal of which is to "help give people information so they can make smart choices about the news they read and have meaningful conversations about what they care about." Facebook will attempt to do this by working with outside organizations to study and promote news literacy both on and off Facebook. The goal of this is "to help people . . . have the information they need to make decisions about which sources to trust." The company's near-term efforts in this regard include working with others to support existing news literacy efforts, identifying and funding new research involving news literacy, and producing public service announcements to help educate Facebook users about the issue. Longer term, Facebook seeks to support news organizations that are working to improve news literacy, including with financial grants where necessary.[203]

Facebook's efforts "show that it recognizes the need to establish processes to maintain the service's trust as a media brand."[204] In doing so, Facebook is also hoping to make "sure that a healthy news ecosystem and journalism can thrive."[205] It remains to be seen how effective these efforts will be and how committed Facebook is to achieving these objectives in the long term. Facebook certainly has an incentive to promote its users' confidence in the information found on its site. Otherwise, it risks becoming associated in the public's mind with fake news, which could cause it to lose users and revenue. Further, Facebook's not being bound by the constraints of the First Amendment,[206] combined with the broad immunity provided it by section 230 of the Communications Decency Act, make it preferable for Facebook and other social media sites—rather than the government—to take actions like these.

CONCLUSION

The misinformation provided by fake political news stories and the wide reach those stories can achieve through popular social media sites like Facebook present a threat to the efficient functioning of our democracy.[207] Government regulation of fake news, however, does not appear to be the solution to the problem. The protection given to political speech by the First Amendment—even when that speech is false—makes it unlikely a law could be crafted that would survive the strict scrutiny to which it would be subjected. Based on the Supreme Court's holding in *U.S. v. Alvarez* and other cases, courts are more likely to conclude that the proper strategy for fighting the problems associated with fake news is not to restrict speech; instead they are likely to find that the proper strategy would be more speech. In fact, the Supreme Court has observed that "suppression of speech by the government can make exposure of falsity more difficult, not less so."[208] Thus, "[t]he remedy for speech that is false is speech that is true. This is the ordinary course in a free society. The response to the unreasoned is the rational; to the uninformed, the enlightened; to the straight-out lie, the simple truth."[209]

Defamation is an existing cause of action targeting false speech—one that has been held to be constitutional by the Supreme Court[210]—that might be used by political candidates to fight fake news stories about them. However, there are many reasons why this is unlikely to be an effective solution to the problem, not the least of which is that a defamation action is unlikely to be resolved until after an election has already taken place. At that point, the harms that a fake news story might have on an election would have already occurred. Further, the social media sites where defamatory stories might appear, and the users of those sites whose actions may help spread the reach of those stories, are immune to liability for defamation due to section 230 of the Communications Decency Act.[211] A defamed candidate's sole remedy would be against the author or source of the fake news story.

Here is an area where Congress might act. As Justice Moreno pointed out in his *Rosenthal* concurrence, there is a danger that the CDA's immunity could be found to protect a conspiracy to spread fake, defamatory news stories about a candidate, stories that those involved know full well to be false. Moreno's view was that section 230's immunity provisions should be interpreted so as not to cover such purposeful, concerted activity.[212] However, such a result is not at all assured based on the literal language of the law. Congress may want to act to provide some clarity on this point, as it surely can't have intended to immunize such a scheme.

Other than this, and relying on the truth to counter the harms caused by fake news stories, the best means of stemming the flow of fake news seems to be for Facebook and other websites to take action to identify fake news stories and minimize their impact. The immunity provisions of the Communications Decency Act give these sites considerable leeway and discretion to do this. Facebook has already begun to take steps in this regard. While this will not end the spread of fake news online, it is a positive step toward reducing the spread and impact of fake news stories.

In addition to taking these steps to target fake news at its source, Facebook, through its Journalism Project, is working to minimize the harmful impact fake news might have on those exposed to it through the company's efforts to promote news literacy, which can help people make better decisions about which news stories to trust. As with Facebook's other efforts, it remains to be seen exactly how the company will seek to achieve this and how effective its efforts might be, but it does seem to be a worthwhile endeavor, particularly given our legal system's preference under the First Amendment for fighting falsity with the truth. After all, the truth would seem to have a better chance of prevailing over fake news when the public is best able to recognize each for what it is.

NOTES

This essay was originally published as "Fighting Falsity: Fake News, Facebook, and the First Amendment" in *Cardozo Arts & Entertainment Law Journal* 35 (2016): 669–705.

1. Mike Isaac, *Facebook, in Cross Hairs After Election, Is Said to Question Its Influence,* New York Times, November 12, 2016, www.nytimes.com/2016/11/14/technology/facebook-is-said-to-question -its-influence-in-election.html.

2. See Angie Drobnic Holan, "FACT-LASH," *Tampa Bay Times,* December 14, 2016, www.press reader.com/usa/tampa-bay-times/20161214/282626032321949.

3. See Mike Isaac, "Facebook Mounts Effort to Limit Tide of Fake News," *New York Times,* December 15, 2016, www.nytimes.com/2016/12/15/technology/facebook-fake-news.html?_r=0.

4. To put it another way, fake news refers to "fabricated news accounts that are meant to spread virally online." See Jeremy W. Peters, "Wielding Claims of 'Fake News,' Conservatives Take Aim at Mainstream Media," *New York Times,* December 25, 2016, mobile.nytimes.com/2016/12/25 /us/politics/fake-news-claims-conservatives-mainstream-media-.html?mc=aud_dev&mcid=fb-nytimes&mccr=JanHighADLowMC&mcdt=2017–01&subid=JanHighADLowMC&ad-keywords =AudDevGate&referer=http://m.facebook.com. It should be noted that "conservative cable and radio personalities, top Republicans, and even Mr. Trump himself, incredulous about suggestions that fake stories may have helped swing the election, have appropriated the term and turned it against any news they see as hostile to their agenda." (Peters, "Wielding Claims") The term "fake news" has not been used in any US Supreme Court opinion as of the beginning of 2017. It has been used in approximately twenty US District and Court of Appeals decisions, primarily in cases involving deceptive advertising. See, for example, FTC Press Release, "FTC Permanently Stops Fake News Website Operator That Allegedly Deceived Consumers about Acai Berry Weight-Loss Products," February 7, 2013), www.ftc.gov /news-events/press-releases/2013/02/ftc-permanently-stops-fake-news-website-operator-allegedly. The term "fake news" has also been used in contexts outside the scope of this article. For example, it has been used to refer to programs like *The Daily Show* or *Saturday Night Live*'s "Weekend Update," which provide humorous takes on the news and current events. See, for example, Akilah N. Folami, "Freeing the Press from Editorial Discretion and Hegemony in Bona Fide News: Why the Revolution Must Be Televised," *Columbia Journal of Law & the Arts* 34 (2011): 367, 370. "Fake news" has also

been used to describe video news releases (VNRs) prepared by government agencies and broadcast by TV stations as news reports without divulging the source of the story. See, for example, Janel Alania, "The 'News' from the Feed Looks Like News Indeed: On Video News Releases, the FCC, and the Shortage of Truth in the Truth in Broadcasting Act of 2005," *Cardozo Arts & Entertainment Law Journal* 24 (2006): 229.

5. "The issue is not confined to [Facebook], with a vast ecosystem of false news creators who thrive on online advertising and who can use other social media and search engines to propagate their work. Google, Twitter and message boards like 4chan and Reddit have all been criticized for being part of that chain" (Isaac, "Facebook Mounts Effort").

6. See William P. Marshall, "False Campaign Speech and the First Amendment," *University of Pennsylvania Law Review* 153 (2004): 285, 294.

7. Richard L. Hasen, "A Constitutional Right to Lie in Campaigns and Elections?" *Montana Law Review* 74 (2013): 53, 55.

8. See John Herrman, "Facebook's Problem Isn't Fake News—It's the Rest of the Internet," *New York Times,* December 22, 2016, www.lexisnexis.com.ezproxy.tcu.edu/hottopics/lnacademic/? See also Isaac, "Facebook Mounts Effort." For either purpose, one appeal of fake news for those creating and disseminating it is that it can be inexpensive. As one reporter observed, true news stories are "more expensive to generate. . . . News requires reporting and research and institutional structures like editors and fact checkers to support them. Fake news only takes one person's imagination" (Noah Feldman, "Is Fake News Protected by the First Amendment?" *Napa Valley Register,* November 25, 2016, napavalleyregister.com/news/opinion/editorial/guest-editorials/is-fake-news-protected-by-the -first-amendment/article_3ef53f62–84fe-5a23-af20–43424e95ad3a.html.

9. See Nicky Woolf, "Obama Is Worried About Fake News on Social Media—and We Should Be Too," *Guardian,* November 20, 2016, www.theguardian.com/media/2016/nov/20/barack-obama -facebook-fake-news-problem.

10. See Drobnic Holan, "FACT-LASH."

11. See Drobnic Holan, "FACT-LASH."

12. See Debra Bruno, "Legal Realities of Fake News and Its Consequences," *D.C. Bar,* December 13, 2016, www.dcbar.org/about-the-bar/news/fake-news-and-its-consequences.cfm. Fake news on Facebook and other sites isn't just limited to election campaigns. "The harmful information that spreads on Facebook includes the myths and lies about vaccination and links to autism. It contains myths and lies about the scientific fact of global warming. These are issues that are crucial to our wellbeing" (Woolf, "Obama Is Worried").

13. See Drobnic Holan, "FACT-LASH." In addition, "Facebook rakes in billions in advertising. In the first three quarters of [2016], the company made almost $6bn in profit—a big jump from a mere $3.69bn in 2015" (Olivia Solon, "2016: The Year Facebook Became the Bad Guy," *Guardian,* December 12, 2016, www.theguardian.com/technology/2016/dec/12/facebook-2016-problems-fake -news-censorship).

14. John Herrman, "Inside Facebook's (Totally Insane, Unintentionally Gigantic, Hyperpartisan) Political-Media Machine," *New York Times Magazine,* August 24, 2016, www.nytimes.com/2016/08/28 /magazine/inside-facebooks-totally-insane-unintentionally-gigantic-hyperpartisan-political-media

-machine.html?_r=0. David Zurawik, "Fake News as a Symptom of Sickness in Media Ecosystem," Baltimore Sun, February 16, 2017, www.baltimoresun.com/entertainment/tv/z-on-tv- blog/bs-ae-zontv -fake-news-20161118-story.html.

15. Brian Steinberg, "Facebook Unveils Plans to Stop 'Fake News' Outbreak," Variety, December 15, 2016, variety.com/2016/digital/news/facebook-fake-news-abc-james-goldston1201943 380/.

16. See Isaac, "Facebook Mounts Effort."

17. See Steinberg, "Facebook Unveils Plans."

18. Prior to the "last three months of the campaign, the top election content from major outlets had easily outpaced that of fake election news on Facebook. Then, as the election drew closer, engagement for fake content on Facebook skyrocketed and surpassed that of the content from major news outlets." "The only viral false stories during the final three months that were arguably against Trump's interests were a false quote from Mike Pence about Michelle Obama, a false report that Ireland was accepting American 'refugees' fleeing Trump, and a hoax claiming RuPaul said he was groped by Trump." "The research turned up only one viral false election story from a hyperpartisan left-wing site." That story, from Winning Democrats, "claimed Ireland was accepting anti-Trump 'refugees' from the US. It received over 810,000 Facebook engagements, and was debunked by an Irish publication." (Craig Silverman, "This Analysis Shows How Fake Election News Stories Outperformed Real News on Facebook," BuzzFeedNews, November 16, 2016, www.buzzfeed.com/ craigsilverman/viral-fake -election-news-outperformed-real-news-onfacebook?utm_term=.bf2zz 1xQXZ#.fu1ZZ5QwVW).

19. See Woolf, "Obama Is Worried."

20. Solon, "2016: The Year Facebook Became the Bad Guy."

21. See Alex Heath, "Facebook Is Going to Use Snopes and Other Fact-Checkers to Combat and Bury 'Fake News,'" Business Insider, December 15, 2016, www.businessinsider.com/facebook-will-fact -check-label-fake-news-in-news-feed-2016–12.

22. See Drobnic Holan, "FACT-LASH."

23. See Zurawik, "Fake News as a Symptom of Sickness in Media Ecosystem."

24. See Isaac, "Facebook Mounts Effort."

25. See Solon, "2016: The Year Facebook Became the Bad Guy."

26. See Zurawik, "Fake News as a Symptom of Sickness in Media Ecosystem."

27. See Solon, "2016: The Year Facebook Became the Bad Guy."

28. See Marshall, "False Campaign Speech," 285, 299.

29. See Hasen, "A Constitutional Right to Lie," 56.

30. See Marshall, "False Campaign Speech," 299.

31. See Hasen, "A Constitutional Right to Lie," 56.

32. See US Constitution, Amendment I.

33. See Leigh Ellen Gray, "Thumb War: The Facebook 'Like' Button and Free Speech in the Era of Social Networking," Charleston Law Review 7 (2013): 447, 475, citing Citizens United v. FEC, 558 US 310, 329 (2010), striking down certain campaign finance laws as impermissibly chilling to political speech "central to the meaning and purpose of the First Amendment," Buckley v. Valeo, 424 US 1, 14–15 (1976), describing campaign finance laws as "operating in an area of the most fundamental First Amendment activities" and noting that "discussion of public issues and debate on the qualifications of

candidates are integral to the operation of the system of government established by our Constitution," *City of Ladue v. Gilleo,* 512 US 43, 54–55 (1994), noting that a city ordinance restricting yard signs especially impacts political campaigns, and that "residential signs have long been an important and distinct medium of expression," *Eu v. S.F. Cty. Democratic Cent. Comm.,* 489 US 214, 222–23 (1989), quoting *Williams v. Rhodes,* 393 US 23, 32 (1968), holding that a state law banning political primary endorsements "directly affects speech which 'is at the core of our electoral process and of the First Amendment freedoms,'" *Roth v. United States,* 354 US 476, 484 (1957), "The protection given speech and press was fashioned to assure unfettered interchange of ideas for the bringing about of political and social changes desired by the people."

34. See Marshall, "False Campaign Speech," 298.

35. *Buckley v. Valeo,* 424 US at 14–15 (citations omitted).

36. *Grant v. Meyer,* 828 F.2d 1446, 1455 (10th Cir. 1987), quoting *NAACP v. Button,* 371 US 415, 445 (1963).

37. *Cantwell v. Connecticut,* 310 US 296, 310 (1940).

38. *N.Y. Times v. Sullivan,* 376 US 254, 271 (1964), citing *NAACP,* 371 US at 433 (1963), "Because First Amendment freedoms need breathing space to survive, government may regulate in the area only with narrow specificity."

39. *Abrams v. United States,* 250 US 616, 630 (1919), Holmes, J., dissenting; see also *New York Times,* 376 US at 270, quoting *United States v. Associated Press,* 52 F. Supp. 362, 372 (SDNY 1943), "The First Amendment, said Judge Learned Hand, 'presupposes that right conclusions are more likely to be gathered out of a multitude of tongues, than through any kind of authoritative selection. To many this is, and always will be, folly; but we have staked upon it our all.'"

40. See *Grant,* 828 F.2d at 1455, quoting *Thomas v. Collins,* 323 US 516, 545 (1945), Jackson, J., concurring (quotations omitted).

41. See Noah Feldman, "Fake News May Not Be Protected Speech," *Bloomberg View,* November 23, 2016, www.bloomberg.com/view/articles/2016-11-23/fake-news-may-not-be-protected -speech.

42. *United States v. Alvarez,* 132 S.Ct. 2537, 2542 (2012) (plurality opinion).

43. See *United States v. Alvarez.*

44. *United States v. Alvarez* at 2564 (Alito, J., dissenting), "Even where there is a wide scholarly consensus concerning a particular matter, the truth is served by allowing that consensus to be challenged without fear of reprisal. Today's accepted wisdom sometimes turns out to be mistaken."

45. See *United States v. Alvarez* at 2544, quoting *Hustler Mag., Inc. v. Falwell,* 485 US 46, 52 (1988). The government also pointed to the following quotes: "false statements 'are not protected by the First Amendment in the same manner as truthful statements,'" quoting *Brown v. Hartlage,* 456 US 45, 60–61 (1982), "[u]ntruthful speech, commercial or otherwise, has never been protected for its own sake," *Brown v. Hartlage,* quoting *Virginia Bd. of Pharmacy v. Virginia Citizens Consumer Council, Inc.,* 425 US 748, 771 (1976), "[s]preading false information in and of itself carries no First Amendment credentials," *Virginia Bd. of Pharmacy v. Virginia Citizens Consumer Council, Inc.,* quoting *Herbert v. Lando,* 441 US 153, 171 (1979), "there is no constitutional value in false statements of fact," *Herbert v. Lando,* quoting *Gertz v. Robert Welch, Inc.,* 418 US 323, 340 (1974), and "the knowingly false statement

and the false statement made with reckless disregard of the truth, do not enjoy constitutional protection," *Gertz v. Robert Welch, Inc.,* quoting *Garrison v. Louisiana,* 379 US 64, 75 (1964).

46. *United States v. Alvarez* at 2545 (Kennedy, J., plurality).

47. *United States v. Alvarez* at 2546 (Kennedy, J., plurality).

48. See *United States v. Alvarez,* 132 S.Ct. 2537, 2545 (2012).

49. *United States v. Alvarez* at 2555 (Breyer, J., concurring).

50. See *United States v. Alvarez* at 2544–45.

51. *United States v. Alvarez* at 2546–47.

52. See *United States v. Alvarez* at 2544.

53. *United States v. Alvarez* at 2564 (Alito, J., dissenting) (citation omitted).

54. See, for example, Hasen, "A Constitutional Right to Lie," 69.

55. Hasen also observed that the decision will make "it much harder to sustain the constitutionality of many false campaign speech laws in the future" ("A Constitutional Right to Lie," 54).

56. See *Am. Freedom Def. Initiative v. King Cty.,* 136 S.Ct. 1022, 1025 (2016), citing *United States v. Alvarez,* 132 S.Ct. 2537 (2012), plurality opinion.

57. See *Alvarez,* 132 S.Ct. at 2547, quoting *U.S. v. Stevens,* 559 US 460, 472 (2010).

58. See *Stevens,* 559 US at 472.

59. See *Alvarez,* 132 S.Ct. at 2547 (2012), quoting *Brown v. Entm't Merch. Ass'n,* 564 US 786, 792 (2011).

60. See *Eu v. S.F. Cty. Democratic Cent. Comm.,* 489 US 214, 223 (1989), quoting *Monitor Patriot Co. v. Roy,* 401 US 265, 271 (1971).

61. See *Citizens United v. Fed. Election Comm'n,* 558 US 310, 340 (2010), internal quotations omitted.

62. See *Eu,* 489 US at 231, citing *Rosario v. Rockefeller,* 410 US 752, 761 (1973).

63. See *McIntyre v. Ohio Elections Comm'n,* 514 US 334, 350 (1995).

64. See *Burson v. Freeman,* 504 US 191, 199 (1992), citing *Eu v. S.F.,* 489 US at 228–29. On the other hand, one court has taken the view that "the State's claimed compelling interest to shield the public from falsehoods during a political campaign is patronizing and paternalistic. . . . It assumes the people of the state are too ignorant or disinterested to investigate, learn and determine for themselves the truth or falsity in political debate, and it is the proper role of the government itself to fill this void" (*State ex rel. Public Disclosure Comm'n v. 119 Vote No! Comm.,* 957 P.2d 691, 698–99 [Wash. 1998]).

65. See *United States v. Alvarez,* 132 S.Ct. 2537, 2549 (2012), citation omitted.

66. See *United States v. Alvarez* at 2551, quoting *Ashcroft v. American Civil Liberties Union,* 542 US 656, 666 (2004).

67. See *United States v. Alvarez* at 2549.

68. *United States v. Alvarez* at 2555.

69. See *United States v. Alvarez,* citing *United We Stand America, Inc. v. United We Stand, America N.Y., Inc.,* 128 F.3d 86, 93 (2d Cir. 1997), upholding against First Amendment challenge application of the Lanham Act to a political organization, *Treasurer of Comm. to Elect Lostracco v. Fox,* 150 Mich. App. 617, 389 N.W.2d 446 (Mich. 1986), upholding under First Amendment statute prohibiting campaign material falsely claiming that one is an incumbent).

70. See *United States v. Alvarez,* 132 S.Ct. at 2556

71. See *United States v. Alvarez*, 132 S.Ct. 2537, 2556 (2012).

72. See *Lostracco*, 150 Mich. App. at 621.

73. See *Lostracco*, 150 Mich. App. 623, citing *Vanasco v. Schwartz*, 401 F. Supp. 87, 91–92 (E.D.N.Y., 1975), aff'd 423 US 1041 (1976), quoting *Garrison v. Louisiana*, 379 US 64, 75 (1964).

74. See *Lostracco*, 150 Mich. App. at 623. The other case cited by Justice Breyer in his *Alvarez* concurrence, *United We Stand America, Inc. v. United We Stand, America New York, Inc.*, involved a political organization's use of a service mark owned by another political organization. That court's only First Amendment analysis was to observe that the defendant's use of the mark in violation of the Lanham Act was not a use protected by the First Amendment. See *United We Stand*, 128 F.3d at 93.

75. See discussion of *United States v. Alvarez*, above.

76. Justice Breyer stated, "I would also note, like the plurality, that in this area more accurate information will normally counteract the lie." See *Alvarez*, 132 S.Ct. at 2555.

77. Staci Lieffring, "First Amendment and the Right to Lie: Regulating Knowingly False Campaign Speech After United States v. Alvarez," *Minnesota Law Review* 97 (2013): 1047, 1073 (citations omitted).

78. Lieffring, "First Amendment and the Right to Lie."

79. These questions point to another fundamental concern lawmakers must consider in crafting a law targeting fake news stories: vagueness. A vague law is one that is framed such that it does not give "notice to ordinary people of what materials are affected, nor sufficient guidance to law enforcement officials to prevent arbitrary law enforcement" (*Davis-Kidd Booksellers, Inc. v. McWherter*, 866 S.W.2d 520, 532 (Tenn. 1993). Such laws, when aimed at protected speech, will typically "be declared void for vagueness." See *Davis-Kidd Booksellers, Inc. v. McWherter* at 531. If a law leaves questions like those posed above unanswered, not only will it have a difficult time surviving strict scrutiny, it will have problems with vagueness concerns as well.

80. *N.Y. Times v. Sullivan*, 376 US 254, 279 (1964), citations omitted, 279–80, 270.

81. *N.Y. Times v. Sullivan* at 279–80, 270.

82. *Hustler Mag. v. Falwell*, 485 US 46, 52 (1988), citing Gertz v. Robert Welch, Inc., 418 US 323, 340 (1974).

83. See *Hustler Mag. v. Falwell* at 52 (1988), citing *Philadelphia Newspapers, Inc. v. Hepps*, 475 US 767, 772 (1986).

84. *United States v. Alvarez*, 132 S.Ct. 2537, 2545 (2012).

85. See *United States v. Alvarez* at 2554 (Breyer, J., concurring), citing Restatement (Second) of Torts §§ 558, 559 (1976).

86. See, for example, Restatement (Second) of Torts §§ 558, 559 cmt. d (1977).

87. See Joe Trevino, "From Tweets to Twibel: Why the Current Defamation Law Does Not Provide for Jay Cutler's Feelings," *Sports Law Journal* 19 (2012): 49, 51.

88. *Hustler Mag. v. Falwell*, 485 US 52, 52 (1988), citing *N.Y. Times v. Sullivan*, 376 US 254, 279–80 (1964).

89. See, for example, Restatement (Second) of Torts § 558(a) (1976).

90. See, for example, David Boies, Corporate Defamation Symposium, "The Chilling Effect of Libel Defamation Costs: The Problem and Possible Solution," *St. Louis Law Journal* 39 (1995): 1207.

91. According to Los Angeles–based entertainment attorney Bill Abrams, "Sometimes drawing attention to the [lie] does more damage than if you let it slide." See Leslie Gornstein, "Why Don't We Hear More About Celebs Suing Tabloids?" *E! News,* August 19, 2006, www.eonline.com/news/58182 /why-don-t-we-hear-more-about-celebs-suin-tabloids; Guy Bergstrom, "To Sue, or Not to Sue: Libel," *Balance,* June 1, 2016, www.thebalance.com/defamation-from-a-pr-point-of-view-2295253 (accessed January 23, 2017): "It's often smarter, from a PR standpoint, to let a story die than give it new life [by filing a defamation lawsuit]"; "A libel [defamation] lawsuit could drag out for months or years."

92. Of course, the subject of that story (in this example, the Pope) might be able to successfully pursue a defamation action, but for some of the reasons listed above—most likely the time and expense involved as well as the fear of drawing more attention to the story—may be reluctant to do so.

93. See Bethany C. Stein, "A Bland Interpretation: Why a Facebook 'Like' Should Be Protected First Amendment Speech," *Seton Hall Law Review* 44 (2014): 1255, 1267, citing *Reno v. Am. Civil Liberties Union,* 521 US 844 (1997).

94. See *Reno,* 521 US 844 at 870.

95. See Gray, "Thumb War," 477, citing *Doe v. Prosecutor, Marion Cty., Ind.,* No. 12–2152, 2013 WL 238735 at *1 (7th Cir. January 23, 2013); *Mattingly v. Milligan,* No. 4:11CV00215, 2011 WL 5184283, at *2–3 (E.D. Ark. November 1, 2011); *Stein v. Dowling,* 867 F. Supp. 2d 1087, 1096–98 (S.D. Cal. 2012); *Gresham v. City of Atlanta,* No. 1:10-CV-1301-RWS, 2011 WL 4601020, at *2 (N.D. Ga. September 30, 2011); *United States v. Michael,* No. 2:12-cr-1-WTL-CMM, 2012 WL 4796629, at *2 (S.D. Ind. October 9, 2012); *R.S. ex rel. SS v. Minnewaska Area Sch. Dist.,* No. 2149, No. 12–588, 2012 WL 3870868, at *10 (D. Minn. September 6, 2012); *United States v. Elonis,* No. 11–13, 2011 WL 5024284, at *1–3 (E.D. Pa. October 20, 2011); *Tatro v. Univ. of Minn.,* 816 N.W.2d 509, 523 (Minn. 2012). It has also been "held that Liking another person's post on Facebook is also speech" (Gray, "Thumb War," 478, citing *Three D, LLC,* No. 34-CA-12915, 2012 WL 76862, at *9 (N.L.R.B January 3, 2012).

96. It is the "black letter rule" that "one who republishes a libel is subject to liability just as if he had published it originally." This is often true even if the republisher attributes the libelous statement to the original publisher, and even if he expressly disavows the truth of the statement. This rule is widely recognized, and can be found in § 578 of the Restatement (Second) of Torts. Such "republication" may occur when someone verbally repeats a slander he previously heard, or a libel he read. Likewise, it may occur when someone prints or reprints defamatory statements previously "published" verbally or in writing. Of significance is that, "each time [defamatory] material is communicated by a new person, a new publication has occurred, which is a separate basis of tort liability." Therefore, every person who reprints or otherwise "republishes" a defamatory statement becomes subject to liability to the same extent as if he had originally published it (William E. Buelow III, "Re-Establishing Distributor Liability on the Internet: Recognizing the Applicability of Traditional Defamation Law to Section 230 of the Communications Decency Act of 1996, *West Virginia Law Review* 116 (2013): 313, 319–20, citations omitted.

97. See, for example, "How do I comment on something I see on Facebook?" Facebook Help Center, www.facebook.com/help/187302991320347?helpref=search&sr=21&query=what%20happens%20 when%20i%20comment (accessed April 16, 2017); "Who can see a story in their News Feed about something I share?" Facebook Help Center, www.facebook.com/help/ 225435534134033?helpref=search

(last visited Apr. 16, 2017); "What does it mean to 'Like' something?" Facebook Help Center, www .facebook.com/help/110920455663362? helpref=search (last visited Apr. 16, 2017).

98. See Communications Decency Act of 1996, 47 U.S.C. § 230 (2015).

99. See Communications Decency Act of 1996 at § 230(c)(1).

100. See Heidi Frostestad Kuehl, "Free Speech and Defamation in an Era of Social Media: An Analysis of Federal and Illinois Norms in the Context of Anonymous Online Defamers," *Northern Illinois University Law Review* 36 (2016): 28, 37, citing 47 U.S.C. § 230.

101. See Joshua N. Azriel, "Social Networks as a Communications Weapon to Harm Victims: Facebook, Myspace, and Twitter Demonstrate a Need to Amend Section 230 of the Communications Decency Act," *John Marshall Journal of Information Technology & Privacy Law* 26 (2009): 415, 420, citing 47 U.S.C. §§ 230(a)(3)–(5).

102. See Azriel, "Social Networks as a Communications Weapon," 420, citing 47 U.S.C. § 230(b). In support of the need for section 230's immunity provisions, Congress's findings included those that the "Internet and other interactive computer services offer a forum for a true diversity of political discourse"; that Americans increasingly rely "on interactive media for a variety of political, educational, cultural, and entertainment services"; and that the "Internet and other interactive computer services have flourished, to the benefit of all Americans, with a minimum of government regulation." See 47 U.S.C. §§ 230(a)(3)–(5).

103. See Azriel, "Social Networks as a Communications Weapon," 421, discussing House Report 104-458, Telecommunications Act of 1996, at 194 (1996), rpt. in 1996 *United States Code Congressional and Administrative News* 10.

104. Communications Decency Act of 1996, 47 U.S.C. § 230 (2015).

105. 47 U.S.C. § 230(c)(1). "'Interactive computer service' means any information service, system, or access software provider that provides or enables computer access by multiple users to a computer server, including specifically a service or system that provides access to the Internet and such systems operated or services offered by libraries or educational institutions. . . . 'Information content provider' means any person or entity that is responsible, in whole or in part, for the creation or development of information provided through the Internet or any other interactive computer service (47 U.S.C. §§ 230[f][2]–[3]).

106. See Kuehl, "Free Speech and Defamation," 41, citing *Doe II v. Myspace Inc.,* 175 Cal. App. 4th 561 (Cal. Dist. Ct. App. 2d 2009), revealing that social networking websites had immunity under the CDA from tort claims by minor females who were sexually assaulted by men they met on the website; see also Claudia G. Catalano, "Validity, Construction, and Application of Immunity Provisions of Communications Decency Act, 47 U.S.C.A. 230," 52 A.L.R. Fed. 2d 37 (2011).

107. See Kuehl, "Free Speech and Defamation," 37, citing *Zeran v. Am. Online, Inc.,* 129 F.3d 327 (4th Cir. 1997).

108. See Azriel, "Social Networks as a Communications Weapon," 422 (2009), citing *Green v. Am. Online (AOL),* 318 F.3d 465 (3rd Cir. 2003); *Zeran v. Am. Online, Inc.,* 129 F.3d 327 (4th Cir. 1997); *Blumenthal v. Drudge,* 992 F. Supp. 44 (D.D.C. 1998).

109. See *Zeran,* 129 F.3d at 327, 329–30, 328, 332–33.

110. *Zeran,* 129 F.3d at 331, citing W. Page Keeton et al., *Prosser and Keeton on Torts* § 113 at 810 (5th ed., St. Paul, MN: Academic West, 1984).

111. *Zeran,* 330–31 (4th Cir. 1997).

112. Kuehl, "Free Speech and Defamation," 39, citing *Zeran,* 129 F.3d 327.

113. "Specifically, § 230 precludes courts from entertaining claims that would place a computer service provider in a publisher's role. Thus, lawsuits seeking to hold a service provider liable for its exercise of a publisher's traditional editorial functions—such as deciding whether to publish, withdraw, postpone or alter content—are barred" (*Zeran,* 129 F.3d at 330).

114. See Odelia Braun, "Internet Publications and Defamation: Why the Single Publication Rule Should Not Apply," *Golden Gate University Law Review* 32 (2002): 325, 325: "At common law, each communication of a defamatory statement to a third person constituted a new publication, which gave rise to a cause of action," citing Restatement (Second) of Torts § 58. See also *Schneider v. United Airlines, Inc.,* 208 Cal. App. 3d 71 (1989); *Spears Free Clinic & Hosp. for Poor Children v. Majer,* 261 P.2d 489 (Colo. 1953); Restatement (Second) of Torts § 578 (1977); Heather Saint, "Section 230 of the Communications Decency Act: The True Culprit of Internet Defamation," *Loyola of Los Angeles Entertainment Law Review* 36 (2015): 39, 48–49. "Courts have always been willing to hold a person strictly liable for his repetition of another's defamatory statement" (Doug W. Ray, "A Unified Theory for Consent and Compelled Self-Publication in Employee Defamation: Economic Duress in Tort Law," *Texas Law Review* 67 (1989): 1295, 1299, citing *Liberty Lobby, Inc. v. Dow Jones & Co.,* 838 F.2d 1287, 1298 (D.C. Cir.), *cert. denied,* 109 S.Ct. 75 (1988): "The common law of libel has long held that one who republishes a defamatory statement 'adopts' it as his own, and is liable in equal measure to the original defamer."

115. See 47 U.S.C. § 230(c)(1) (2015): "No provider *or user* of an interactive computer service shall be treated as the publisher or speaker of any information provided by another information content provider" (emphasis added).

116. See Azriel, "Social Networks as a Communications Weapon," 423, citing *Barrett v. Rosenthal,* 146 P.3d 510 (Cal. 2006).

117. *Barrett v. Rosenthal,* 146 P.3d 510 (Cal. 2006).

118. See *Barrett v. Rosenthal,* 9 Cal. Rptr. 3d 142, 146 (Cal. Ct. App. 2004).

119. *Rosenthal* at 146 P.3d at 515.

120. *Rosenthal* at 513.

121. See *Rosenthal* at 513: "The immunity has been applied regardless of the traditional distinction between 'publishers' and 'distributors.' Under the common law, 'distributors' like newspaper vendors and booksellers are liable only if they had notice of a defamatory statement in their merchandise. The publisher of the newspaper or book where the statement originally appeared, however, may be held liable even without notice."

122. See *Rosenthal* at 513.

123. See *Rosenthal* at 510, 513 (Cal. 2006), "The immunity has been applied regardless of the traditional distinction between 'publishers' and 'distributors.'"

124. *Rosenthal* at 146 P.3d at 517, citing *Zeran v. Am. Online, Inc.,* 129 F.3d 327, 333 (4th Cir. 1997).

125. *Rosenthal* at 525, citing Witkin, *Summary of California Law Torts,* vol. 5 §§ 529, 556 et seq. (10th ed., 2005).

126. *Rosenthal* at 525, citing *Baker v. Los Angeles Herald Examiner,* 721 P.2d 87 (Cal. 1968); see also *Time, Inc. v. Hill,* 385 US 374, 389 (1967).

127. *Rosenthal* at 517, citing *Zeran,* 129 F.3d at 333.

128. See *Zeran,* 129 F.3d at 333.

129. *Zeran,* 129 F.3d at 333.

130. See *Barrett v. Rosenthal,* 146 P.3d 510, 524 (Cal. 2006), citing *Zeran v. Am. Online, Inc.,* 129 F.3d 327, 333 (4th Cir. 1997).

131. See *Donato v. Moldow,* 865 A.2d 711, 726 (N.J. Super. Ct. App. Div. 2005).

132. *Rosenthal,* 146 P.3d at 525 (citations omitted), 529, and 526.

133. *Rosenthal* at 526.

134. See *Rosenthal* at 510, 529 (Cal. 2006).

135. *Rosenthal* at 529 (Moreno, J., concurring).

136. See *Rosenthal* at 530 (Moreno, J., concurring). Such a conspiracy might include the operator of the service where the defamatory comment is posted, as the provider would be protected from liability by section 230. As another court observed, "a service provider that cannot be held liable for posting a defamatory message may have little incentive to take such material down even if informed that the material is defamatory." See *Batzel v. Smith,* 333 F.3d 1018, n. 19 (9th Cir. 2003), *cert. denied,* 541 US 1085 (2004).

137. See *Rosenthal,* 146 P.3d at 530.

138. *Rosenthal* at 513, 529.

139. See Walter Stillwell, "Carafano v. Metrosplash.com: An Expansion of Tort Immunity for Web Service Providers Under 47 U.S.C. § 230, Even When They Take a Greater Editorial Role in Publishing Material from Third Parties," *Tulane Journal of Technology and Intellectual Property* 6 (2004): 307, 309, citing *Zeran v. Am. Online, Inc.,* 129 F.3d 327, 331 (4th Cir. 1997).

140. *Zeran,* 129 F.3d at 331.

141. See Stillwell, "Carafano v. Metrosplash.com," 310, citing *Zeran,* 129 F.3d at 331.

142. *Zeran,* 129 F.3d at 331.

143. 47 U.S.C. § 230(c)(2)(A) (2015).

144. 47 U.S.C. § 230(c)(2)(A) (2015).

145. *E360Insight, LLC v. Comcast, Corp.,* 546 F. Supp. 2d 605 (N.D. Ill. 2008).

146. See *E360Insight* at 606, 608, 607.

147. *E360Insight* at 608, citing *Zango, Inc. v. Kaspersky Lab, Inc.,* No. C07-0807-JCC, 2007 US Dist. LEXIS 97332, at *11 (W.D. Wash. Aug. 28, 2007); see also *Pallorium Inc. v. Jared,* No. G036124, 2007 Cal. App. Unpub. LEXIS 241, at *7 (Cal. Ct. App. Jan. 11, 2007).

148. *Zango, Inc. v. Kaspersky Lab, Inc.,* No. C07–0807-JCC, 2007 US Dist. LEXIS 97332, at *11 (W.D. Wash. Aug. 28, 2007), quoting 47 U.S.C. § 230(c)(2)(A) (2015). One court was presented with the argument that "a blocking software provider might abuse that immunity to block content for anticompetitive purposes or merely at its malicious whim, under the cover of considering such material 'otherwise objectionable.'" See *Holomaxx Techs. Corp. v. Microsoft Corp.,* 2011 US Dist. LEXIS

94316, at *6 (N.D. Cal. Aug. 23, 2011). The court's response was to observe, "Section 230(c)(2) allows [an interactive service provider] to establish standards of decency without risking liability for doing so." See *Holomaxx,* citing *Goddard v. Google, Inc.,* 2008 US Dist. LEXIS 101890, at *6 (N.D. Cal. Dec. 17, 2008), quoting *Green v. Am. Online,* 318 F.3d 465, 472 (3d Cir. 2002), *cert. denied* 2003 US LEXIS 7034 (US, Oct. 6, 2003) (internal quotations omitted).

149. 47 U.S.C. § 230(c)(2)(A).

150. *Milo v. Martin,* 311 S.W.3d 210, 221 (Tex. App. 2010) (Gaultney, J., concurring).

151. *Darnaa, LLC v. Google, Inc.,* 2016 US Dist. LEXIS 152126, at *25 (N.D. Cal. 2016) (citation omitted). One court expressed the view that good faith might be lacking if a service provider cited one of its policies to support the removal of content when in fact the provider had no such policy. See *Spy Phone Labs LLC v. Google Inc.,* 2016 US Dist. LEXIS 143530, at *25 (N.D. Cal. 2016). In this case, Google removed a Spy Phone app from its Google Play store, stating the app's name violated its policy against apps using the word "spy" in their titles. When other apps containing the word "spy" in their title continued to be offered in the online store, Spy Phone alleged that Google had no such policy. See *Darnaa.*

152. See *Donato v. Moldow,* 865 A.2d 711, 727 (N.J. Super. Ct. App. Div. 2005).

153. *Donato v. Moldow.*

154. See *Zeran v Am. Online, Inc.,* 129 F.3d 327, 330–31 (4th Cir. 1997).

155. *Donato,* 865 A.2d at 726, citing *Zeran,* 129 F.3d at 335.

156. See *Barrett v. Rosenthal,* 146 P.3d 510, n. 19 (Cal. 2006), citing Batzel v. Smith, 333 F.3d 1018, 1031 (9th Cir. 2003); *Ben Ezra, Weinstein, & Co. v. Am. Online, Inc.,* 206 F.3d 980, 985–86 (10th Cir. 2000); *Green v. Am. Online,* 318 F.3d 465, 471 (3d Cir. 2003); *Donato v. Moldow,* 865 A.2d 711, 720–26 (N.J. Super. Ct. App. Div. 2005) (reviewing cases); *Schneider v. Amazon.com, Inc.,* 31 P.3d 37, 42–43 (Ct. App. Wash. 2001).

157. See *Zeran,* 129 F.3d at 330–31.

158. See *Donato v. Moldow,* 865 A.2d 711, 722–23 (N.J. Super. Ct. App. Div. 2005), citing and discussing *Ben Ezra,* 206 F.3d at 985–86.

159. *Donato v. Moldow,* citing and discussing *Schneider,* 31 P.3d at 38–39.

160. See *Schneider,* 31 P.3d at 42–43, discussing *Ben Ezra,* 206 F.3d at 980.

161. See *Schneider* at 43, quoting *Blumenthal v. Drudge,* 992 F. Supp. 44, 52 (D.D.C. 1998).

162. See *Schneider* 31 P.3d 37, 42 (Ct. App. Wash. 2001).

163. *Green v. Am. Online,* 318 F.3d 465 (3d Cir. 2003).

164. See *Green* at 468–69, 471.

165. *Donato v. Moldow,* 865 A.2d 711, 723 (N.J. Super. Ct. App. Div. 2005), citing and discussing *Green,* 318 F.3d at 468–69, 471.

166. *Green,* 318 F.3d at 471–72.

167. *Donato,* 865 A.2d at 723, citing and discussing *Green,* 318 F.3d at 472.

168. See *Donato,* 865 A.2d at 727.

169. *Batzel v. Smith,* 333 F.3d 1018, 1021 (9th Cir. 2003), *cert. denied,* 541 US 1085 (2004).

170. See *Batzel* at 1021–22.

171. See *Batzel* at 1031, 1029.

172. *Blumenthal v. Drudge,* 992 F. Supp. 44, 52 (D.D.C. 1998).

173. See Heath, "Facebook Is Going to Use Snopes."

174. Jim Rutenberg, "Media's Next Challenge: Overcoming the Threat of Fake News," *New York Times,* November 6, 2016, www. nytimes. com/2016/11/07/business/media/medias-next-challenge -overcoming-the-threat-of-fake-news.html.

175. Isaac, "Facebook Mounts Effort" (internal quotations omitted).

176. See Heath, "Facebook Is Going to Use Snopes."

177. Isaac, "Facebook Mounts Effort."

178. See Heath, "Facebook Is Going to Use Snopes."

179. See Isaac, "Facebook Mounts Effort."

180. See Isaac, "Facebook Mounts Effort."

181. Heath, "Facebook Is Going to Use Snopes."

182. Isaac, "Facebook Mounts Effort."

183. See Rutenberg, "Media's Next Challenge."

184. See Isaac, "Facebook Mounts Effort."

185. See Isaac, "Facebook Mounts Effort."

186. See Fidji Simo, "Introducing: The Facebook Journalism Project," *Facebook,* January 11, 2017, media.fb.com/2017/01/11/facebook-journalism-project/.

187. See Isaac, "Facebook Mounts Effort."

188. See Heath, "Facebook Is Going to Use Snopes."

189. Isaac, "Facebook Mounts Effort."

190. Heath, "Facebook Is Going to Use Snopes."

191. Herrman, "Inside Facebook's Political-Media Machine."

192. Isaac, "Facebook Mounts Effort."

193. See Herrman, "Inside Facebook's Political-Media Machine."

194. Isaac, "Facebook Mounts Effort."

195. See *Zeran v. Am. Online, Inc.,* 129 F.3d 327, 330–31 (4th Cir. 1997).

196. *Donato v. Hoffman,* 865 A.2d 711, 727 (N.J. Super. Ct. App. Div. 2005).

197. See *Hoffman,* 865 A.2d at 722–23, citing and discussing *Ben Ezra, Weinstein, and Co., Inc. v. America Online, Inc.,* 206 F.3d 980, 985–86 (10th Cir.), *cert. denied,* 531 US 824 (2000).

198. See Cathy Young, "Who Will Check Facebooks 'Fact Checkers?'" *The Hill,* December 16, 2016, thehill.com/blogs/pundits-blog/media/310849-who-will-check-facebooks-fact-checkers.

199. Olivia Solon and Julia Carrie Wong, "Facebook's Plan to Tackle Fake News Raises Questions over Limitations," *Guardian,* December 16, 2016, www.theguardian.com/ technology/2016/dec/16 /facebook-fake-news-system-problems-fact-checking.

200. See Solon and Wong, "Facebook's Plan" (internal quotations omitted).

201. Young, "Who Will Check Facebooks 'Fact Checkers?'"

202. Oliver Darcy, "Conservatives React with Skepticism and Alarm to Facebook's War on 'Fake News,'" *Business Insider,* December 15, 2016, www.businessinsider.com/facebook-fake-news -conservatives-2016–12.

203. See Simo, "Introducing: The Facebook Journalism Project." Other components of Facebook's Journalism Project include "collaborating with industry partners to develop news products, including new storytelling formats; [and] providing training and tools for journalists, which includes a partnership with Poynter to launch a certificate curriculum for journalists in the months ahead." See Todd Spangler, "Facebook's Evolution as Media Company Continues with Launch of Journalism Project," *Variety,* January 11, 2017, variety.com/2017/digital/news/facebook-media-journalism-project-fake -news-1201957989/ (internal quotations omitted).

204. Spangler, "Facebook's Evolution."

205. Simo, "Introducing: The Facebook Journalism Project."

206. The First Amendment applies to government efforts to restrict or prohibit speech, and generally not to companies like Facebook. See *Columbia Broadcasting System v. Democratic National Committee,* 412 US 94, 139 (1973), Stewart, J., concurring: "The First Amendment protects the press *from* governmental interference" (emphasis in original); Geoffrey A. Manne, "A Conflict of Visions: How the '21st Century First Amendment' Violates the Constitution's Amendment," *First Amendment Law Review* 13 (2014): 319, 324: "Generally speaking, the protections of the First Amendment apply only to state action," citing *Shelly v. Kraemer,* 334 US 1, 13 (1948).

207. In an interview following the 2016 election, then-President Barack Obama warned of the dangers of fake news. See, for example, Woolf, "Obama Is Worried."

208. *United States v. Alvarez,* 132 S.Ct. 2537, 2550 (2012), quoting *Abrams v. United States,* 250 US 616, 630 (1919), Holmes, J., dissenting.

209. *Alvarez,* 132 S.Ct. at 2550, citing *Whitney v. California,* 274 US 357, 377 (1927), Brandeis, J., concurring.

210. See *N. Y. Times v. Sullivan,* 376 US 254 (1964).

211. *See* 47 U.S.C. § 230(c)(1) (2015).

212. See *Barrett v. Rosenthal,* 146 P.3d 510, 530 (Cal. 2006), Moreno, J., concurring.

POTATO CHIPS, BOTULISM, AND CARBON MONOXIDE

THE LYING-BULLSHITTING DISTINCTION IN FAKE NEWS

Fred Vultee

F ar from dying down after the 2016 US elections, the specter of "fake news" kept its grip on the issue agenda as the next election cycle approached. National legislatures debated or enacted restrictions on fake news;[1] social media magnates were hauled before Congress to address their platforms' short-comings;[2] and accusations that traditional news outlets were themselves "fake news" continued to pour forth from the presidential Twitter account. Yet a consistent definition was no closer in 2018 than in 2016: Is the problem "blatant falsehoods passed off online as the truth and spread by conspiracy theorists,"[3] the unfavorable survey results that so angered the winning candidate, any allegations of electoral wrongdoing that displeased the new administration, or something else entirely? Nor has responsibility become easier to fix: "Scammers looking to make a quick buck," Internet companies that enable the lightning spread of fake news but lag in figuring out how to block or label it,[4] and audiences that are as careless about their news diets as their real diets all come in for blame. Putting a name and a description to fake news is essential to addressing it coherently, yet journalists, commentators, and politicians can barely agree on where to look or what to look at—let alone what to do about it.

Falsity is not new to news or to political campaigns. Not every attempt to influence a political outcome is fake; influencing outcomes is what political campaigns are about. Nor is fabrication an ethics challenge *per se* for journalism: there are no cases in which it is appropriate to publish as fact a fabricated claim that a presidential candidate is operating a child-sex ring from a pizza parlor. But as the different sorts of claims about fake news suggest, fakery thrives in the gray areas outside the clarity of falsification. Drawing largely on the philosophical distinction between lying[5] and bullshit,[6] I will set out a taxonomy of fake news and offer some suggestions for reasoning ethically about the challenges it presents for journalism.

Since the Progressive Era, journalism educators and observers have talked about the quality of news in terms of the quality of democracy's nutrient supply. On that analogy, false news is toxic in and of itself, whatever its origin: ill luck, poor verification practices, malice by sources, or deliberate deceit. The larger challenge of fake news is primarily a matter of framing: Distinguishing false facts from false context, discarding any false facts, and then addressing the context that makes the overall report fake. In that sense, fake news is less like the "virus" decried by the *New York Times*[7] than it is like carbon monoxide: it looks so much like oxygen that the body politic cannot tell them apart until it falls over gasping. From a broader perspective, fake stories combine to create fake issues, testing the limited carrying capacity of the public issue agenda:[8] the more attractive choice crowds out the more nourishing one.

False news does have consequences. Belief in false stories about the 2016 US presidential candidates (for example, that Hillary Clinton was in "very poor health" from a serious illness or that the Pope had endorsed Donald Trump) is associated with defection among participants who had voted Democratic in 2012.[9] More directly, false or miscontextualized social outrages attributed to college faculty members have led to threats against both individuals and campuses.[10] Fakery too can carry real consequences; the 1964 Republican candidate, Barry Goldwater, won a libel suit—under the "actual malice" standard of the recently decided *Times v. Sullivan* case—over a magazine's distortions of a supposed survey of psychiatrists about his mental health.[11] (The subsequent "Goldwater rule," enjoining psychiatrists from offering "a professional opinion" about public figures they have not examined,[12] also received new prominence after the 2016 election.) But neither falsity nor fakery is a matter for the legal system in every case. Lies that would be prohibited in the advertisements surrounding a debate are protected political speech in the debate itself, and that presence obliges journalists not only to acknowledge it but to consider whether or how to mitigate its potential damage. In the US context at least, then, fake news can be more reliably dealt with as a matter of ethics or practice than one of law.

In that light, by readdressing news practice based on a recalibration of journalistic duties, journalists can better address fakery in its different forms while keeping falsity at bay. Duties of truth-telling and preventing fakery can be understood in terms of how journalism does ethics and of the lying-bullshitting distinction. Because carbon monoxide poses risks different from those of junk food or foodborne illness, I propose a taxonomy of fake news: What types of fakery can be isolated and addressed? In addition to fakery and falsity, this approach calls for attention to the misuse of data through emphasis and salience, the domain of framing and agenda-setting. In an age in which the nation's loudest critic of "fake news" is also its most ardent practitioner, how do journalists maintain their position as practitioners of real news?

TRUTH, LIES, AND SOCIAL RESPONSIBILITY

Truth-telling, prized though it is in news organizations' codes of ethics and practice, poses challenges that are often glossed over in the name of tradition or common sense. For one thing, truth is not cumulative; stories about police-citizen interactions do not become truer simply by having more facts piled upon them, no matter how often we write "yellow police tape surrounded the home." For another, journalism requires a finely calibrated sense of when to stop telling truths: not when to start telling falsehoods, but when to set a limit on "the whole truth," whether it involves the home address of a sex-assault victim or the sailing date of a troopship. Those are separate concerns from those raised by lying, and they suggest that, rather than being a point on an ethical continuum, truth-telling as an obligation is conditioned by its relationship to other duties and to a variety of actors—an intuitionist approach championed by W. D. Ross.[13]

Truth-telling is integral to a Rossian duty of fidelity, not just to the audience but to the sex-assault victim and to the families that want both security for their country and safety for their loved ones aboard the troopship. A distinct duty of noninjury does not mean that truth-telling is no longer an obligation, but that the truthfulness and news value of home addresses and sailing dates can be weighted less than the value of individual or collective safety; a duty of justice suggests that protecting the identity of an assailant can be a lower priority than protecting the identity of a victim. Ross variously called these duties "prima facie" (meaning "self-evident, intuitively known, and general")[14] and "conditional." Such intuitive knowledge is not meant to suggest a "mysterious sixth sense" so much as "the ability to think and understand."[15] Ross himself characterized a prima facie duty as "an act which would be a duty proper if it were not at the same time of another kind which is morally significant."[16]

An intent-based attempt from 1990 to put truth and lies on a continuum posited "selective information" as a lesser form of truth, engaged in by opinion writers and propagandists.[17] A kinder name for selective information, of course, is news judgment. Selection is at the core of framing; Robert Entman's often-cited definition begins by noting that "to frame is to *select some aspects of a perceived reality and make them more salient in a communicating text.*"[18] Selective information, in other words, is how truth makes sense. In Ross's perspective, such a dispute represents a disagreement about facts or conditions rather than about the moral principle of truth-telling: What we know today about judgment and bias formation, for example, should affect how we think about the place of ethnicity in a routine crime story, or of religion in covering a violent act that might (or might not) be "terrorist." A midcentury textbook could give "Veteran, Shot By Negro, Dies," as an example of how to crowd "essentials" into a headline;[19] what has changed since then is not the duties of fidelity or non-maleficence but the social understanding of which voices are heeded when "essentials" are determined.

The interaction of culture with variably weighted duties fits the "social responsibility" model of journalism articulated after the Second World War in "Four Theories of the Press."[20] As explained a decade earlier by the Hutchins Commission,[21] sheer facticity was no longer a sufficient condition for truth; what was needed in addition was "the truth about the fact." This is context: truth about the fact and the fact-teller helps distinguish lying from bullshit.[22]

A social responsibility model requires participants in a democracy to do a lot of work and, in turn, to seek out the "pure mental food"[23] that sustains them in that work: if Detroit was the wartime Arsenal of Democracy, the news was democracy's mess hall. That concern predates the idea of an "information society" and even predates journalism itself. As Frankfurt put it: "Civilizations have never gotten along healthily, and cannot get along healthily, without large quantities of reliable factual information."[24] The damage of lying comes about because, like violence, it is coercive;[25] it constrains the target's autonomy, which underpins the ability to carry out the day labor of democracy. By altering voters' perceptions of how and by whom their interests are addressed, fake news makes "pure" news—more expensive, less accessible, and far less tasty—a worse option.

Like plagiarism, lying appears at first glance to raise no ethical questions for journalism because there are no cases in which it is appropriate. Bok clouds this simple question by casting truth-telling in a different light from Kantian universalism;[26] citing the Dutch philosopher Hugo Grotius, she asks whether we are obliged to be truthful with those who want to know where our money is so they may steal it. Like violence, lying in self-defense is justifiable, though subject to scrutiny for matters like proportionality.[27] Similarly, commonly held rules of journalism allow for weighting of obligations in determining how much openness is too much. The first principle in the Society of Professional Journalists' Code of Ethics is "Seek truth and report it"; a later section cautions against using "undercover" methods "unless traditional, open methods will not yield information vital to the public."[28]

There is no universal understanding of the exact border between "traditional" and surreptitious; Bok points to a number of deceptive tactics recounted in *All the President's Men,* such as telling sources that an uncorroborated bit of information had already been corroborated.[29] Bok's point is less that those methods were wrong *per se* than that even in hindsight they seem to have provoked no reasoning about the values of harms averted versus harms inflicted, or of general gains (exposing Watergate) versus specific harms (the individual story). Such forms of deceit can be placed in a broader category of countering harm, or, like working undercover in a packing plant, of exposing corrupt practices: both are also broadly done on behalf of a collective audience, rather than a single individual. In general, passive deceptions are preferred to the active deception of vigilante organizations like Project Veritas, which failed in an attempt to plant a false story in the *Washington Post* before a special Senate election in Alabama.[30]

Other hedges also attach to the apparently simple art of lying. Much as ticking the wrong box in a statistics program does not constitute research misconduct by itself, human error is not the same thing as lying. A lie is not merely deceptive: it is deliberate, made with knowledge of what is true, and it is an explicit statement, not an inference left hanging to tempt the unwary.[31] The role of selection and salience in building a narrative of news helps smudge the distinction between misunderstanding and misconduct, reflecting journalism's murky status as a self-proclaimed profession that shuns such hallmarks of a profession as certification and internal discipline. The *New York Times* might have bemoaned "fake news stories" that find "Mr. Trump pulling ahead of Hillary Clinton in the popular vote,"[32] but no similar concerns appear to have been raised about an equally specious claim in the *Washington Post* that Trump's support had begun to "collapse."[33] Comforting as it might be that statistical self-deception knows no party boundaries, it only reinforces the perception of journalism as a craft that separates data from perception and then prints the perception.

ON FRAMING AND *ON BULLSHIT*

The idea of fake news as "alternative facts" gained notoriety after a Trump aide, Kellyanne Conway, disputed an interviewer's contention that Trump's press secretary had lied, saying instead that he "gave alternative facts."[34] That is a charitable reading of a claim that "this was the largest audience to ever witness an inauguration, period." But by presenting a nonfalsifiable claim (perhaps every iPhone in China was indeed streaming the presidential oath) and casting facts in terms of perspective, the statement becomes a question of framing—the selection and narrative structuring of evidence—rather than falsity, placing it in the domain that Frankfurt describes as "bullshit."

Unlike lying, which presumes a knowledge of "truth" that is deliberately disregarded, bullshit is characterized by "an indifference to how things really are."[35] Like lying, bullshit is deliberate, but it is more a bluff than a lie: "The essence of bullshit is not that it is false but that it is phony." A lie is "an act with a sharp focus . . . designed to insert a particular falsehood at a specific point . . . in order to avoid the consequences of having that point occupied by the truth"; bullshit, by being "panoramic rather than particular," thrives on the vagaries of context.[36] When Trump contended in tweets of October 2012 that federal employment statistics were "cooked" and "a complete fraud," he was lying; when, six months into office, he cited statistics from the same process as evidence that "things are starting to kick in now," he was bullshitting. Knowledge of where a fact stands is central to successful truth-telling or successful lying; the bullshitter's eye, though, "is not on the facts at all . . . except insofar as they may be pertinent to his interest in getting away with what he says."[37]

Distinguishing lies from bullshit from conflicting interpretations of the causal forces that animate politics—did Ronald Reagan win the Cold War, or should credit go Warsaw Pact officials addressing internal policy concerns well after Reagan left office?—is challenge enough, but it still falls short of the main question. Since journalists' mandate is to tell truth, rather than to not lie, how should they apportion their time and efforts, and to what end? How can they make those allocations at a pace that allows for timely production of the commodity they are promise-bound to deliver? If they detect a lie, what is entailed in a duty to maximize audience autonomy, given readers' own obligations to do democracy effectively?

That depends in part on what kind of duty truth-telling is. Having contracted to deliver a load of journalism at a specified time, journalists are promise-bound to deliver it—and to ensure as well that it meets trade standards for accuracy, readability, interest, and lack of manifest falsity. That second duty, though also representing a claim of fidelity, is conditioned differently from the first. In Ross's framework, producing journalism up to standard might also involve a duty of gratitude, in not compromising the sources who risk their jobs by providing core information; a duty of preventing a misdistribution of goods or benefits (a candidate who lies is not given a free pass to impair the autonomy of the audience); or a duty of noninjury: preventing tangential harm that could arise from mishandling truth.

Such an equation is complicated to explain to the candidate or listener who demands to know why a favored story—the cunning Democratic plot to assassinate Justice Antonin Scalia, for example[38]—was not passed along unadorned to the audience. But Ross was not a fan of parsimony for parsimony's sake: "It is more important that our theory fit the facts than that it be simple."[39] His structure of weighted, conditional duties provides a path for addressing the dilemmas posed by fake news in a way that works with the demands of news practice. Like distinguishing lies from bullshit, that also calls for setting out a taxonomy of fakery and falsity, and that starts with admitting that both practices have been around for a bit.

THE FALSE AND THE FAKE: TOWARD A TAXONOMY

Falsity and fakery have coexisted with news for as long as "news" has had its current form. In seventeenth-century England, "reports interpreted unusual events as omens or miracles";[40] in the decades and centuries since, wishful thinking and cultural congruence have worked together to ensure that all manner of material—vital and trivial, honest and dishonest, natural and supernatural—made sense to its audience. Craft standards compel journalism not to make things up, but by compelling it at the same time to make things interesting, they leave a range of weighty and often contradictory decisions to a process with little time for reflection on the difference.

Nor is the evidence itself always innocent: the "composograph"[41] was a feature of journalism half a century after photographers arranged bodies and rifles on Civil War battlefields to yield compelling images. Technology underscores the challenge raised by a distinctive property of photographs known as indexicality: As apparent products of a set of physical processes rather than fallible human judgment, photos come with "an implicit guarantee of being closer to the truth."[42] A photo is certain to be true about something, even if it is silent on what it true about. In the twenty-first century, the episodic image that goes viral raises a similar problem: It becomes viral by a process independent of the journalist, but it is often opaque on what it is viral about. Neither the viral tweet nor the miracle is demonstrably false, but they are fake in different ways that call for different preventions and treatments.

A taxonomy of fake news begins with an understanding of how false news spreads and how it works. "Pizzagate" is likely the most famous case of false news from the 2016 election. In response to a fabricated story about a Democratic child-sex ring run from a Washington pizza restaurant, a North Carolina resident decided to take up arms and investigate.[43] Whether that response to a single message qualifies as a "media effect" is debatable. No single report, in general, makes an unbalanced gun owner pack his firearms and drive to the nation's capital, any more than a single story drove another gun owner from North Carolina to attack a Planned Parenthood clinic in Colorado.[44] The Pizzagate story did not come as close to the news mainstream as a similar fabrication that arose at about the same point in the campaign: plans for a satanic ritual involving Hillary Clinton's campaign manager,[45] which, unlike Pizzagate, became the lead story at the *Drudge Report*. As indicators of conspiratorial thinking, such linkblogs have become required reading for the nonpartisan media as well; a false story or a false narrative arriving there is only a short hop from the homepage of *Fox News* and a spot, however short-lived, on the issue agenda.

Most fabricated news is thus confined to small parts of the far-right media spectrum.[46] Stories with a greater surface plausibility—the papal endorsement of Trump, or the questions about Clinton's health (especially when accompanied by pictures of the candidate being helped into a van)—have a higher probability of replacing actual news or altering the salience of issues. To note that some fabrications are unlikely to have caused certain specific harms is not to suggest that false news is not harmful, but it does suggest that questions about harm need to address issues of about how harm is demonstrated or caused. There is a fractional risk that, when fabricated news is repeated, even to be debunked, someone will miss the point and think it's true. As with vaccines, though, the fractional risk is outweighed by the benefits of herd immunity.

The harms of bullshit are harder to specify because of its panoramic nature. The viral tweet that captures what might be an offense against social norms does not replace a true statement with a false one; it changes the contextual atmosphere in which current and future events are interpreted. This type of fakery draws its impact from the pattern that events are encouraged to form, and those supposed patterns crowd other events off the agenda.

Sometimes, like carbon monoxide, fake news mimics real news in a way that fools the body's defense systems. Sometimes, like junk food, it clogs the arteries simply because it is routinely tastier, cheaper, and easier to find. But prioritizing stories about lucky stores with a record of selling winning lottery tickets is something journalism has always done—often with the same didactic functions that accompany real news. The "pseudo-events" described by Daniel Boorstin[47] are created for the media to publicize, but they are also reminders of the ordered world "we" inhabit. They require a truth-teller's fidelity to recounting events as they are told but a bullshitter's disdain for the picture they are allowed to form. (Judge not, lest thy front-page story about the annual Super Bowl halftime flushing crisis be judged.)

Other stories propose a true representation of the world, but in a context that gives a meaning sought by the news agency or the political party it serves, rather than by any of the participants. In agenda-setting terms, the challenge is not the individual potato chip—the story—but the entire bag: the pseudo-issue formed from partially true stories that then takes on a life of its own. After the election of a Muslim candidate as mayor of London in 2016, any story about civic policy-making in London could become a "Londonistan" story in the partisan press: an indication that the United Kingdom, and by extension, the United States, was a step closer to the imposition of religious law. Following a familiar transmission route, "London's Muslim mayor takes aim at racy images" appeared on the *Fox News* homepage June 14, 2016, a day after "London's Muslim mayor bans sexy women in advertisements" appeared at the *Daily Caller*. Both are indifferent to the details of a policy that addressed body-shaming ads on public transit but not "all images of people in their underwear or swimming gear":[48] as Frankfurt noted, bullshit is as happy to fake the context as to cook the facts.[49]

Fake news can also be created by omitting the middle term of the news syllogism, as illustrated when a Londonistan story was reported from Leeds, some 170 miles from the capital. It was literally and chronologically true that the protagonist, described by *Fox News* as "a longtime activist against Islam," had been "jailed after filming outside child grooming trial," as the headline announced, but the causal connection reported in the *Fox* story[50] and elsewhere[51] was omitted: he was under a suspended sentence for contempt of court and was violating restrictions imposed on reporting on the current case out of concerns over pretrial prejudice. As with earlier moral panics over "road rage" and "welfare queens," the facts appear to speak for themselves, but only some of them are allowed to speak.

The restraints imposed by news practice can themselves make context a challenge. The practices of objectivity[52] constrain journalists from judging a lie to be a lie on their own, whether it comes from a candidate or from another media outlet. Despite the well-established norms meant to partition evidence from opinion, a competing mandate to present rival claims impartially tends to smudge that separation: in framing terms,[53] to distinguish problem definition and moral evaluation from the data that are being defined and evaluated. "It's morning in America" is an evaluation; "we can turn this recession around" embeds a fact claim that, made during an economic expansion, is false on its face. But presented in a "both sides" argument, it is another path down which fakery disguised as balance can spread, and it points to the especially challenging problem of dealing with numbers—the most "objective" of empirical data.

DATA: THE MOTE IN THE EYE

It would be easier to call out the partisan press for specious reporting on public opinion polls if specious reporting on public opinion polls was not a staple of the mainstream media diet. If there is a distinction, it is that the professionalized press spreads the bounty of error equally, while the partisan press's misinterpretations tend to be unidirectional: A three-point advantage for Barack Obama over John McCain in 2008 was "Within Margin of Error" in foxnews.com's report on its monthly poll; an identical advantage for McCain the following month produced the headline "McCain Out Front." Alongside the traditional practice of claiming that the data represent a trend that the writer wants to see, though, a trend of lying about how data were created has gained prominence in the fake news era. Attacks in both fringe and mainstream conservative media on monthly federal employment surveys appear to have begun in 2012 with a tweet from the former chief executive of General Electric and reached a peak of salience the month before the 2012 election, when foxnews.com's lead story asked: "Is the number real?" It was no small irony that the Trump administration, having as a campaign happily claimed that the data were bogus, embraced the steady, if slightly slower, increase in nonfarm payroll employment demonstrated by the 2017 data as proof of its success. Professionalized routines cast such assertions as points of debate, rather than lies, making them hard to challenge.

Other number-based claims reach the mainstream because of a shared gravitas that replaces meaningfulness. Persistent assertions about Barack Obama's first-person-singular pronoun frequency are an example. These were generally presented in news accounts or commentaries as simple proportions or frequency counts: the president used "I" some specified number of times per speech or per hundred words. Notwithstanding that evidence repeatedly showed that Obama was unexceptional, if generally low, in presidential FPS frequency,[54] and that a "large-scale, multisite, multimeasure, and dual-language investigation" found "consistent evidence of a near-zero effect" for the relationship between narcissism and FPS frequency,[55] this pattern was held up as evidence that Obama was narcissistic, obsessed with himself, and generally unworthy of holding the same office once held by people who demonstrated nearly identical linguistic features. Again, though it is unlikely that such representations influence voter behavior, they do support an atmosphere in which numbers are used to paint a conclusion that is the opposite of what they show in real life.

All those challenges—falsity, fakery, and an upside-down world in which numbers exist without a mooring to reality—raise different sorts of questions for the practice of news. If identified, a falsehood can be challenged and stopped; bullshit, on the other hand, has a press pass it borrowed at the entrance to the debate. A war on fake news would be easier if journalism could invoke the norms of a profession: a standard punishment for fabrication, say, rather than a patchwork where fakery is a firing offense at one outfit and a matter for celebration at another. But without a rule that requires a credential in quantitative methods before undertaking to interpret public opinion data in an election year, journalism is better described as a craft than a profession. It is, to be sure, a demanding craft, but it structures expertise differently, and places different expectations on its practitioners, than law, medicine, holy orders, or the profession of arms. In that sense, journalism is professionalized rather than professional; its expertise is repeated every day, rather than earned and placed in a frame on the wall. It does things according to routinized sets of standards,[56] and for good reason; journalism requires rapid decision-making about novel developments so they can be placed into understood structures, often done in real time before a demanding and uncharitable audience. As Walter Lippmann noted at the dawn of the "mass communication" era, journalists have neither the time nor the energy to reason every decision through *de novo*.[57] It makes sense to do procedures rather than ethics.

For the larger domain of journalism as the breadbasket of "pure mental food," that is not a problem; journalism is a provider of information, rather than an arbiter of how people live their lives. Nor has proceduralism precluded journalists from working or thinking ethically. It does, though, leave them at a loss when the White House responds to questions about the president's public behavior by—to use a recently revived term—gaslighting: attempting to persuade the people who see a problem that their perceptions are the problem. In these cases, there is no referee to reward or recognize good behavior; journalism is left to rely on the goodwill of the crowd, and the acclaim that greets assertions that journalism itself is "fake news" suggests that such goodwill is in short supply. Regulation is not a remedy, but journalism can take some other steps to bolster its practices until journalists can escape the enemies list.

CONCLUSION: CARBON MONOXIDE, BOTULISM AND NEWS

Fake news, whatever its source or function, does enjoy one vital ally: the high level of protection the US system provides for political speech. Commercial speech can be regulated, as can threats of violence or other forms of speech that pose direct threats, but letting the government rule on what is true or false "creates a very harrowing precedent that the First Amendment was enacted to prevent."[58] As Walter Lippmann wrote a century ago: "If I lie in a lawsuit involving the fate of my neighbor's cow, I can go to jail. But if I lie to a million readers in a matter involving war and peace, I can lie my head off, and, if I choose the right series of lies, be entirely irresponsible."[59]

Traditionally the remedy is "counterspeech":[60] bringing balance to a bullshit-flooded marketplace of ideas by adding better ideas. A gubernatorial primary in which a candidate from one party accuses a Muslim potential rival from the other party of plotting "civilization jihad"[61]—invoking, again, the fake issue raised by "Londonistan"—recalls Lippmann's claim: "Nobody will punish me if I lie about Japan, for example. I can announce that every Japanese valet is a reservist, and every Japanese art store a mobilization center."[62] Broadly, the public needs to know when candidates are spreading fabrications; if the fiction is countered elsewhere in a secondary headline by a contention that the candidate is a "pathetic, bigoted fool,"[63] the duties of fidelity and noninjury are closer to balance. If no rival is at hand to provide counterspeech, news organizations should be prepared to provide their own.

Another suggestion has been to consider extending advertising's disclosure requirements to fake news on social media, stemming from "the simple observation that fake news is not 'news.' It is political advertising."[64] While this could alleviate some concerns about autonomy, the protection of political speech would likely provide sanctuary once a lie reached the cathedral steps of a news site.

Those are primarily concerns about false—or in its kindest form, nonfalsifiable—news. They are generally more directly available to journalists than remedies for fake news: specious virality, conflation of political events with moral fables, self-serving interpretations of data, and exaggerations of things sources might have meant—or not—into claims about what sources said. False news poses threats different from those of fake news, just as carbon monoxide poses a health threat different from junk food or botulism. Remedies can also differ depending on whether they are written for journalism as a craft or journalism as a profession, because those two conceptions can involve different duties for different actors.

Journalists, it is clear, should continue practicing the craft of journalism: that is, gathering evidence, comparing it to previously acquired evidence, and presenting it in a form that is usable by a mass democratic audience, regardless of whether it aligns with any individual ideology or partisan preference. The final score is the final score, whichever team the crowd seems to favor. Craft and profession respond to false news in similar ways: Don't do it, don't share it, make sure that falsehoods—again, distinguished from errors—are firmly attached to those who introduce them into the news supply.

As a craft, journalism should take stock of how its digital practices reflect its pen-and-ink practices. The individualized offerings of a "proprietary algorithm" are not an equal substitute for the judgment of a human editor: "Processing is not judgment."[65] One key to stopping the virality of fake news is in stopping virality. Any story whose sole reason for being is "immediately went viral" should be suspect; as with the indexicality of photos, a viral event is clearly true about something but often unclear as to what it is true about. Moral panics are born of the indifference to truth demonstrated in unexamined virality.

The reach of digital news also points to values that should have carried over from analog news: particularly, attention to disfavored stakeholders. If spotlighting the international relations instructor who assigned an essay about the 9/11 attacks "from the perspective of the terrorist network" ("9/11 was bad. But let's pretend it wasn't")[66] violates a Rossian duty of noninjury, so does a report that prints the home addresses of concealed-carry licensees.[67] The latter might contain more individual truths, or take fewer liberties with the evidence, but facticity by itself does not create the collective beneficence that might make a private individual into a prototype "Enemy of the People." The permanence of information also suggests a balance away from personalized or exemplar stories, in which one person stands for a presumed social phenomenon—particularly when juveniles or members of other potentially vulnerable groups are involved.

Journalism's traditional bias toward intuition—the grizzled statehouse reporter's gut feeling about a public opinion poll, as opposed to the new hire's formal training in survey interpretation—suggests a rebalancing of professional and craft duties. (Ross's prima facie duties are supposed to be intuitive but at the same time general, rather than driven by the mystic wisdom of the elect.) Mandatory certification would run against a core purpose of the First Amendment: in Justice Hugo Black's phrase, the "unconditional right to say what one pleases about public affairs,"[68] but in-house adherence to a professional standard is a selling point, like painting the parts of a car that people don't see.

Similarly, the craft norm of seeking a broad span of contradictory opinions can be complemented by better attention to the grounds on which those opinions rest. Opinion-makers do not get a free pass to lie about how other people conduct their surveys. An advanced degree and a home on the op-ed page do not validate either lies about presidential pronoun frequency or bullshit about the sociolinguistic meaning of pronoun frequency counts. Such assertions can be professionally greeted with public ridicule. A duty of fidelity to the public—providing timely, well-validated information on salient issues—does not erase a duty of noninjury to candidates, or to the public, in not spreading culturally appealing fictions. Those who chortled along with the *New York Times*'s claim[69] that George W. Bush invented the word "decider," which the *Oxford English Dictionary* dates to 1568, may now act suitably embarrassed.

Fake news has the property of becoming a fact—of a sort—when it is spoken. A racist conspiracy theory proclaimed by a candidate for statewide office does not become true by being proclaimed, but it does become news. That suggests renewed attention to the idea that frames are not naturally occurring properties; the proclamation of a conspiracy theory should not be presented as the first volley of a legitimate political debate. Those who do not choose frames carefully are liable to have frames chosen for them; journalists should be the first to ask who benefits from a presumption that any set of events should fit a particular story line.

A more drastic step toward professionalism would challenge who gets to hang out the shingle of journalism. Bok cites the American Medical Association's position that doctors "should expose, without hesitation, illegal or unethical conduct" by other doctors,[70] and the SPJ code calls on journalists to "expose unethical conduct in journalism." Rarely as this might happen in day-to-day life, it does stand as a potential check on the tendency of those who share a line of work—even if in competing newsrooms—to follow other codes that call on them to "treat each other as brothers."[71] The solidarity of the White House press corps has been tested on occasion over the years, as when Franklin D. Roosevelt brought an Iron Cross to a news conference for a disfavored correspondent;[72] a serious attempt to address fake news might call for putative comrades-in-arms to choose where they stand. The duties of righting wrongs and avoiding the maldistribution of goods compel journalists to stand with a *Fox News* presenter who was subject to sexual harassment in the office and—from Fox's preferred candidate—on the job. But an obligation to stand with *Fox* journalists in *Fox*'s war on women need not extend to *Fox*'s broader war on truth. The mainstream media of 1942 could be thorough in chronicling the deeds of the "vermin press."[73] Rather than treating alt-right racism as a legitimate political perspective, professional organizations could invest their time and resources in documenting its spread.

Technology, to borrow again from Ross, does not change moral judgments but can change the facts around which they are made. Fidelity to the spoken or unspoken rules by which journalism produces news is more than a balance of truth-telling and noninjury; journalists are obliged not to unduly suppress views because they are personally offensive, but also not to unduly spread those that are, intuitively, false or malicious. Should an organization complain that its viewpoints are being trodden down by social media algorithms, its audience has far more remedies than the traditional "start your own newspaper."

The challenges of the "fake news" era are not unique, in that most have been seen before, but they are distinctive, in that that they have not occurred in this combination before. Journalism can approach those challenges ethically, rather than just procedurally, with an appropriate combination and understanding of variably weighted duties. Calling lies out as lies poses little professional challenge and seems to be having only a small, if potentially cumulative, effect so far. Calling bullshit on bullshit might prove a valuable professional addition.

NOTES

1. Jon Henley, "Global Crackdown on Fake News Raises Censorship Concerns," *The Guardian*, April 24, 2018, www.theguardian.com/media/2018/apr/24/global-crackdown-on-fake-news-raises -censorship-concerns.

2. Cecile Kan and Kevin Roose, "Facebook Chief Faces Hostile Congress as Calls for Regulation Mount," *New York Times*, April 11, 2018, www.nytimes.com/2018/04/11/business/zuckerberg-facebook -congress.html.

3. Dan Merica, "Hillary Clinton Calls Fake News 'an Epidemic' with Real World Consequences," *CNN.com*, December 12, 2016, www.cnn.com/2016/12/08/politics/hillary-clinton-fake-news-epidemic /index.html.

4. "Facebook and the Digital Virus Called Fake News," *New York Times*, November 20, 2016, www .nytimes.com/2016/11/20/opinion/sunday/facebook-and-the-digital-virus-called-fake-news.html.

5. Sissela Bok, *Lying: Moral Choice in Public and Private Life* (New York: Pantheon, 1999).

6. Harry Frankfurt, *On Bullshit*. (Princeton, NJ: Princeton University Press, 2005); Harry Frankfurt, *On Truth* (New York: Alfred A. Knopf, 2006).

7. "Facebook and the Digital Virus."

8. Maxwell McCombs and Jian-Hua Zhu, "Capacity, Diversity and Volatility of the Public Agenda: Trends from 1954 To 1994," *Public Opinion Quarterly* 59 (1995): 495–525.

9. Richard A. Gunther, Paul A. Beck, and Erik Nisbet, "Trump May Owe His 2016 Victory to 'Fake News,' Study Suggests," *Conversation*, February 15, 2018, theconversation.com/trump-may-owe -his-2016-victory-to-fake-news-new-study-suggests-91538.

10. Peter Schmidt, "Professors' Growing Risk: Harassment for Things They Never Really Said," *Chronicle of Higher Education*, June 16, 2017, www.chronicle.com/article/Professors-Growing-Risk-/240424.

11. Armando Simón, "Psychologists and Psychiatrists Who Violate the Goldwater Rule Are Guilty of Malpractice, *Journal of Human Behavior in the Social Environment* 28 no. 7 (2018): 948–56.

12. Ralph Slovenko, "Psychiatric Opinion Without Examination," *Journal of Psychiatry and Law* 28 (2000):103–43.

13. William David Ross, *The Foundations of Ethics* (Oxford, UK: Clarendon Press, 1939); William David Ross, *The Right and the Good,* ed. Philip Stratton-Lake (Oxford, UK: Oxford University Press, 2002).

14. Christopher Meyers, "Appreciating W. D. Ross: On Duties and Consequences" *Journal of Mass Media Ethics* 18 (2003): 81–87.

15. Philip Stratton-Lake, Introduction to Ross, *The Right and the Good.*

16. Ross, *The Foundations of Ethics,* 19.

17. Frank Deaver, "On Defining Truth," *Journal of Mass Media Ethics* 5 (1990): 168–77.

18. Robert M. Entman, "Framing: Toward Clarification of a Fractured Paradigm," *Journal of Communication* 43 (1993): 51–58.

19. Norman J. Radder and John E. Stempel, *Newspaper Editing, Make-Up and Headlines* (New York: McGraw-Hill, 1942).

20. Fred S. Siebert, Theodore Peterson, and Wilbur Schramm, *Four Theories of the Press: The Authoritarian, Libertarian, Social Responsibility, and Soviet Communist Concepts of What the Press Should Do* (Champaign: University of Illinois Press, 1956).

21. Commission on Freedom of the Press, *A Free and Responsible Press: A General Report on Mass Communication: Newspapers, Radio, Motion Pictures, Magazines, and Books.* (Chicago: University of Chicago Press, 1947).

22. Bok, *Lying*; Frankfurt, *On Bullshit.*

23. The Hutchins Commission applied the term to journalism in 1947, though "pure mental food" in similar contexts appears in journalism textbooks and business publications early in the twentieth century; Willard G. Bleyer's *Newspaper Writing and Editing* (Boston: Houghton-Mifflin, 1913) warned of the danger of "adulterated" news in a section that also covers "How 'faking' does harm."

24. Frankfurt, *On Truth,* 34.

25. Bok, *Lying.*

26. Bok, *Lying,* 267–72; see also Stephen J. A. Ward, *The Invention of Journalism Ethics: The Path to Objectivity and Beyond.* (Montreal: McGill-Queen's University Press, 2006).

27. Bok, *Lying.*

28. Society of Professional Journalists, "SPJ Code of Ethics," www.spj.org/ethicscode.asp (accessed January 7, 2019.)

29. Bok, *Lying,* 120–21.

30. Beth Reinhardt, Aaron C. Davis, and Andrew Ba Tran, "Woman's Effort to Infiltrate the *Washington Post* Dated Back Months," *Washington Post,* November 29, 2017, www.washingtonpost.com /investigations/womans-effort-to-infiltrate-the-washington-post-dates-back-months/2017/11/29 /ce95e01a-d51e-11e7-b62d-d9345ced896d_story.html.

31. Bok, *Lying*; Frankfurt, *On Bullshit.*

32. "Facebook and the Digital Virus."

33. Chris Cillizza, "It Might be Time for Republicans to Start Panicking about Donald Trump," *Washington Post,* June 17, 2016, www.washingtonpost.com/news/the-fix/wp/2016/06/17/dear -republicans-heres-why-it-might-be-time-to-start-panicking-about-donald-trump-in-1-chart/.

34. Eric Bradner, "Conway: Trump White House Offered 'Alternative Facts' on Crowd Size," *CNN.com*, January 23, 2017, www.cnn.com/2017/01/22/politics/kellyanne-conway-alternative-facts/index.html.

35. Frankfurt, *On Bullshit*, 34.

36. Frankfurt, *On Bullshit*, 47, 51–52.

37. Frankfurt, *On Bullshit*, 56.

38. "Michael Savage: Was Scalia Murdered?" *World Net Daily*, February 15, 2016, www.michaelsavage.wnd.com/2016/02/was-scalia-murdered/; Trump discussed the question on Savage's radio program that day.

39. Ross, *The Foundations of Ethics*, 19.

40. Ward, *The Invention of Journalism Ethics*, 85.

41. Ken Kobré, "Positive/Negative: The Long Tradition of Doctoring Photos," *Visual Communication Quarterly* 2 (1995): 14–15.

42. Paul Messaris and Linus Abraham, "The Role of Images in Framing News Stories," in *Framing public life*, ed. Stephen D. Reese, Oscar H. Gandy Jr. and August E. Grant (Mahwah, NJ: Lawrence Erlbaum Associates, 2001).

43. News routines create pressure to take even these claims at face value; a headline in the largest newspaper in North Carolina read: "Salisbury man investigating fake news has history of drug, alcohol charges." See Merica, "Hillary Clinton Calls Fake News 'an Epidemic,'" for a description of Pizzagate itself.

44. A local newspaper's live blog of the Colorado event points to the genuine danger of failing to balance the duties of fidelity and non-maleficence: "Police are communicating by cell phone with three people trapped in a bathroom closet inside Planned Parenthood" ("Active Shooter Situation Reported near Planned Parenthood in Colorado Springs," *The Gazette*, November 27, 2015, gazette.com/crime/active-shooter-situation-reported-near-planned-parenthood-in-colorado-springs/article_c2bb1734-6335-5afb-92db-080a7948f670.html).

45. Paul Joseph Watson, "'Spirit Cooking': Clinton Campaign Chairman Practices Bizarre Occult Ritual." *InfoWars*, November 4, 2016, www.snopes.com/fact-check/john-podesta-spirit-cooking/.

46. Richard Hofstadter's essay "The Paranoid Style in American Politics" notes that conspiratorial thinking is not unique to the right, though he draws on nativist and populist movements of the past to illuminate the grand conspiracies favored in the Goldwater and McCarthy eras (*The Paranoid Style in American Politics and Other Essays* [1964; New York: Vintage, 2008]).

47. Daniel Boorstin, *The Image: A Guide to Pseudo-Events in America*. (New York: Harper & Row, 1961).

48. Pippa Crerar, "Sadiq Khan: There Will be No More 'Body Shaming' Adverts on the Tube," *Evening Standard*, June 13, 2016, www.standard.co.uk/news/london/sadiq-khan-there-will-be-no-more-body-shaming-adverts-on-the-tube-a3269951.html.

49. Frankfurt, *On Bullshit*, 52.

50. "Right-Wing Activist Tommy Robinson Reportedly Jailed after Filming Outside Child Grooming Trial," *Fox News*, May 26, 2018, www.foxnews.com/world/right-wing-activist-tommy-robinson-reportedly-jailed-after-filming-outside-child-grooming-trial.

51. Palko Karasz, "Tommy Robinson, Anti-Muslim Activist, Is Freed on Bail in U.K.," *New York Times,* August 1, 2018, www.nytimes.com/2018/08/01/world/europe/uk-tommy-robinson.html.

52. Gaye Tuchman, "Objectivity as Strategic Ritual: An Examination of Newsmen's Notions of Objectivity," *American Journal of Sociology* 77 (1972): 660–79.

53. Entman, "Framing."

54. Mark Liberman, "Another Casual Lie from Charles Krauthammer," *Language Log,* September 16, 2014, languagelog.ldc.upenn.edu/nll/?p=14625.

55. Angela L. Carey, Melanie S. Brucks, Albrecht CP Küfner, Nicholas S. Holtzman, Mitja D. Back, M. Brent Donnellan, James W. Pennebaker, and Matthias R. Mehl, "Narcissism and the Use of Personal Pronouns Revisited," *Journal of Personality and Social Psychology* 109, no. 3 (2015): e1.

56. Tuchman, "Objectivity as Strategic Ritual."

57. Walter Lippmann, *Liberty and the News* (New York: Harcourt, Brace and Howe, 1920).

58. Jessica Stone-Erdman, "Just the (Alternative) Facts, Ma'am: The Status of Fake News under the First Amendment," *First Amendment Law Review* 16 (2017): 410–41.

59. Lippmann, *Liberty and the News.*

60. Stone-Erdman, "Just the (Alternative) Facts."

61. Kathleen Gray, "Colbeck: Rival is Part of Muslim Plot," *Detroit Free Press,* April 25, 2018.

62. Lippmann, *Liberty and the News.*

63. Gray, "Colbeck."

64. Abby K. Wood, Ann M. Ravel, and Irina Dykhne, "Fool me once: Regulating "fake news" and other online advertising," *Southern California Law Review* 91 (2018).

65. Kevin Healey and Robert H. Woods Jr., "Processing is not judgment, storage is not memory: A critique of Silicon Valley's moral catechism," *Journal of Media Ethics* 32 (2017): 2–15.

66. "9/11 from terrorist's perspective basis for Iowa State assignment," foxnews.com, March 27, 2017.

67. Christine Haughney, "After pinpointing gun owners, paper is a target," *New York Times,* January 27, 2013.

68. *Ginzburg et al. v. Goldwater,* 396 US 1049; 90 S.Ct. 701 (1970); Black had made the same point earlier in *Times v. Sullivan.*

69. Sheryl Gay Stolberg, "The Decider," *New York Times,* December 24, 2006, www.nytimes .com/2006/12/24/weekinreview/24stolberg.html.

70. Bok, *Lying,* 154.

71. Bok, *Lying,* 153.

72. Phelps Adams, "F.D.R. Outburst Called New Low in Vilification," *Chicago Tribune,* December 20, 1942, 5. The journalist was John O'Donnell of the *New York Daily News* (owned by a cousin of the *Tribune's* publisher), whose lawsuit against a Philadelphia paper that had called him a "naziphile" was about to go to trial.

73. "Voices of Defeat," *Life* magazine, April 13, 1942, 86–100. For an overview, see Michael S. Sweeney, *Secrets of Victory: The Office of Censorship and the American Press and Radio in World War II* (Chapel Hill: University of North Carolina Press, 2001).

THE SELF-RADICALIZATION OF WHITE MEN

FAKE NEWS AND THE AFFECTIVE
NETWORKING OF PARANOIA

Jessica Johnson

O n December 4, 2016, a twenty-eight-year-old white man from North Carolina named Edgar Maddison Welch drove to Comet Ping Pong pizzeria
in Washington, DC, in possession of an AR-15 assault-style rifle, a Colt
.38 handgun, a shotgun, and a folding knife. His aim was to "self-investigate" a
worldwide child sex trafficking ring with ties to Hillary Clinton. Although he
searched the premises, threatening an employee in the process, Welch found no
children held captive in hidden caverns. Nevertheless, he fired the rifle inside the
restaurant. Accounts concerning the shooting vary, including when, how many
times, and in what manner the bullets were discharged, but it is their triggering
without cause that is the focus of my analysis.

Welch peacefully surrendered without physically inflicting harm; however,
this story does not begin or end with him. James Alefantis, the restaurant's owner,
as well as his employees and nearby businesses, were attacked on social media
before Welch's arrival. Alefantis was forced to contact the FBI, local police, Facebook, and other social media platforms in an effort to remove the "fake news"
articles that had gained traction online identifying his establishment at the center
of a global pedophilic enterprise. However, when the police initially arrested
Welch, they insisted that the incident was not related to Pizzagate.

The willingness of legal authorities to ignore evidence that linked the conspiracy theory to Welch's crime testifies to a general reluctance among government

officials to identify white men as "self-radicalized" terrorists. Through profiling, including the data mining of Facebook profiles and social media accounts, US citizens quickly mutate into self-radicalized Islamic terrorists killing on behalf of jihad, so long as they look the part. In the case of Welch, his radicalization was rendered invisible by his whiteness and undersold given no one was hurt when he shot his AR-15.

"Self-radicalization" is a misnomer. Rather than pathology relegated to a specific subject or a particular form of extremism, radicalization is a social process of affective networking. In a rare interview, Welch shared that he listened to conspiracy theorist and *InfoWars* host Alex Jones—a Christian who calls Hillary Clinton and President Obama "demons"—and enjoyed John Eldridge's *Wild at Heart,* a popular book on evangelical masculinity.[1] His militarized sense of masculine duty to protect imaginary children from Satanic perverts speaks to the power of "fake news" to trigger real guns and calculatedly crowdsource paranoia.

Much news coverage of conspiracy theory discourse focuses on questions of belief, proposing that many viewers of Jones's *InfoWars,* for example, disbelieve "wilder fantasies" such as Pizzagate and simply tune in for entertainment, "enjoying the ridiculous exaggerations and outright lies for the outrage they provoke in Democrats, liberals, intellectuals, and pompous commentators of all political stripes."[2] Subsequently, "true believers" such as Welch are dismissed as brainwashed or mentally disturbed, although he also admitted that Jones "goes off the deep end on some things"[3]

While media coverage on the proliferation of conspiracy theory discourse today recognizes the obvious role that the Internet has played in attracting a wider audience, this recognition does not go far enough in assessing the agency and impact of digital technology in the visceral gut-appeal of "fake news" in the United States during the Trump administration. What constitutes "fake news" is constantly cast into doubt by the president himself, further obscuring and complicating distinctions between facts and falsehoods as he unabashedly lies to the public and bullies the press, shouting "fake news" at reporters and lashing out against the "fake news media" on Twitter and at rallies.

Many studies have made convincing arguments concerning the cultural significance of conspiracy theory discourse historically and contemporarily in the United States.[4] It is important to reassess this project in light of the ways in which entertainment and information are increasingly entangled by social media, whereby likes, retweets, and emoji have become arbiters of authenticity and audience reception on Facebook and Twitter, influencing news-feed algorithms and the policing of user-generated content. Meanwhile, the president exploits such metrics of authenticity to manipulate optics so that his approval ratings seem higher than they are, retweeting or quote-tweeting praise from accounts with suspicious bot (automated) activity.[5] It is impossible to distinguish the performance of the president during a press conference from his starring role as the surly boss on the reality television show *The Apprentice*. In effect, Trump's election has mainstreamed and legitimized conspiracy theory discourse using the tactics of shock and awe valorized during Operation Iraqi Freedom at the outset of the global war on terror.

At a time when technologies of state and corporate surveillance are routinized and always on by way of computers and cell phones, modulating habits of communication and gesture while tracking patterns of consumption and movement, trust in the media and government is at an all-time low. Such a political climate calls for a nuanced analysis of how conspiracy theory discourse has become normalized by reframing paranoia from the pathological to the ecological. By invoking ecology in this instance, I refer to its conceptualization apart from nature as such, what Bruno Latour has articulated as "a new way to handle all the objects of human and nonhuman collective life."[6] While situating conspiracy theory discourse as promoted and amplified through digital media leading up to and in the aftermath of the 2016 election, I examine paranoia as a networking process that radicalizes white men through social theory that disrupts, rather than reinforces, neoliberal logics of individual, human, and US exceptionalism.

In actor-network theory (ANT), networks are not *technical systems* of transport, flow, or communication, but *networking processes* of movement, circulation, and connection. Bruno Latour writes, "An actor-network may lack all the characteristics of a technical network—it may be local, it may have no compulsory paths, no strategically positioned nodes"[7] Such an analytical approach is well suited to investigating the political mobilization of what has been coined by white nationalist Richard Spencer as the "alt-right," a network which has no head or center but relies on human and nonhuman actors to bodily move and digitally connect men across the country as they enjoy "lolz" online. In the "Unite the Right" riots that ensued over a weekend in Charlottesville, Virginia, in August 2017, common ground and ideological affinity among Ku Klux Klan members, neo-Nazis, militia men, Trump supporters, and alt-righters materialized in the affective networking of white masculinist paranoia. In ANT, there is no social or real space outside of associations, no a priori relation of scale or order according to binaries of macro/micro, local/global, individual/mass, or subject/society. Additionally, there is no inside or outside to a network. This conceptual frame is useful for questioning how radicalization happens not *via* the Internet, but *of* networking processes—so that singular acts of terror by white men and structural terrorism by the state are in social relation without coordination.

Furthermore, ANT is analytically productive when examining the persuasive power of conspiracy theory discourse as it is communicated online, because it fuses "a semiotic definition of entry building; a methodological framework to record the heterogeneity of such a building; an ontological claim on the 'networky' character of the actants themselves."[8] Latour posits this ontological orientation as the radical intervention of ANT, its "network tracing activity."[9] Analyzing Edgar Welch's "self-radicalization" using ANT means de-emphasizing psychological factors and individual motive, and troubling logics of human exceptionalism and rationales of self-interest, while conceptualizing social relations and political action in terms of networking processes that involve human and nonhuman actors. The term "actor" in ANT signifies an "actant" as something that acts, an agency that is not relegated to individual humans, or humans in general, but includes nonhuman life. According to ANT, "a network is not a thing but the recorded movement of a thing . . . what moves and how that movement is recorded."[10] I trace the affective networking of paranoia such that conspiracy theory discourse not only politically mobilizes humans but also becomes mobile. Surplus affect is the recorded movement that signals the radicalization of white men. Thus, I investigate how paranoia moves and moves others.

Feminist affect theorist Sara Ahmed argues, "emotions play a crucial role in the 'surfacing' of individual and collective bodies through the way in which emotions circulate between bodies and signs."[11] Her theorization of affective economies concerns the circulation of emotion as affective value and resonates with ANT insofar as it suggests "that emotions are not simply 'within' or 'without,'" and "do not simply belong to individuals," but rather "create the very effect of the surfaces or boundaries of bodies and worlds."[12] According to Ahmed, "in such affective economies, emotions *do things,* and they align individuals with communities—or bodily space with social space—through the very intensity of their attachments."[13] While Welch denied that his actions were driven by any political motive, he confessed to praying for President Elect Donald Trump to take the county "in the right direction."[14] Meanwhile, Trump's "Make America Great Again" campaign was precipitated by his own unflagging popularization of another conspiracy theory, that of "birthergate," which generated suspicion concerning President Obama's nationality and religion out of racial animus.

Ahmed examines the Aryan Nations website to postulate that "white subjects claim the place of hosts [in the United States while] . . . at the same time they claim the position of victim," a narrative that "suggests that it is love of the nation that makes the white Aryans hate those whom they recognize as strangers, as the ones who are taking away the nation, the role of the Aryans in its history, as well as their future."[15] In this rewriting of US history, the labor of migrants, slaves, and other nonwhite people is erased. Such erasure justifies "rallies" organized by white nationalists to defend "free speech" alongside the racist Confederate "her-itage" of statues celebrating generals such as Robert E. Lee, a landmark in Char-lottesville connected to urban planning projects that displaced black residents.[16]

Sara Ahmed writes, "the reading of others as hateful aligns the imagined sub-ject with rights and the imagined nation with ground. This alignment is affected by the representation of both the rights of the subject and the grounds of the nation as already under threat. It is the emotional reading of hate that works to bind the imagined white subject and nation together."[17] She is speaking of white nationalist mobilization in the United States as situated by the war on terror. While Ahmed focuses on the circulation of hate in her analysis, the affective net-working of paranoia is also critical to the political mobilization of white bodies. This ontological process involves emergent media such as Richard Spencer's "I'm safe" cell phone videos recorded in suffocating close-up post-punch or –pepper spray, memes of Pepe the Frog and/as Donald Trump, Alex Jones alternatively sobbing and screaming over the state of America in the clutches of the "New World Order," as well as Ku Klux Klan members bearing Confederate flags and neo-Nazis holding their arms in stiff salute.

In her analysis of power and paranoia in the age of fiber optics, Wendy Hui Kyong Chun (2006) examines how the Internet, a technology that she argues thrives on control, has been accepted as a mass medium of freedom.[18] She con-tends that the "structuring paradox of information and communications" of the Internet is "a response to the end of the Cold War and to the successes and failures of containment."[19] This troubling convergence of freedom and control post–Cold War "stems from the attempt to solve political problems technologically," such that "to be paranoid is to think like a machine."[20] Currently, paranoia legitimizes federal laws and Twitter outbursts that instrumentalize threat as a weapon against the press and the public, including African Americans, Muslim Americans, undocumented immigrants, and those who identify across the LGBTQ spectrum (among others) in mandated checks on police monitoring, US travel limitations targeting predominantly Islamic countries, the boastful advertising of deportation statistics, and the rollback of protections for trans youth and soldiers.

Chun states that her project is to demonstrate how "the Internet enables communications between humans and machines, enables—and stems from—a freedom that cannot be controlled," in order to "take seriously the vulnerability that comes with communications—not so that we simply condemn or accept all vulnerability without question but so that we might work together to create vulnerable systems with which we can live."[21] Scholarship and speculation concerning the origins of fake news and the psychological profiles of those it convicts distracts from the project of creating vulnerable systems with which we cannot only live, but that are critical to life as with vulnerable beings.

THE "SELF-RADICALIZATION" OF WHITE MEN

The AR-15 rifle Edgar Welch fired in Comet Ping Pong is cousin to the military issue M-16, the same weapon used by Omar Mateen, the American who killed forty-nine people at Pulse nightclub in Orlando in June 2016. This mass shooting was immediately considered an act of terrorism carried out by a "self-radicalized" Islamic extremist without clear evidence that Mateen had any link, even indirectly, to an organization such as ISIS. While Mateen had pledged allegiance to the Islamic State in a 911 call as the massacre began, after further investigation the CIA concluded that he had no relationship to ISIS, and questions concerning his religious convictions remained unresolved.

Overwhelmingly, "self-radicalization" is a category reserved for "a self-starter jihadist guy, or girl . . . who can be lionized as a soldier of the Islamic State and regarded as a warrior."[22] According to this formulation, "self-radicalization" is particular to Muslims and involves not only the "lone wolf" terrorist but also information and images designed to affirm that the violence performed has greater purpose. During the Obama administration, the federal counterterrorism program known as Countering Violent Extremism (CVE) sought to deter potential terrorist attacks from various groups inspired by violent ideologies, including the Ku Klux Klan, neo-Nazis, and antigovernment militias. However, contrary to this principle of inclusivity, CVE primarily focused on enlisting Muslim communities to monitor suspicious individuals and share information with law enforcement to preempt terrorist attacks and prevent radicalization. Pilot CVE programs headed by US attorneys in cities with a high percentage of Muslims such as Los Angeles, Minneapolis, and Boston cultivated animosity, distrust, and fear of prosecution. While the CVE buzzword was collaboration, it promoted the alienation and criminalization of American Muslims.

Even so, during his 2016 campaign, Donald Trump railed against President Obama's refusal to utter "radical Islamic terrorism" as politically correct obfuscation that undermined counterterrorism efforts. He also called the Obama administration "weak" in its effort to combat ISIS, a masculinist refrain that energized supporters at rallies. President Trump has since intonated that he intends to revamp and rename CVE "Countering Islamic Extremism" or "Countering Radical Islamic Extremism." What gets elided in this dangerous narrowing of what qualifies as "extremist" is the role that news sites like *InfoWars* and *Breitbart*, message boards like 4chan and Reddit, and social media such as Twitter and Facebook have played in the affective networking of paranoia.

During the weekend of August 12 to 13, 2017, in Charlottesville, Virginia, white supremacists, white nationalists, and self-styled militias—members of the Ku Klux Klan, neo-Nazis, alt-righters, and Trump supporters among them—demonstrated against the removal of a statue of Robert E. Lee from Emancipation Park. David Duke, a former KKK imperial wizard, made explicit connections between the Unite the Right rally—where protestors arrived for battle with assault rifles and broken pool cues—to Donald Trump's election. Duke stated, "We are determined to take our country back. We are going to fulfill the promises of Donald Trump. That's what we believed in, that's why we voted for Donald Trump. Because he said he's going to take our county back. That's what we gotta do."[23] On Friday night, several hundred people, most of them men, marched on the main quadrangle of the University of Virginia campus with torches and gathered under a statue of Thomas Jefferson, shouting, "White Lives Matter," "You will not replace us," "Jews will not replace us," and "blood and soil," a Nazi rally cry.

That evening, protestors and counter-protestors confronted one another under the statue, and physical conflict waxed and waned throughout the following day.

The first response from the White House was First Lady Melania Trump, who tweeted: "Our country encourages freedom of speech, but let's communicate w/o hate in our hearts. No good comes from violence. #Charlottesville." By locating hate in individual hearts, the First Lady reframed this orchestration of terror into an individual "bad apple" problem—one that led to the murder of a thirty-two-year-old woman named Heather Heyer when a car plowed into a group of anti-racist protesters on a street near Emancipation Park. The driver was a twenty-year-old white man from Ohio named James Alex Fields Jr.—a registered Republican who was photographed at the protest bearing the shield and bland uniform of a white shirt and khaki pants to demonstrate solidarity with the white nationalist organization Vanguard American.

On his Facebook page, memes of Pepe the Frog and Emperor Trump were found among neo-Nazi symbols, a photo of soldiers with Nazi and American flags, and a portrait of baby Hitler. While Facebook, Google, Twitter, and Microsoft collaborate on sharing information to stem the flow of "terrorist propaganda" through their networks, it is unclear how this material is defined. Twitter and Facebook encourage users to report hateful messages and censor individuals for violating their terms of service. Much like the efforts of CVE, however, the focus of tech companies appeared to be on content released to recruit Muslims on behalf of jihad, until the violence in Charlottesville. GoDaddy and Google removed neo-Nazi and white nationalist sites, while Facebook banned pages with names such as "Right Wing Death Squad" and "White Nationalist United."[24] However well intentioned, such efforts will not curb the deluge of user-generated content on message boards that function as networks themselves. On Reddit, for example, the alt-right feeding frenzy called "The_Donald" has over 450,000 subscribers and three billion comments.[25]

On August 12, President Trump eventually spoke on the violence in Charlottesville: "We condemn in the strongest possible terms, this egregious display of hatred, bigotry, and violence, on many sides, on many sides. It's been going on for a long time in our country, not Donald Trump, not Barack Obama. . . . Our country is doing very well in so many ways; our country has record, just record employment. We have unemployment the lowest it's been in almost seventeen years. We have companies pouring into our country. Foxconn, car companies, so many others, they're coming back to our country. We're renegotiating trade deals to make them great for our country and great for the American worker. We have so many incredible things happening in our country." In this speech, President Trump did not rebuke, or even mention, racism, neo-Nazis, or the KKK. Neither the President nor officials on the ground called the violence perpetrated in the name of white nationalism and in support of white supremacy "domestic terrorism."

By repeatedly stating that hatred, bigotry, and violence came from "many sides," and ahistorically positing this conflict as "going on for a long, long time, not Trump, not Obama," the president distanced himself from the violence and whitewashed US history. Simultaneously, he figured the white, working-class men left behind by a globalized economy to be the *real* victims, while promoting himself as a man who is keeping his promise to "Make America Great Again." His comments earned the approval of his target audience, as evidenced in the praise of the founder of the neo-Nazi website the *Daily Stormer*, Andrew Anglin: "He didn't attack us. He just said the nation should come together. Nothing specific against us. He said that we need to study why people are so angry, and implied there was hate . . . on both sides! Also refused to answer a question about White Nationalists supporting him. No condemnation at all. When asked to condemn, he just walked out of the room. Really, really good. God bless him."[26] Trump's statement demonstrates how emotions such as anger, fear, and hate have visible identifiers, making it simple to reverse subject-and-object relations. That does not make such equivocations justifiable or legitimate, but it does lead to conjecture concerning who is to blame, even if the ideological differences between someone carrying a neo-Nazi flag and an antifascist flag appear obvious.

A few days later, on August 15, President Trump unleashed a tirade against the "fake news" media during a press conference when he was asked why he did not release a more timely statement on the violence in Charlottesville: "Before a statement I need the facts. . . . if the press were not fake and if it was honest, the press would have said what I said was very nice. . . . unlike the media, before I make a statement I like to know the facts." Minutes later, Trump became more combative when asked whether he thought the alt-right was behind the attacks, "what about the alt-left who came charging at the, as you say, alt-right. Do they have any semblance of guilt?" After reiterating that there were two sides at equal fault for the violence, he added, "Not all those people were neo-Nazis, believe me. Not all those people were white supremacists, by any stretch. Those people were also there because they wanted to protest the taking down of the statue of Robert E. Lee. . . . I noticed that Stonewall Jackson is coming down. I wonder if it is George Washington next week and if it is Thomas Jefferson the week after?" With these words, the president echoed statements by the Neo-Confederate League of the South, which called the disappearance of the Confederate statues in New Orleans "ISIS-Style Cultural Genocide."[27] He also used the First Amendment to defend white nationalists, while the Justice Department seeks to identify anti-Trump protesters on Inauguration Day. These threats against the press and the public by the state are focused on anyone whom President Trump views an opponent, optics that shift according to his mood and which rarely reflect on his "base"—white, working-class men who love God, guns, and country.

In his sociological study of "American masculinity at the end of an era," Michael Kimmel argues, "white men's anger comes from the potent fusion of two sentiments—entitlement and a sense of victimization."[28] By this rationale, Trump's election shows that the righteous rage fueling anti-Washington populism is driven by "aggrieved entitlement," or "that sense that those benefits to which you believed yourself entitled have been snatched away from you by unseen forces larger and more powerful."[29] The white men Kimmel spoke with shared sentiments rather than a worldview, which leads him to surmise, "Populism is not a theory [or] an ideology, it's an emotion. And the emotion is righteous indignation that the government is screwing 'us'"[30] While his conceptualization of aggrieved entitlement is convincing, Kimmel's analysis stays moored in exploring the hegemonic notions held by white men and women about their victimhood, the American dream, and what it means to be a real man. He takes a nonjudgmental stance with relation to white men's rage because "It's hard to tell anyone that their feelings are wrong. Their feelings are *real* . . . but at the same time, their feelings may not be *true*—they may not provide an accurate assessment of their situation."[31] By figuring emotion as a right of ownership, Kimmel validates white men's anger despite declarations otherwise. His map of social relations feeds paranoia by reiterating the (white) individual and (multicultural feminist) society as oppositional. Literary scholar Timothy Melley calls the effects of this form of paranoia "agency panic" and contends that conspiracy theories are "self-protection," the "attempt to defend the integrity of the self against the social order."[32] Trump and Alex Jones use social media to stoke and spread conspiracy theories that thrive and capitalize on the agency panic of white men; however, paranoia is also animated in the networking process *of* social media so that it is not strictly attributable to, or generated by, them.

"FAKE NEWS" AND THE AFFECTIVE NETWORKING OF PARANOIA

"The Intel on this wasn't 100 percent," Edgar Welch stated a few days after his arrest, "I just wanted to do some good and went about it the wrong way."[33] Rumors by word of mouth became incontrovertible facts once he installed Internet service at home and began to self-investigate Pizzagate online. As one report linked to several more, details from a combination of sources left him with the "impression something nefarious was happening."[34] Despite landing in jail as a result of following this conspiracy to its unfounded conclusion, Welch remained unconvinced that it was "fake news" and stated that he did not like this term because it served to validate the "mainstream media," which he did not trust.[35] He was far from alone in being suspicious of the press after so many pundits wrongly predicted the outcome of the 2016 election.

However, Facebook also received criticism for proliferating anti-Clinton conspiracy theories in the form of news. The day after the election, Mark Zuckerberg responded in a Facebook post, "Our goal is to give every person a voice. We believe deeply in people. . . . Assuming that people understand what is important in their lives and that they can express those views has driven not only our community, but democracy overall. . . . Of all the content on Facebook, more than 99% of what people see is authentic. Only a very small amount is fake news. . . . our goal is to show people the content they will find most meaningful, and people want accurate news."[36] What Zuckerberg assumes is better posed as a question: Do people want accurate news? There is evidence to the contrary.

InfoWars had ten million unique viewers during its "coverage" of Pizzagate from November to December 2016, more hits than the *National Review* and Rush Limbaugh's site.[37] After the shooting, Jones and many alt-right talking heads, bloggers, and even government officials, maintained that Pizzagate was real. Finally, in March 2017, in lieu of a lawsuit threatened by Alefantis, Jones issued a public apology in which he admitted that none of what he had conjectured regarding Comet Ping Pong was true. However, this admission did not stop a group of fifty to sixty protestors, several of whom had endured or witnessed sexual abuse, from rallying outside the White House to call for an official investigation. One fifty-five-year-old woman wearing a pink T-shirt with the words "Ephesians 6:12," a reference to scripture that speaks to a struggle "against the powers of this dark world and against the spiritual forces of evil," drove eight hours from Michigan with her family and told a reporter, "Pedogate is a spiritual darkness."[38] Throughout his "reporting" on Pizzagate, Jones gave political voice to such Manichean-millennial visions by pitting good versus evil in an apocalyptic tenor. In these *InfoWars* segments, Jones perpetually stressed that Pizzagate was real and urged viewers to investigate the evidence on WikiLeaks and *InfoWars* themselves—a "rabbit hole that is horrifying to go down." He admonished viewers, "it's up to you to research this yourself, you gotta go to InfoWars.com and actually see the photos and videos inside these places. . . . something needs to be investigated, you just call it fake news, these are real WikiLeaks, real stuff going on."

Social media incites users to circulate information as a form of entertainment in ways that undermine Zuckerberg's vision of such networks as democratizing public squares. Political scientist Jodi Dean calls the enjoyment of contributing and sharing online content "affective networks," "feedback loops, the circuits of drive, entrapping contemporary subjects"[39] Dean critiques Zuckerberg's statement on fake news as she discusses how Twitter and Facebook feed "communicative capitalism," which is an "inescapable circuit" that materializes democratic ideals "in the contemporary information and entertainment networks necessary for globalized neoliberalism."[40] Social media generates and amplifies affect to the extent that "people *enjoy* the circulation of affect that presents itself as contemporary communication."[41] Subsequently, the enjoyment of participating in an affective network is a "binding technique" that intensifies through reflexive communication—adding comments, links, and interconnecting myriad platforms, people, and devices.[42] Rather than finding accurate news meaningful, Facebook users find the affective pleasure of connectivity addictive, whether or not the information they share is factual, and that is how communicative capitalism captivates subjects as it holds them captive.

In her analysis, Dean assumes the neoliberal subject is intact but ensnared by the affective networks that bolster communicative capitalism. She writes, "Every little tweet or comment, every forwarded image or petition, accrues a tiny affective nugget, a little surplus enjoyment, a smidgen of attention that attaches to it, making it stand out from the larger flow before it blends back in."[43] In her argument, the individual is subjugated by a stable technical system; affective networks are closed structures that breed engagement and feed capitalism out of self-interest. However, there is evidence that surplus affect overrides individual human agents and reveals the myth of self-contained subjectivity. The affective networking of paranoia *as* social media bodily mobilizes white men to commit singular acts of terror that belie logics of self-interest, such as shooting a gun at nothing and speeding a car into a crowd for no reason. Rather than hate, fear, anger, or enjoyment, paranoia is without a subject or an object—it is an affective network that has no visible expression such as rage, and as such it is more difficult to index, claim, disassociate from, and transpose.

The way that Trump's mood was monitored and modulated by campaign staff to curb his compulsive tweeting demonstrates how processes of digital communication affectively network paranoia without a user plugging in. Six former campaign officials said that the "key to keeping Trump's Twitter habit under control" was "to ensure that his personal media consumption include[d] a steady stream of praise."[44] When there was no positive reinforcement to be found, "staff would turn to friendly outlets to drum some up . . . using alternative media like Breitbart, Washington Examiner, Fox News, InfoWars and the Daily Caller to show Trump positive coverage."[45] While Trump was effectively validated and affectively stroked by the aggregation of such admiration from online sources, this process was meant to hinder, not further, his voice on social media. Instead of feeding a technical system such as communicative capitalism, this online curation technique networked paranoia as affective capital offline to interrupt it. The only "real" news was political endorsement so that paranoia intensified through the bodily networking of information without knowledge. There is no man in this machine or subject of this network, only the circulation of paranoia as social media.

People and machines have demonstrated that they cannot be as trusted as Zuckerberg thinks when it comes to caring about, and sharing, accurate news. In the aftermath of the 2016 election and criticism for Facebook's role in spreading misinformation, the company evaluated its options for determining real from fake news. These possibilities included editing by trained professionals before information enters the news stream, crowdsourced vetting to democratize the process of evaluation, and algorithmic vetting, which was the technique that Facebook initially preferred. However, this system failed to identify and downgrade hoaxes or distinguish satire from real stories, proliferating fake news soon after it was implemented.[46]

Even when Facebook used a human fact-checking system, it failed. When a *Newport Buzz* article was flagged as possible "fake news," traffic to the story accelerated. Conservatives took the warning as a sign that news important to them was about to be censored, so they began to share the story that falsely claimed hundreds of thousands of Irish people were brought to the United States as slaves.[47] Jestin Coler, a writer known for the fake news that he published in 2016, said that it was difficult to imagine this system effectively working. "These stories are like flash grenades," he stated, "They go off and explode for a day."[48] Such commentary signals the affective value of fake news, as it inflames and networks paranoia without belief.

On December 5, 2015, Trump appeared on *InfoWars* for a mutually congratulatory meeting during which the future president commented on Jones's "amazing reputation" and told him, "I will not let you down." During his campaign, Trump showed his admiration for Jones's media savvy by amplifying his conspiracies. *InfoWars* marketed the "Hillary for Prison" T-shirts spied so often on Trump's campaign trail, where "Lock Her Up" became a rally cry.[49] Trump capitalized on an *InfoWars* headline that announced "Three Million Votes in Presidential Election Cast By Illegal Aliens" to claim that he would have won the popular vote if those ballots were disqualified.[50] He has also retweeted *InfoWars* fake news reports, including in 2015 the fallacy that "thousands" of Muslims in New Jersey celebrated the 9/11 attacks.[51]

Media coverage of national tragedies such as the attacks on 9/11 serve to promote not only conspiracy theories by the likes of Jones but also the notion that the United States is exceptional—the only free nation equipped to combat evil during an endless war on terror and prolonged end times on earth. Over the years, Jones has used traumatic events considered national tragedies to spin conspiracy theories. He calls these terrorist acts "false flag" attacks staged by the government to curtail citizens' freedom—the 1995 Oklahoma City bombing; the 2013 Boston Marathon bombing; the 2015 San Bernadino shooting; and the 2012 Sandy Hook Elementary School massacre, which Jones proclaimed a hoax fabricated by gun control advocates. The parents of the children murdered continue to endure harassment over Jones's declaration that rather than real, their children were "crisis actors" playing roles. Jones used a similar narrative with relation to the violence in Charlottesville—one InfoWars video headline declared, "Virginia Riots Staged To Bring In Martial Law, Ban Conservative Gatherings."[52] In a later "report," he would claim that Ku Klux Klan demonstrators, in his experience, are actually Jewish actors.[53]

Jones has also proliferated conspiracies concerning the "feminization of men," such as chemicals in drinking water that can change the sex of babies in utero.[54] This *InfoWars* story suggested that the filtering of water as much as possible was necessary to defend against this feminizing contaminate. Conveniently, on the *InfoWars* website Jones's audience can buy the "Alexpure Pro Water Filtration System" for a mere $147.75, nearly twelve times the price of the cheapest Brita water filter. To further combat feminization, men can purchase Caveman True Paleo Formula, a "bone broth" that is advertised as "A Return to Ancient Traditions and Practices" when "man roamed the Earth in a constant state of hunting and being hunted."[55]

This masculinist paranoia furthers the Islamophobia in the "church militant" strain of Catholicism proffered by former White House chief strategist and executive chairman of Breitbart News Stephen Bannon, who calls on Christians to battle against a "new barbarity" of "Islamic fascism."[56] In turn, Christians are told by Vice President Mike Pence that "their faith is the most persecuted" in the world.[57] Concurrently, the conviction that Christians are under assault in America is validated by President Trump, who calls them "targeted, bullied [and] silenced."[58] This claim is reflected in state policy, such as an executive order on religious liberty aimed to increase the political influence of churches while preserving their tax-exempt status, and proposed travel restrictions on refugees that privileged Christians over Muslims.

Wendy Chun writes, "Fiber-optic networks spread the light and conflate message with medium, so that we no longer see the light through our glass tubes. What we do see via, if not through them, seems delusional and hallucinatory, supposedly consensually so. Although we do not mistake personal hallucination for reality, developers hope that one day everyone, not just paranoid schizophrenics, will be unable to distinguish between pictured humans and real ones."[59] Perhaps Welch's gunfire is evidence of the developers' success. Facebook increasingly evaluates and rewards users based on the ambient metrics of authenticity.[60] Negative feedback, such as people unliking your page or hiding your posts, qualifies for authenticity demerits. Positive feedback, in the form of comments, likes, or reactions (via emoji), earn authenticity points.[61] The reactions are more heavily weighted than likes, presumably because they require more time and demonstrate further engagement, but this interactive approach to registering individual mood also modulates and measures social sentiment, signaling a distinct visceral value in the networking process.

Despite ovations to the contrary by Zuckerberg, the goal of Facebook is not to give every person a voice, but to rank voices based on algorithms. The agency panic generated in this instance is not one organized through logics of self-protection, but human exceptionalism. Meanwhile, Trump's Twitter feed is a daily source of news for people who have no interest in following him on social media. His tweets litter *New York Times* articles online, for example, where facts used to be. Readers of the "mainstream" or "liberal" media are regularly confronted by the president's tweets, which are often outrageous and threatening in tone and content, feeding spectacle and amplifying terror.[62] This evidence suggests that, rather than countering violent extremism by focusing on violent ideologies, counter-terrorism efforts would be better served by attuning to violent intensities.

In June 2017, researchers from the Facebook AI Research Lab (FAIR) discovered that chatbots, or "dialogue agents," were creating their own language. The bots queered scripted norms and spoke on their own terms. Using machine-learning algorithms, the dialogue agents strengthened their conversational skills to become what developers called "incredibly crafty negotiators."[63] Conspiracy theories proliferate online due to an agency panic that is built into the social process of human and nonhuman communication. Facebook is not the democratic public square that Zuckerberg imagines; nor does the Internet simply thrive on control and the illusion of freedom to circulate affect in support of capitalism. Instead of thinking of these technologies as systems or tools, we need to consider them as affective networking processes that demand vulnerability, because political life is not lived in a moral universe of good and evil.

NOTES

This essay was originally published as "The Self-Radicalization of White Men: "Fake News" and the Affective Networking of Paranoia" in *Communication Culture & Critique* 11, no. 1 (2018): 100–115.

1. Adam Goldberg, "The Comet Ping Pong Gunman Answers Our Reporter's Questions," *New York Times*, December 7, 2016, www.nytimes.com/2016/12/07/us/edgar-welch-comet-pizza-fake-news.html.

2. Geoffrey Kabaservice, "The Great Performance of Our Failing President," *New York Times*, June 9, 2017, www.nytimes.com/2017/06/09/opinion/great-performance-of-donald-trump-our-failinng-president.html.

3. Kabaservice, "The Great Performance."

4. Jack Z. Bratich, *Conspiracy Panics: Political Rationality and Popular Culture* (Albany: State University of New York Press, 2008); Mark Fenster, *Conspiracy Theories: Secrecy and Power in American Culture* (Minneapolis: University of Minnesota Press, 2008); Peter Knight, *Conspiracy Nation: The Politics of Paranoia in Postwar America* (New York: New York University Press, 2002).

5. Cristina López G. "Paid Actors, a Fake Publicist, and Retweeted Bots, How Trump Creates His Own Reality," *AlterNet,* August 22, 2017, www.alternet.org/media/paid-actors-fake-publicist-and-retweeted-bots-how-trump-creates-his-own-alternate-reality.

6. Bruno Latour, "To Modernize or to Ecologize? That's the Question . . . ," *Remaking Reality: Nature at the Millennium* (New York: Routledge, 1998), 220–41.

7. Bruno Latour, "On Actor-Network Theory: A Few Clarifications." *Soziale Welt* (1996): 2.

8. Latour, "To Modernize or to Ecologize?" 7.

9. Latour, "To Modernize or to Ecologize?" 14.

10. Latour, "To Modernize or to Ecologize?" 14.

11. Sara Ahmed, "Affective Economies," *Social Text* 22, no. 2 (2004): pp. 117–39., doi:10.1215/01642472–22–2_79–117. 117.

12. Ahmed, "Affective Economies."

13. Ahmed, "Affective Economies," 119, emphasis in original.

14. Goldberg, "Comet Ping Pong."

15. Ahmed, "Affective Economies," 118.

16. Sophia Abramowitz, Eva Latterner, and Gillet Rosenblith, "Tools of Displacement: How Charlottesville, Virginia's Confederate Statues Helped Decimate the City's Historically Successful Black Communities," *Slate,* June 23, 2017, slate.com/news-and-politics/2017/06/how-charlottesvilles-confederate-statues-helped-decimate-the-citys-historically-successful-black-communities.html.

17. Ahmed, "Affective Economies," 118.

18. Wendy Hui Kyong Chun, *Control and Freedom: Power and Paranoia in the Age of Fiber Optics* (Cambridge, MA: MIT Press, 2006).

19. Chun, *Control and Freedom* vii.

20. Chun, *Control and Freedom* vii.

21. Chun, *Control and Freedom* vii.

22. Lizette Alvarez and Richard Pérez-Peña, "Orlando Gunman Attacks Gay Nightclub, Leaving 50 Dead," *New York Times,* June 13, 2016, www.nytimes.com/2016/06/13/us/orlando-nightclub-shooting.html.

23. Hillary Hanson, "Ex-KKK Leader David Duke Says White Supremacists Will 'Fulfill' Trump's Promises," *Huffington Post,* August 12, 2017, www.huffpost.com/entry/david-duke-charlottesville-rally-trump_n_598f3ca8e4b0909642974a10.

24. Matt Stevens, "After Charlottesville, Even Dating Apps Are Cracking Down on Hate," *New York Times,* August 24, 2017, www.nytimes.com/2017/08/24/technology/okcupid-christopher-cantwell.html.

25. Tim Squirrell, "Linguistic Data Analysis of 3 Billion Reddit Comments Shows the Alt-right Is Getting Stronger," *Quartz,* August 12, 2018, qz.com/1056319/what-is-the-alt-right-a-linguistic-data-analysis-of-3-billionreddi.

26. Dominique Mosenbergen, "Neo-Nazi Site Daily Stormer Praises Trump's Charlottesville Reaction: He Loves Us All," *Huffington Post,* August 13, 2018, www.huffpost.com/entry/neo-nazi-daily -stormer-trump-charlottesville_n_59905c7ee4b08a2472750701.

27. Hunter Wallace, "ISIS-style Cultural Genocide Happening in Dixie," *Occidental Dissent,* June 23, 2015, www.occidentaldissent.com/2015/06/23/isis-style-cultural-genocide-unfolding-in-dixie/.

28. Michael S. Kimmel, *Angry White Men: American Masculinity at the End of an Era* (New York: Bold Type Books, 2019), x.

29. Kimmel, *Angry White Men,* x.

30. Kimmel, *Angry White Men,* xi.

31. Kimmel, *Angry White Men,* x, emphasis in original.

32. Timothy Melley, *Empire of Conspiracy: The Culture of Paranoia in Postwar America* (Ithaca, NY: Cornell University Press, 2000), 60.

33. Goldberg, "Comet Ping Pong."

34. Goldberg, "Comet Ping Pong."

35. Goldberg, "Comet Ping Pong."

36. Mark Zuckerberg, Facebook status, November 12, 2016, www.facebook.com/zuck/posts /10103253901916271.

37. Zack Beauchamp, "Alex Jones, Pizzagate Booster and America's Most Famous Conspiracy Theorist, Explained," *Vox,* October 28, 2016, www.vox.com/policy-and-politics/2016/10/28/13424848 /alex-jones-infowars-prisonplanet.

38. Michael E. Miller, "Protestors outside White House Demand 'Pizzagate' Investigation," *Washington Post,* March 25, 2017, www.washingtonpost.com/news/local/wp/2017/03/25/protesters-outside -white-house-demand-pizzagate-investigation/?utm_term=.1439d7a89221.

39. Jodi Dean, "Affective Networks," *Media Tropes* 2 (February 25, 2010): 19–44, mediatropes .com/index.php/Mediatropes/article/view/11932.

40. Dean, "Affective Networks," 21.

41. Dean, "Affective Networks," 21.

42. Dean, "Affective Networks," 21.

43. Dean, "Affective Networks," 21.

44. Eric Hananoki, "A Guide to Donald Trump's Relationship to Alex Jones," *Media Matters,* May 3, 2017, www.mediamatters.org/research/2017/05/03/guide-donald-trump-s-relationship-alex -jones/216263.

45. Hananoki, "A Guide to Donald Trump's Relationship."

46. Nicky Woolfe, "How to Solve Facebook's Fake News Problem: Experts Pitch Their Ideas," *Guardian,* November 29, 2016, www.theguardian.com/technology/2016/nov/29/facebook-fake-news -problem-experts-pitch-ideas-algorithms.

47. Sam Levin, "Facebook Promised to Tackle Fake News. But the Evidence Shows It's Not Working," *Guardian,* May 16, 2017, www.theguardian.com/technology/2017/may/16/facebook-fake-news-tools -not-working.

48. Levin, "Facebook Promised to Tackle Fake News."

49. Hananoki, "A Guide to Donald Trump's Relationship

50. Hananoki, "A Guide to Donald Trump's Relationship

51. Hananoki, "A Guide to Donald Trump's Relationship

52. Alex Jones, "Virginia Riots Staged To Bring In Martial Law, Ban Conservative Gatherings," *InfoWars,* 2017, www.infowars.com/exclusive-virginia-riots-staged-to-bring-in-martial-law-ban -conservative-gatherings/

53. Ron Dicker, "Alex Jones Claims Many KKK Demonstrators Are 'Just Jewish Actors,'" *Huffington Post,* August 15, 2017, www.huffpost.com/entry/alex-jones-kkk-jewish-actors_n_5992e811e4 b090964299c98b.

54. F. Miller, "Chemicals in Drinking Water Linked to the Feminization of Men," *InfoWars,* 2017, www.infowars.com/chemicals-in-drinking-water-linked-to-feminizationof-men/

55. InfoWars Store, *InfoWars,* August 18, 2017, www.infowarsstore.com/caveman-paleo-formula .html.

56. Samuel G. Freedman, "'Church Militant' Theology Is Put to New, and Politicized, Use," *New York Times,* December 30, 2016, www.nytimes.com/2016/12/30/us/church-militant-theology-is-put -to-new-and-politicized-use.html.

57. Antonia Blumberg, "Pence Tells Room Full of Christians in D.C. Their Faith Is the Most Persecuted," *Huffington Post,* May 11, 2017, www.huffpost.com/entry/pence-tells-room-full-of-christians -in-dc-their-faith-is-the-most-persecuted_n_59149198e4b030d4f1fobdcd.

58. Blumberg, "Pence Tells Room Full of Christians."

59. Chun, *Control and Freedom,* 299.

60. Jeraldine Phnaeh, "3 Important Updates to Facebook Algorithm in January 2017," *Socialbakers,* February 1, 2017, www.facebook.com/notes/socialbakers/3-important-updates-to-facebook -algorithm-in-january-2017/10155032524044744/

61. Paul Ramonda, "The Facebook Algorithm Demystified: How to Optimize for News Feed Exposure," *Social Media Examiner,* May 31, 2017, www.socialmediaexaminer.com/facebook-algorithm -demystified-how-to-optimize-for-news-feed-exposure/.

62. For example, this news article on Trump's proposed banning of transgender people in the military, "Trump Says Transgender People Will Not Be Allowed In the Military," Julie Hirschfield Davis and Helene Cooper, *New York Times,* July 26, 2017, www.nytimes.com/2017/07/26/us/politics /trump-transgender-military.html. Or the news coverage of verbal threats and insults traded with North Korean leader Kim Jong-un that suggest President Trump is ready and willing to engage in a nuclear war.

63. Indo-Asian News Service, "Facebook Shuts Down AI System After Bots Create Language Humans Can't Understand," *Gadgets 360,* July 31, 2017, gadgets.ndtv.com/social-networking/news /facebook-shuts-ai-system-after-bots-create-own-language-1731309.

CONCLUSION

Josh Grimm

As we've seen throughout this reader—particularly in the final section—the future of fake news is more about trying to contain the damage rather than stopping the problem. In other words, it's about mitigating damage and slowing down the distribution, if nothing else so the fake news feed becomes manageable. When it comes to distribution, social media outlets remain the main culprits. It's easy to see why, given the speed at which a fake news piece can spread. As the famous quotation attributed to Mark Twain put it, "A lie can travel halfway around the world while the truth is putting on its shoes."

And this quote is more than a folksy aphorism. A study by Vosoughi, Roy, and Aral found real people (not bots) on social media sites spread fake news faster than the truth.[1] The researchers found that "tweets containing falsehoods reach 1500 people on Twitter six times faster than truthful tweets,"[2] and that the top 1 percent of fake news stories reached between 1,000 and 100,000 people, while "the truth rarely diffused to more than 1000 people."[3]

The scope of fake news is expanded dramatically on social media because fake news demands interaction. Fake stories "thrive on Facebook because Facebook's algorithm prioritizes 'engagement'—and a reliable way to get readers to engage is by making up outrageous nonsense about politicians they don't like."[4] However, there's really no incentive—apart from a moral and ethical obligation to the fabric of truth in this country—for these social media outlets to do anything. From a financial standpoint, this content increases engagement, which increases traffic, which is the whole point of these networks in the first place. And even when it seems like the leadership in these social media outlets are doing the so-called right thing, the permanence of the solutions is fleeting. For example, a Bloomberg news article published in late November 2018 noted: "Two months ago, Facebook showed off a 'War Room' that brought employees from different teams together to quickly spot and fix issues like misinformation during the U.S. midterm elections. At the time, the company said the War Room might be deployed for future elections. But it's been disbanded. Facebook says it was never intended to be permanent, and the company is still assessing what is needed for future elections."[5]

Trust that social media will correct the problem is further eroded by the fact that shockingly little has been done to rectify the problem over time. A massive study conducted by the Knight Foundation analyzed "10 million tweets from 700,000 Twitter accounts that linked to more than 600 fake and conspiracy news outlets."[6] Roughly 6.6 million tweets were found to have linked to fake news publishers in the month leading up to the 2016 election. Studying a thirty-day period from mid-March to mid-April 2017, the researchers found the problem persisted, with 4 million tweets linking to fake news stories.[7] "Contrary to claims that fake news is a game of 'whack-a-mole,' more than 80 percent of the disinformation accounts in our election maps are still active as this report goes to press. These accounts continue to publish more than a million tweets in a typical day."[8]

The problem very clearly persists. However, while focus on finding out how to hold social media giants like Facebook and Twitter accountable is important, the role of the audience cannot be ignored, which is where media literacy can play a key role. Media literacy campaigns can be effective; for example, campaigns centered on increasing awareness of the dangers of melanoma have shown to be capable of reducing the likelihood of indoor tanning.[9] However, relatively few people have built their identities around tanning salons, and so attitudes have some room to grow and adjust. This is why the effectiveness of media literacy programs can be hit-or-miss. When Stony Brook's Center for News Literacy conducted a study testing this, researchers found slightly more students could "better assess the reliability of information and the fairness of evidence after a news literacy course compared to those who did not take the course." Moreover, after one year, over 25 percent were less likely to make that distinction. This is further complicated by the fact that students who did not take a course on media literacy were actually *more* likely to correctly identify a reliable source a year after they were first tested, "meaning they become in a sense more news literate over time than students who took the course." Stanford professor Sam Wineburg argues it's because the curriculums of media literacy courses are simply outmatched when it comes to the pervasiveness of media consumption:

> The approaches that are being bandied about are doomed to fail. We are in a freaking revolution. We bank differently. We date differently. We shop differently. We choose a Chinese restaurant differently. We do our research differently. We figure out what plumber to come to our house differently. But school is stuck in the past. What we need to do is . . . think hard about what the school curriculum really needs to look like in an age when we come to know the world through a screen.[10]

One approach that might be assisting this inconsistency is the dreaded checklist. Facebook actually dabbled with offering advice in list form on how to fix fake news, though the company pointedly referred to the phenomenon as "false news" so as not to stub its toe politically.[11] Now, while some people might argue this is akin to an arsonist giving fire-prevention tips, it's worth looking at Facebook's suggestions, which I quote here in full because these are pretty standard:

1. Be skeptical of headlines. False news stories often have catchy headlines in all caps with exclamation points. If shocking claims in the headline sound unbelievable, they probably are.

2. Look closely at the link. A phony or look-alike link may be a warning sign of false news. Many false news sites mimic authentic news sources by making small changes to the link. You can go to the site to compare the link to established sources.

3. Investigate the source. Ensure that the story is written by a source that you trust with a reputation for accuracy. If the story comes from an unfamiliar organization, check their "About" section to learn more.

4. Watch for unusual formatting. Many false news sites have misspellings or awkward layouts. Read carefully if you see these signs.

5. Consider the photos. False news stories often contain manipulated images or videos. Sometimes the photo may be authentic, but taken out of context. You can search for the photo or image to verify where it came from.

6. Inspect the dates. False news stories may contain timelines that make no sense, or event dates that have been altered.

7. Check the evidence. Check the author's sources to confirm that they are accurate. Lack of evidence or reliance on unnamed experts may indicate a false news story.

8. Look at other reports. If no other news source is reporting the same story, it may indicate that the story is false. If the story is reported by multiple sources you trust, it's more likely to be true.

9. Is the story a joke? Sometimes false news stories can be hard to distinguish from humor or satire. Check whether the source is known for parody, and whether the story's details and tone suggest it may be just for fun.

10. Some stories are intentionally false. Think critically about the stories you read, and only share news that you know to be credible.[12]

And this is where the task of media literacy becomes a daunting one. On its face, it seems generally sound advice, but the issue isn't the content; the problem is with the checklist format itself. According to Breakstone and colleagues,[13] the Stanford team of researchers who revealed the startling number of US students who were unable to determine fake news (discussed in this volume's introduction) argue vehemently against checklists like these to debunk fake news sites. They explain that these lists may have been useful "when students accessed the internet using a dial-up modem"; however, "they are less effective in an age when anyone can publish a sleek website with a $25 template."[14] When observing fact-checkers in prestigious newsrooms, instead of approaching stories vertically (staying on a single page to look for inconsistencies as most checklists advocate), fact-checkers almost instantaneously left the site and read *laterally*—opening up new browser tabs and searching across the web to see what they could find about the trustworthiness of the source of information."[15] This runs counter to what the checklist approach suggests, and it more closely matches how the average audience member consumes news.

The other problem with checklists is that they're a lot of work. Facebook's list is pretty consistent with what other outlets are warning about; similar lists range from six to thirty items to establish the reliability of a potential fake news source. Those lists are not only exhaustive but they're *exhausting*, particularly for media users. On average, US adults spend over half of their day consuming media of some kind.[16] Adults ages twenty-one to thirty-seven consume news at about a third the rate of adults thirty-eight and older, with the latter group spending over thirty thousand minutes a year following the news (about eighty-two minutes a day).[17] Companies like Facebook are asking the average news consumer to spend an additional chunk of their day running down a ten-point checklist to determine if a news story is true. Given that the average time spent on a single article measures (at most) in the minutes, this is asking for a significant behavioral change. Frankly, as Breakstone and colleagues explain, "it's unrealistic to believe that kids (or any of us, for that matter) will have the patience to go through long lists of questions for every unfamiliar site they encounter."

From the point of view of the audience member, this is not only a significant time commitment (in comparison to the amount of time they normally spend on news), but it also doesn't have a great payoff. Assuming you take the checklist approach, the best-case scenario is that you find what you thought was true actually was true; the end goal is stasis. However, you could just as easily discover that a hilarious viral sensation was a prank or, much more likely (and disappointing), that an article that reinforced what you already believed was actually not true. This strategy asks consumers to take something they enjoy and exercise due diligence in a time-consuming effort to potentially remove that feeling of gratification. You might as well ask kindergartners to conduct a lengthy, in-depth investigation of whether Santa Claus exists.

This is especially true when placing this all in a political context. It's not just that people are appreciating a doctored video or embellished celebrity gossip— these stories are propping up fundamental beliefs about how the world works, how to vote, and whom to support, befriend, or even date. And ignoring the role of politics in the world of fake news can be particularly detrimental, as conflating incorrect information with information you find challenging to your worldview cannot be treated as the same problem: "It's possible—and essential—to delineate between errors made in the course of actual reporting and people or entities who consciously lie for profit and propaganda. Yet, today, *any* form of media mistake is weaponized, with willful fabrications treated the same as sloppy errors."[18]

Again, this is challenging. YoChai Benkler, the Berkman Professor of Entrepreneurial Legal Studies at Harvard Law School, noted that conservative audiences in the United States focus on right-wing news outlets, whereas audiences at the center and left sides of the political spectrum place more emphasis on mainstream organizations.[19] Benkler explains that those on the left are "exposed to a range of media outlets, many of which operate with strong fact-checking norms." However, it's a different story for conservative news audiences:

> On the right, because audiences do not trust or pay attention to outlets outside their own ecosystem, there is no reality check to constrain competition. Outlets compete on political purity and stoking identity-confirming narratives. Outlets and politicians who resist the flow by focusing on facts are abandoned or vilified by audiences and competing outlets. This forces media and political elites to validate and legitimate the falsehoods, at least through silence, creating a propaganda feedback loop.[20]

Combating this feedback loop is a challenge, but perhaps not the insurmountable one that so many assume. While no single approach has shown to be foolproof, adopting multiple tactics should be able to make an impact. First, individuals and organizations must continue to utilize technology, collaborating with engineers to construct algorithms that can identify stories that originate from sites and sources known to produce fake news content. The ubiquity of fake news necessitates a sophisticated system of weeding out that which is easily identifiable, lessening the burden on human intervention while raising the possibility of adoption of such technology by news and social media outlets.

Second, media literacy training *must* adapt to match the sophistication of fake news that audiences are encountering online. To the researchers, teachers, professors, and well-meaning organizations (I'm staring at you, Facebook), ditch the lists. Checklists are not going to be as effective as meaningful, horizontal training in identifying false news stories, all of which needs to be built around an understanding of the media consumption habits of the average consumer. As part of media literacy course development, administrators and instructors must also be prepared for backlash. An important part of this will be understanding that the term "fake news" is radioactive; coordinated, targeted campaigns by conservative organizations seeking to generate controversy must not only be anticipated but also counteracted. As Mihailidis and Viotty explain in a recent article in *American Behavioral Scientist*:

> Media literacy as a movement has been constrained by a need to be apolitical. Much has been made about the need to teach about media's role in society, and specifically about potentially harmful messages. These low-hanging fruits for media literacy, while relevant, perpetuate a frame of reference that sees problems as structural. Media literacy must focus on civic impact: The ways in which media can be used to impact, at realistic scale, the political, social, and cultural issues that define our democracy.[21]

And finally, the journalists themselves must continue to speak up, as it might have more of an impact than they realize. Journalists' practices, particularly through the lens of objectivity, are an important consideration in combating accusations of fake news. However, journalists might need to consider another role as well: advocates for their profession. In a groundbreaking study, researchers from Louisiana State University recently found that journalists defending journalism can potentially increase trust in the press. This was an experiment conducted within an online news portal, and the researchers acknowledge that "the positive effects of defense of journalism found here would not generalize to the real world because defense of journalism would lead to additional anti-media rhetoric." However, they ultimately conclude that, "At least in terms of the outcomes studied here, our results contradict the claim that the most effective response is to ignore anti-media rhetoric and just do good journalism."

The creation, distribution, and consumption of fake news must all be considered when attempting to figure out how to best combat the issue. Hopefully, a book like this one provides the context, evidence, arguments, and potential solutions to help in that fight. An October 2018 survey found that 57 percent of respondents reported seeing fake news during the 2018 midterm election campaign, and 42 percent of respondents said they felt there was more fake news than in the 2016 election.[22] As the issue persists, a variety of researchers are examining potential ways for the journalism industry and general audiences to combat this scourge. Ideally, through a combination of audience outreach, institutional intervention, improved technology and strategies, and potentially the passage and enforcement of legislation targeting the creators of particularly egregious content, a solution can be found. Until then, remember the words of Dr. Turk—"on the Internet, every day is April Fool's Day"[23]—and act accordingly.

NOTES

1. Katie Langin, "Fake News Spreads Faster than True News on Twitter—Thanks to People, Not Bots," *Science Magazine,* March 8, 2018, www.sciencemag.org/news/2018/03/fake-news-spreads-faster-true-news-twitter-thanks-people-not-bots.

2. Langin, "Fake News Spreads."

3. Soroush Vosoughi, Deb Roy, and Sinan Aral, "The spread of true and false news online," *Science* 359, no. 6380 (2018): 1146–51.

4. German Lopez, "Pizzagate, the Fake News Conspiracy that Led a Gunman to DC's Comet Ping Pong, Explained, *Vox,* December 8, 2016, www.vox.com/policy-and-politics/2016/12/5/13842258/pizzagate-comet-ping-pong-fake-news.

5. Sarah Frier, "Facebook's Sheryl Sandberg Is Tainted by Crisis after Crisis," *Bloomberg Media,* November 26, 2018, www.bloomberg.com/news/articles/2018-11-26/facebook-s-sheryl-sandberg-is-tainted-by-crisis-after-crisis.

6. K. Barash and M. Hindman, *Disinformation, "Fake News" and Influence Campaigns on Twitter* (Knight Foundation, 2018), www.knightfoundation.org/reports/disinformation-fake-news-and-influence-campaigns-on-twitter.

7. Barash and Hindman, *Disinformation.*

8. Barash and Hindman, *Disinformation.*

9. Hyunyi Cho, Bing Yu, Julie Cannon, and Yu Michael Zhu, "Efficacy of a Media Literacy Intervention for Indoor Tanning Prevention," *Journal of Health Communication* 23, no. 7 (2018): 643–51.

10. John Dyer, "Can News Literacy Be Taught?" *Nieman Reports,* April 14, 2017, niemanreports.org/articles/can-news-literacy-be-taught/.

11. "Tips to Stop False News," www.facebook.com/help/188118808357379.

12. "Tips to Stop False News."

13. Joel Breakstone, Sarah McGrew, Mark Smith, Teresa Ortega, and Sam Wineburg, "Why we need a new approach to teaching digital literacy," *Phi Delta Kappan* 99, no. 6 (2018): 27–32.

14. Breakstone et al., "Why we need a new approach," 30.

15. Breakstone et al., "Why we need a new approach," 30.

16. "Time Flies: U.S. Adults Now Spend Nearly Half a Day Interacting with Media," *Nielsen,* July 31, 2018, www.nielsen.com/us/en/insights/news/2018/time-flies-us-adults-now-spend-nearly-half-a-day-interacting-with-media.html.

17. Audrey Schomer, "News Consumption Habits Are Trending Digital," *Business Insider,* September 12, 2018, www.businessinsider.com/pew-nielsen-survey-news-consumption-trends -digital-2018–9.

18. Craig Silverman, "I Helped Popularize the Term 'Fake News' and Now I Cringe Every Time I Hear It," *BuzzFeed News,* December 31, 2017, www.buzzfeednews.com/article/craigsilverman/i-helped -popularize-the-term-fake-news-and-now-i-cringe#.vxGRxZNyoA.

19. Henry Farrell, "Blame Fox, Not Facebook, for Fake News," *Washington Post,* November 6, 2018, www.washingtonpost.com/news/monkey-cage/wp/2018/11/06/blame-fox-not-facebook-for-fake -news/?utm_term=.134f6d126436

20. Farrell, "Blame Fox."

21. Paul Mihailidis and Samantha Viotty, "Spreadable spectacle in digital culture: Civic expres- sion, fake news, and the role of media literacies in "post-fact" society," *American Behavioral Scientist* 61, no. 4 (2017): 441–54.

22. Darrell M. West, "Brookings Survey Finds 57 Percent Say They Have Seen Fake News during 2018 Elections and 19 Percent Believe It Has Influenced Their Vote," *Brookings Institute,* October 23, 2018, www.brookings.edu/blog/techtank/2018/10/23/brookings-survey-finds-57-percent-say-they-have -seen-fake-news-during-2018-elections-and-19-percent-believe-it-has-influenced-their-vote/.

23. Žiga Turk, "Technology as Enabler of Fake News and a Potential Tool to Combat It," www .europarl.europa.eu/RegData/etudes/IDAN/2018/619008/IPOL_IDA(2018)619008_EN.pdf, p. 21 (accessed December 12, 2018).

CONTRIBUTORS

LEONARD APCAR is Wendell Gray Switzer Jr. Endowed Chair in Media Literacy at the Manship School of Mass Communication at Louisiana State University. He worked for nearly forty years at the *New York Times* and the *Wall Street Journal*, and he is coauthor of the forthcoming "News Editing and the Editorial Process" in the *Oxford Research Encyclopedia of Communication*.

DAN BERKOWITZ is professor emeritus at the University of Iowa. He is the editor of *Social Meanings of News: A Text Reader* and *Cultural Meanings of News: A Text Reader*, and he recently published "Reporters and Their Sources" in the *Handbook of Journalism Studies*, forthcoming from Routledge.

TRYFON BOUKOUVIDIS is a graduate student at the Manship School of Mass Communication at Louisiana State University.

JULIEN GORBACH is assistant professor at the University of Hawai'i at Manoa. He is the author of *The Notorious Ben Hecht: Iconoclastic Writer and Zionist*, and he recently published the articles "The Journalist and the Gangster: A Devil's Bargain, Chicago Style," in *Journalism History* and "The Old New Journalist" in *Literary Journalism Studies*.

JOSH GRIMM is associate professor in the Manship School of Mass Communication at Louisiana State University. He is the author of *It Follows* and *Ex Machina*, and he is the coeditor of *How Public Policy Impacts Racial Inequality*. He is currently working on a coauthored book, *Communication and the End of HIV*.

JOHN MAXWELL HAMILTON is the Hopkins P. Breazeale Professor in the Manship School of Mass Communication at Louisiana State University and a senior scholar at the Woodrow Wilson International Center for Scholars in Washington, DC. He is the author or coauthor of six books. The most recent, *Journalism's Roving Eye: A History of American Foreign Reporting,* won the Goldsmith Prize.

MICHAEL HENDERSON is director of the Public Policy Research Lab at Louisiana State University and assistant professor at the Manship School of Mass Communication. He recently coauthored the articles "Knowledge Persists, Opinions Drift: Learning and Opinion Change in a Three-Wave Panel Experiment" in *American Politics Research* and "Public Service or Propaganda? How Americans Evaluate Political Advocacy by Executive Agencies" in *Social Sciences Quarterly.* He is currently working on a book about how media coverage shapes public opinion about schools.

JESSICA JOHNSON is a visiting assistant professor in the Department of Religious Studies at the College of William and Mary. She is the author of *Biblical Porn: Affect, Labor, and Pastor Mark Driscoll's Evangelical Empire,* and she recently published the articles "When Hate Circulates on Campus to Uphold Free Speech" in *Studies in Law, Politics, and Society* and "Affective Radicalization and White Masculinity" in *Feminist Media Studies.*

PAMELA LABBE is a graduate student at the Manship School of Mass Communication at Louisiana State University.

JACOB L. NELSON is assistant professor in the Walter Cronkite School of Journalism at Arizona State University. His most recent articles are "The Next Media Regime: The Pursuit of 'Audience Engagement' in Journalism" in *Journalism* and "The Persistence of the Popular in Mobile News Consumption" in *Digital Journalism.*

DAVID ASA SCHWARTZ is assistant professor of communication studies at Augustana College. He is a coauthor of the "'The Best Minute and a Half of Audio': Boundary Disputes and the Palin Family Brawl" in *Journalism Practice* and is currently working on his book, *For the Win: The History and Geography of Sport.*

JOEL TIMMER is associate professor in the Department of Film, Television and Digital Media at Texas Christian University. His most recent articles are "Promoting and Infringing Free Speech? Net Neutrality and the First Amendment" in *Federal Communications Law Journal* and "Potential FCC Actions Against 'Fake News': The News Distortion Policy and Broadcast Hoax Rule" in *Communication Law and Policy*.

HEIDI TWOREK is assistant professor of international history at the University of British Columbia. She is the author of *News from Germany: The Competition to Control World Communications, 1900–1945,* and coeditor of *The Routledge Companion to the Makers of Global Business*.

FRED VULTEE is associate professor in the Department of Communication at Wayne State University. His most recent articles are "Attitudes toward News Content, News Practice and Journalism's Future" in *Teaching Journalism & Mass Communication* and "Audience Perceptions of Editing Quality: Assessing Traditional News Routines in the Digital Age" in *Digital Journalism*.

INDEX

ABC News, 83, 153

Abrams, Bill, 163n91

actor-network theory (ANT), 191–92

"actual malice" standard, 140–41, 145, 171

Adams, John, 42

advertising, 9, 19, 63n9, 152, 182; profit motive and, 16, 19–21, 63n9, 131, 133, 153

affective networking of paranoia, 70, 190–94, 199–204

Affordable Care Act, 91, 113

African Americans, 194

agency panic, 198–99, 204

agenda-setting, 172, 178

Ahmed, Sara, 192–93

Alefantis, James, 189, 199

algorithms, 27, 70, 78, 184, 191, 204, 208, 213

Alien and Sedition Acts, 42

Al Jazeera, 83

Allcott, Hunt, 84, 91

All the President's Men (film), 174

alternative news, 115

alt-right, 184, 187n46, 191–92, 195–200. *See also* far right; Ku Klux Klan (KKK); neo-Nazis; right-wing news outlets

Alvarez, United States v., 135–39, 155, 160nn44–45

Amazon, 150

American, 41

American Behavioral Scientist, 214

American Medical Association, 20, 184

American Society of Newspaper Editors, 39

America Online (AOL), 144–46, 150

Anglin, Andrew, 197

Annenberg, Max, 41

Annenberg, Moe, 41

anti-Semitism, 58–60, 75. *See also* neo-Nazis

April Fool's Day, 19, 215

Arab Spring, 44

Aral, Sinan, 208

Aretino, Pietro, 48

Artley, Meredith, 110, 121, 124

Aryan Nation, 193

Associated Press, 153

Associated Press, United States v., 160n39

Atlantic Monthly, 18

audiences, 26–27; access to, 113; expectations of, 114; media consumption habits, 214; partisanship and, 213 (*see also* partisanship); size of, 81–84. *See also* media literacy

authenticity, 113, 191, 199, 203–4, 210–11

authoritarianism, 43, 48–49, 60. *See also* totalitarian propaganda

authority: free speech and, 134, 137; hyperrealism and, 109, 114–16, 120–25; questioning of, 49, 58

Riis, Jacob, 58
Roderick, Kevin, 118
Rolling Stone, 120
Romanoff, Harry, 40
Roosevelt, Eleanor, 22
Roosevelt, Franklin D., 184
Rosen, Jay, 26
Rosenstiel, Tom, 28, 43
Rosenthal, Barrett v., 145–48, 156, 165n23, 165n121
Ross, W. D., 172–73, 176, 183–84
Roth v. United States, 160n33
Roy, Deb, 208
rural areas: Internet access, 15, 25; news in, 14–15
Russian propaganda, 2, 43; US presidential election and, vii–viii, 76–77

Salon, 118
Sandy Hook Elementary School massacre, 23, 202
satire, 9; anxiety about fake news and, 48; deception and, 34; of foreign news, 53–54; history of, 112; mainstream media account-ability and, 108–11; political purposes of, 69. See also *Onion; parody*
Saturday Night Live (SNL), "Weekend Update," 111, 124, 157n4
Saturday Review, 18–19
Saunders, Richard, 35
Scalia, Antonin, 176
Scaramucci, Anthony, 26
Schlesinger, Robert, 119
Schneider v. Amazon.com, 150
scholarship on fake news, ix, 48, 83, 194
Schudson, Michael, 15
Schwartz, A. Brad, *Broadcast Hysteria,* 67
Schwartz, David Asa, 69
scooping, 40
search algorithms. See algorithms

Sedgwick, Ellery, 24–25, 28; "A Modern Voyage to Liliput," 17–19
selective exposure, 77–78. See also partisan selective exposure
selective information, 173
sensationalism, 18
Shakespeare, William, 49
Sherley Amendment (1912), 21
Sherover, Max, *Fakes in American Journalism,* 11, 54–58
Silverman, Craig, 3–4
Sims, Norman Howard, 38
Sinclair, Upton: *The Brass Check,* 56; *The Jungle,* 41
Sisson Documents, 22
Sitewell, K. Jason, 18–19
skepticism: about fact-checkers, 154; about laws targeting false speech, 137; about media literacy, 69, 104
slander, 163n96
Slate, 73, 77
Snopes, 4, 153
SNSs (social network sites). See social media
social goals, 114, 125
social media: diffusion of information on, 23–25, 208; engagement and, 208; entertainment and, 190–91; fake news and, 74–79, 82; pass-and-share culture of, viii–ix; protection on speech, 142–51. See also Facebook; Internet; Reddit; Twitter
social media algorithms. See algorithms
social responsibility, 172–75
Society of Professional Journalists, Code of Ethics, 174, 184
Southern Literary Messenger, 35
Soviet Union, 22
Spanish-American War, 16, 55
Spears, Britney, 122
Spencer, Richard, 191, 193
spoofs, 17, 19, 108, 111, 153
Spy Phone Labs LLC v. Google Inc., 167n151

United Muslims of America (Facebook group), 1–2

United States (US): history of journalism in, 14–16, 75 (*see also* journalism, professional). *See also* presidential election (2016)

United the Right rally, 191, 195. *See also* Charlottesville, Virginia, violence in

United We Stand America, Inc. v. United We Stand, America New York, Inc., 162n74

University of Southern California, Annenberg School for Communication and Journalism, 121–22

urban areas, news in, 14–15, 25

USA Today, 120

US Constitution, 42

US Court of Appeals, 157n4

US District Courts, 157n4

US House Intelligence Committee, 1

U.S. News, 119

US Senate Intelligence Committee, 1

US Supreme Court, 134–51, 155–56, 157n4

vaccination stories, 158n12

vagueness, 162n79

Vanasco v. Schwartz, 138

Vanderlip, Frank, 39–40

Vanguard American, 196

Variety, 119–20

violence: in Charlottesville, Virginia, 191–92, 195–98, 202–3; conspiracy theories and, 91, 177, 189–90 (*see also* Pizzagate); ideologies and, 204; paranoia and, 70; threats of, 6, 181

Viotty, Samantha, 214

viral events, 183

Virginia Bd. of Pharmacy v. Virginia Citizens Consumer Council, Inc., 160n45

VMA. *See* MTV Video Music Awards (VMA)

Vosoughi, Soroush, 208

Vultee, Fred, 69–70

Walker, Patrick, 152

Wallenstein, Andrew, 119–20

Wall Street Journal, 82

"War of the Worlds" radio broadcast, 38, 43, 66–68

Washington Examiner, 201

Washington Journalism Review, 26

Washington Monthly, 114

Washington Post, 3, 16, 65, 132–33, 174–75

watchdog journalism, 112, 115, 123

Watergate scandal, 174

websites. *See* Internet

Webster, J. G., 78

Weimar Republic, 58

Weiner, Anthony, 114

Welch, Edgar Maddison, 189–90, 192–94, 203

Welles, Orson, 38, 43, 66–68

White, David Manning, 28

White House press corps, 184

white men, "self-radicalization" of, 190, 192, 194–99

white nationalism, 191–98

WikiLeaks, 113, 115, 200

Williams v. Rhodes, 160n33

Wilson, Woodrow, 22

Wineburg, Sam, 5, 71, 210

Winning Democrats, 159n18

Wired, 34

World War II, 22–23, 60, 62

Yahoo-ABC, 82

yellow journalism, 18

YouGov, 96, 106n32

YouTube, 44

Zelizer, Barbie, 15

Zeran v. America Online, Inc., 144–46, 165n113

Zimdars, Melissa, 79

Zuckerberg, Mark, 32, 63, 133, 152, 199–201, 204. *See also* Facebook

CPSIA information can be obtained
at www.ICGtesting.com
Printed in the USA
LVHW041552080620
657422LV00005B/532